BIG GODS

BIG GODS

How Religion Transformed Cooperation and Conflict

Ara Norenzayan

PRINCETON UNIVERSITY PRESS
Princeton and Oxford

Copyright © 2013 by Princeton University Press

Published by Princeton University Press, 41 William Street,

Princeton, New Jersey 08540

In the United Kingdom: Princeton University Press, 6 Oxford Street,

Woodstock, Oxfordshire OX20 1TW

press.princeton.edu

Jacket photograph: Synagogue ceiling detail © Craftvision/Getty Images.

Library of Congress Cataloging-in-Publication Data

    Norenzayan, Ara, 1970–

    Big gods : how religion transformed cooperation and conflict / Ara Norenzayan.

       pages   cm

    Includes bibliographical references and index.

    ISBN-13: 978-0-691-15121-2 (cloth : alk. paper)

    ISBN-10: 0-691-15121-0 (cloth : alk. paper)   1. Psychology, Religious. 2. Psychology—Religious aspects.   3. Faith development—Psychological aspects.   4. Cooperation—Religious aspects.   5. Conflict management—Religious aspects.   I. Title.

    BL53.N634 2013

                  200.1′9—dc23   2013011723

British Library Cataloging-in-Publication Data is available

This book has been composed in Garamond Premier Pro

Printed on acid-free paper. ∞

Printed in the United States of America

10 9 8 7 6 5 4 3 2 1

For Max

Contents

Illustrations

Acknowledgments

Scott Atran, Joseph Henrich, Jonathan Haidt, and Richard Sosis will no doubt recognize the influence of their ideas and our communications in this book. Two of my former students, Azim Shariff and Will Gervais, have been the major players in a great deal of the original research that this book is based on. Much of this book is the result of our fruitful collaborations. I feel privileged to have worked with them, as well as with other former and current graduate students: Ian Hansen, Emma Buchtel, Ilan Dar-Nimrod, Aiyana Willard, Albert Lee, and Rita McNamara. Much of this original research has been generously supported by grants from the Social Sciences and Humanities Research Council of Canada. In particular I thank the Cultural Evolution of Religion Research Consortium, supported by SSHRC. At the early stages, the idea of this book was shaped by sage advice from Russell Weinberger and Katinka Matson. A special thanks goes to Eric Schwartz, my editor at Princeton University Press, for his guidance and support. Also thanks to Ryan Mulligan, Karen Fortgang, and Jennifer Harris for their valuable help turning the manuscript into a book. This book benefited a great deal from Adam Baimel's technical know-how. He helped me save time in myriad ways and stay on the elusive task of finishing this book.

I am grateful to Jonathan Monk, Nicholas Epley, Benjamin Purzycki, Joseph Bulbulia, Hagop Sarkissian, Robert McCauley, Frans de Waal, Scott Atran, Jonathan Haidt, Paul Bloom, and David S. Wilson, for their valuable feedback on an earlier draft. Thanks to Dimitris Xygalatas for providing a firsthand image of the Cavadee ritual, and to Megan Daniels, for pointing me to the archaeological record of religious fraternities in Delos. I could not have asked for a more stimulating and supportive group of colleagues and students at the University of British Columbia, where I have the privilege of working. I am particularly grateful to the gang at the Center for Human Evolution, Cognition, and Culture, Steve Heine, Mark Schaller, Joseph Henrich, Mark Collard, and Ted Slingerland for their friendship and intellectual support. I couldn't have asked for a more supportive group of colleagues, including Jess Tracy, Liz Dunn, Toni Schmader, Darrin Lehman, Alan Kingstone, and two friends and former colleagues, Gregory Miller and Edith Chen. This stellar group would not have come about without the tireless efforts and the creative talents of Darrin Lehman. Whether in the corridors of the Kenny Building at UBC, over lunch, or on the ski slopes outside Vancouver, they challenge me to think harder and deeper, and never allowed for boredom to take root. As a social psychologist interested in all things cultural, I am deeply indebted to the support and influence of several mentors. Robert Levine infected me with the excitement of cross-cultural research during my undergraduate days; Richard Nisbett, my mentor in graduate school, shaped my way of thinking about psychology in profound ways; Norbert Schwarz taught me, among other important things, the art of psychological experimentation; and Scott Atran, through a rare and inspiring postdoctoral training in Paris, planted early seeds that eventually led me to write this book.

The basic outline of the argument in this book in an earlier form can be found in Norenzayan and Shariff, 2008, *Science*. Chapters 4 and 5 draw substantially from Gervais, Shariff, and Norenzayan, 2011, *Journal of Personality and Social Psychology*; and Gervais and Norenzayan, 2012, *Psychological Science*. Parts of chapter 6 are based on Gervais, Willard, Norenzayan, and Henrich, 2010, *Religion*. Chapter 10 partly draws on Norenzayan and Gervais, 2013, *Trends in Cognitive Sciences*. I gratefully acknowledge my coauthors on these original publications.

My parents, Anahid and Ohannes Norenzayan, did everything in their powers to help me and my brother and sister succeed in life. Eva Oberle nurtured me and patiently tolerated and supported what seemed to be an endless writing project, even through the birth of our son, Max. This book was supposed to arrive before Max, but Max arrived first, and set us out on a new adventure. Without Eva, there would be no book.

The Eight Principles of Big Gods

The entire argument in this book can be summarized in eight interrelated principles.

1. *Watched people are nice people.*

2. *Religion is more in the situation than in the person.*

3. *Hell is stronger than heaven.*

4. *Trust people who trust in God.*

5. *Religious actions speak louder than words.*

6. *Unworshipped Gods are impotent Gods.*

7. *Big Gods for Big Groups.*

8. *Religious groups cooperate in order to compete.*

BIG GODS

Chapter 1

Religious Evolution

On June 27, 1844, a man named Joseph Smith died at age 38 in the prairie town of Carthage, Illinois. Fewer than fifteen years earlier, he had experienced visions and subsequently established an obscure religious movement. Smith's movement was just one of hundreds of new religious movements that sprouted in nineteenth-century America and actively competed for adherents. This was a time and place of great religious innovation and fervor. When he died in 1844, Smith could not have known that he had founded what was going to be one of the most enduring religious movements in American history. Initially, the Latter Day Saints Movement had just a few dedicated followers. In the ensuing years, the church moved its headquarters to Utah and grew by leaps and bounds.[1] The Mormon Church, as it is known today, is one of the fastest growing religions not just in the United States, but in the entire world. From its unremarkable origins as an obscure sect, and within a short time span of 170 years, the Mormon Church has spread to all corners of the globe, from Argentina to Zimbabwe. Its membership now exceeds 15 million worldwide. Back-of-the-envelope calculations suggest a phenomenal growth rate of 40 percent per decade, which, in one estimate, approximates Christianity's expansion rates in the early Roman Empire. If the past trend continues, this growth will continue to increase exponentially, reaching the 100-million mark in just a few decades.[2]

The rise of Mormonism is just a recent example of a broader pattern of history. Pentecostalism, a once obscure Christian "charismatic" sect established in Los Angeles in the early part of the twentieth century, has over 125 million followers worldwide and is fast becoming a contender to be the "third" force in Christianity, just behind Catholicism and Protestantism, soon displacing the venerable but demographically stagnating Orthodox branch. Like Mormonism, it is also one of the world's fastest growing religions. On the whole, there are today nearly 2 billion self-proclaimed Christians. Islam, with 1.3 billion people, is thriving too, and fundamentalist strains are making fresh inroads into all three Abrahamic faiths. Christian fundamentalism in particular is spreading like wildfire in places like China and Southeast Asia, and most of all, in sub-Saharan Africa.[3] The United States—the world's most economically powerful society and a scientifically advanced one—is also, anomalously, one of the most religious. Over 90 percent of Americans believe in God, 93 percent and 85 percent believe in heaven and hell, respectively, and close to one in two Americans believe in a literal interpretation of Genesis.[4] These facts and figures point to our first observation about religious evolution: despite many predictions of religion's demise in the last 200 years, most people in most societies in the world still are, and have always been, deeply religious.[5]

The second observation about religious evolution is equally important: religions have always been multiplying, growing, and mutating at a brisk pace. In one estimate, new religions sprout at an average rate of two to three per day. "Many are called, but few are chosen," says the Gospel according to Matthew (22:14). This "Matthew Effect" might as well refer to the iron law of religious evolution, which dictates that while legions of new religious elements are created, most of them die out, save a potent few that endure and flourish.

By one estimate, there are 10,000 religions in the world today.[6] Yet, the vast majority of humanity adheres to a disproportionate few of them: just a handful of religions claim the vast majority of religious minds in the world. This is the third observation that flows from the first two: that most religious people living on the planet today are the cultural descendants of just a few outlier religious movements that won in the cultural marketplace. In the long run, almost all religious movements end in failure. Anthropologist Richard Sosis looked at the group survival rates of a representative set of 200 nineteenth-century utopian communities,[7] both religious and secular. He found a striking but overwhelming pattern. The average life span of the religious communes was a mere 25 years. In 80 years, nine out of ten religious communes had disbanded. Secular communes (mostly socialist) fared even worse: they lasted for an average of 6.4 years, and nine out of ten disappeared in less than 20 years.[8]

This cultural winnowing of religions over time is evident throughout history and is occurring every day. It is easy to miss this dynamic process, because the enduring religious movements are all that we often see in the present. However, this would be an error. It is called *survivor bias*. When groups, entities, or persons undergo a process of competition and selective retention, we see abundant cases of those that "survived" the competition process; the cases that did not survive and flourish are buried in the dark recesses of the past, and are overlooked. To understand how religions propagate, we of course want to put the successful religions under the microscope; but we do not want to forget the unsuccessful ones that did not make it—the reasons for their failures can be equally instructive.[9]

As a typical case of high expectations but disappointing cultural resilience, consider the Perfectionists of Oneida, New York. The Perfectionists believed that Jesus Christ had already returned in the first century CE, which made it possible to enjoy God's Kingdom here on Earth. They practiced complex marriage, such that every adult man was married to every adult woman. Postmenopausal women introduced young men to the pleasures of sex. However, such hedonism was tempered by the practice of mutual criticism, in which every member of the community was regularly subjected to public criticism by a committee, or sometimes by the entire community. The commune lasted about 33 years, splintering soon after its leader, John Humphrey Noyes, unsuccessfully attempted to pass on the leadership of the commune to his son. The Perfectionists certainly could have done better! They did not last very long, although their exacting standards survive on dinner tables to this day: some of their members established what became the giant silverware company Oneida Limited (their motto: "Bring Life to the Table").[10]

While the overwhelming majority of religious movements in history share the fate of the not-so-perfect Oneida commune (and are forgotten by everyone), a few have stood the test of time, and even prospered at the expense of their less successful rivals. There is a deep puzzle lurking behind these winning religions. How is it that, for thousands of years, human beings have been able to organize themselves into large, anonymous, yet cohesive and highly cooperative societies?

The Puzzle of Big Groups

Precise estimates are hard to come by, but if all human beings on the planet represented a crowd of spectators at a soccer match, only one or two of them would be hunter-gatherers. Close to all of humanity—indeed, it is safe to say more than 99.9 percent—lives in very large-scale communities of anonymous strangers.[11] Total strangers regularly depend on each other for livelihood, economic exchange, shelter, and defense. Going backward through time, we see that this feature of modern societies is a remarkable development that begs for an explanation. Its origins can be found in the earliest towns and villages that arose on the Fertile Crescent and the Nile, at the start of the Holocene period. This is the time marked by the agricultural revolution a mere 12,000 years ago, a blip in the vast timescale of human evolution. These communities of a few thousands, not to mention the mega-societies of today numbering in millions, contrast sharply with most of human existence, characterized by the comparatively smaller bands of foragers and hunters tied to each other with the tight bonds of blood and brotherhood driven by face-to-face interactions, and occasionally, some forms of limited interactions with strangers.[12]

Alarmingly, the remaining few hunter-gatherers and foragers are on the verge of extinction. When their way of life vanishes completely, a vast store of knowledge about human origins will disappear with them. While they exist, they give us important, though imperfect, clues about human origins. While many of these groups have fluid memberships and do trade and interact with other groups under some circumstances, suspicion toward most strangers is, and has been common. But at the dawn of the Holocene, and likely starting even earlier, there has been a remarkable and sustained "scaling-up" of human groups over time. In the process of this transformation, human beings have radically altered their own ecological niche, exchanging a hunting and foraging existence of face-to-face societies with an agricultural one of dense populations, followed by an industrial age of machines and mass production, and culminating in an information age of instant and mass communication. To appreciate how strange this is, consider the two explanations from evolutionary biology for the origins of cooperation. These principles can be discerned in how we relate to the two kinds of people we care deeply about—*kith* and *kin*.

First is kin selection. *Hamilton's rule* specifies that genetically related individuals cooperate with each other—and by doing so favor the spread of their shared genes. From social insects to social apes, individuals help others to the degree to which the recipient and the helper are related and the benefits of helping outweigh its costs. This logic also applies to us humans. It should come as no surprise to you that, the world over, a large share of blood, body organs, money, food, and time, are donated between close family members in a manner proportional to the degree of genetic relatedness.[13]

Second is friendly behavior among kith. There is nothing evolutionarily puzzling about genetically unrelated individuals cooperating with each other, as long as these acts are mutually beneficial, individuals can track each other's reputations over time, and cheaters are detected and socially excluded, or threatened with punishment. This is known as *reciprocity*, which governs much of our lives defined by friends, neighbors, and allies. Reciprocity, as long as certain conditions are met, is a building block of human social life. Make your first move a cooperative one, then do unto others what others do unto you, and you will go far in your social life (this is the "tit for tat" rule, one of several successful reciprocity strategies).[14]

In economic game experiments that model everyday interactions, total strangers are placed in cooperative dilemmas, where they are given a certain amount of money, which they can decide to keep or share with others. Mutual cooperation means profit for everyone, but how do you avoid being the sucker who cooperates but never receives anything in return? In such experiments, participants are typically found to cooperate more when they expect to interact with the same person repeatedly in the future, and this occurs right from the first round. That is, people respond to reciprocity incentives; they do not learn to cooperate by trial and error. But it's not just the expectation of future interactions that makes strangers more cooperative. Knowledge of a partner's previous play, even with a different player, or *reputation*, dramatically affects cooperation levels, and so does the threat of punishment. What makes friendships and alliances work, therefore, are reputation, expectations of future interactions, and the opportunity to retaliate selfish acts if necessary. The social imperative to cooperate requires that people eagerly and regularly assess the reputations of others, and be choosy about their interaction partners.[15]

If *freeriding*—the act of receiving benefits without reciprocating—incurs a reliably hefty punitive cost, potential freeriders may restrain their selfish urges. Punishment of selfish acts is an effective strategy that stabilizes cooperation, but it pushes the problem further back: monitoring and punishing freeriders itself can be costly, which means that individuals would rather see someone else punish selfish individuals and enjoy the fruits of cooperative groups. It creates opportunities for people to freeride on their punishment duties.[16] One solution to this problem, of course, is *third-party* punishment—that is, policing institutions. A study done in Switzerland, for example, found that in cantons with genetically homogenous populations, where kinship ties are strong, people rely on the police less. However, in cantons with greater genetic diversity, reliance on police increases, exactly as would be expected if policing institutions were designed to enforce cooperation among strangers.[17]

But in the absence of modern, reliable policing institutions, who will punish those who fail to punish? It is easy to see how this leads to an infinite regress problem. How did human societies find effective (though far from failsafe) punishment mechanisms before the emergence of effective modern institutions such as police and courts? Was belief in supernatural policing an early social tool that provided a solution?

The rise of large cooperative groups is, therefore, a double conundrum. With ever-greater chances of encountering strangers, genetic relatedness subsides geometrically, and without extra safeguards, reciprocal altruism also rapidly reverts to selfishness. Neither kin selection nor reciprocal altruism can explain the rise of large cooperative societies. The puzzle deepens further. This process of "scaling up" of the cooperative sphere has occurred only very recently in human evolution—in the last 12,000 years, and in only one species—no other animal species other than humans is known for such ultra-sociality. No doubt, there is altruism among close relatives in social insects such as ants and bees, and some instances of limited cooperation among strangers under some conditions—for example, reciprocal food sharing among vampire bats, and cases of empathy-driven altruism in chimpanzees such as adoptions.[18] Still, human beings are the only known species that underwent a radical transformation from small, tight-knit groups (*Gemeinschaft*, or community) to large, anonymous societies (*Gesellschaft*, or civil society), which practice sustained cooperation toward anonymous genetic strangers on a massive scale.[19] This is the puzzle of large cooperative groups.[20]

As I shall elaborate in this book, it is a puzzle that gives us important clues about the reasons behind the spread of religious beliefs and practices that reflect credible displays of commitment to supernatural beings with policing powers. It turns out that a big force leading from *Gemeinschaft* to *Gesellschaft* was prosocial religions with Big Gods.

Back to the Puzzle of Prosocial Religions

Now let's go back to the first puzzle that I started with: the worldwide spread of prosocial religions also during the Holocene, the same historical period that saw the rise of large groups. If you are Christian, Muslim, Jewish, Hindu, Buddhist, or even an agnostic or atheist descendant of any of these traditions, you are heir to an extraordinarily successful religious movement that started as an obscure cultural experiment. To appreciate why these two puzzles are fundamentally connected, it is important to take a look at that hallmark of all religions—belief in supernatural beings such as gods, ghosts, and devils.[21] These beliefs and their dramatic cultural evolution in the last 12,000 years both reflect a puzzle in its own right and contain the seeds of a solution to the puzzle of large cooperative groups.[22]

A startling fact about the spirits and deities of foraging and hunter-gatherer societies is that most of them do not have wide moral concern. At first glance, this seems absurd—people steeped in the Abrahamic faiths are so accustomed to seeing religion tied up with morality that it is hard to recognize that this association is a peculiar cultural innovation of the recent ages, and present only in some places. But anthropologists tell us that in small bands resembling ancestral human groups, the gods may want to be appeased with sacrifices and rituals, although they are typically unconcerned about moral transgressions such as theft and exploitation, which preoccupy the Big Gods of major world religions. Many gods and spirits are not even fully omniscient to be good monitors of moral behavior—they perceive things within village boundaries but not beyond; they may be tricked by humans or be manipulated by other rival gods. Religion's early roots did not have a wide moral scope.[23]

We gain appreciation for why this is so when we realize that in these intimate, transparent groups, encountering kin is common, and reputations can be monitored and social transgressions are difficult to hide. Perhaps that's why spirits and gods in these groups typically are not involved in the moral lives of people. Nevertheless, despite their relative infrequency in the supernatural panoply of hunter-gatherer societies, powerful, omniscient, interventionist, morally concerned gods, or as I call them in this book, the *Big Gods* of prosocial religions, proliferated in the last 12,000 years of the Holocene period through cultural diffusion, population expansions, and conquest.[24] Why did these Big Gods colonize the minds of so many people? Were these beliefs part of the network of causes that ushered the worldwide expansion of prosocial religions? Why is it that the majority of believers in the world today worship this particular cultural flavor of supernatural agents?

Outline of a Solution

There is a simple solution to each puzzle, which is that each answers the other.[25] In this book, I present an argument that solves both riddles simultaneously by considering that they gave mutual rise to the *prosocial religions* and *large-scale cooperation*. Prosocial religions, with their Big Gods who watch, intervene, and demand hard-to-fake loyalty displays, facilitated the rise of cooperation in large groups of anonymous strangers. In turn, these expanding groups took their prosocial religious beliefs and practices with them, further ratcheting up large-scale cooperation in a runaway process of cultural evolution.

Weaving the various conceptual threads together, we see the outline of an emerging picture. Religious beliefs and rituals arose as an evolutionary by-product of ordinary cognitive functions that preceded religion.[26] These cognitive functions gave rise to *religious intuitions*—for example, that minds and bodies are separate entities and that the former can exist without the latter. These intuitions support widely held religious beliefs and related practices, such as gods, spirits, and souls of various types and characteristics.[27] Once that happened, the stage was set for rapid cultural evolution—nongenetic, socially transmitted changes in beliefs and behaviors—that eventually led to large societies with Big Gods.

Here is how: Some early mutants in this template were watchful Big Gods with interventionist inclinations. Believers who feared these gods co-operated, trusted, and sacrificed for the group much more than believers in morally indifferent gods or gods lacking omniscience. Displays of devotion and hard-to-fake commitments such as fasts, food taboos, and extravagant rituals further transmitted believers' sincere faith in these gods to others.

In this way, religious hypocrites were prevented from invading and undermining these groups. Through these and other solidarity-promoting mechanisms, religions of Big Gods forged anonymous strangers into large, cohesive moral communities tied together with the sacred bonds of a common supernatural jurisdiction.

Of course, Big Gods were a potent cause, but not the sole cause that led to the social expansion of some groups. Surely there are additional solutions to large-scale cooperation. Moreover, differential cultural success does not imply a moral hierarchy. But these groups would have been larger and more cooperative. These ever-expanding groups with high social solidarity, high fertility rates that ensure demographic expansion, and a stronger capacity to attract converts grew in size often at the expense of other groups. As they spread, they took their religious beliefs and practices with them, ultimately culminating in the morally concerned Big Gods of the major world religions.

And what about the secular societies of today? Only recently, and only in some places, some societies have succeeded in sustaining large-scale cooperation with institutions such as courts, police, and mechanisms for enforcing contracts. In some parts of the world such as Northern Europe, especially Scandinavia, these institutions have precipitated religion's decline by usurping its community-building functions. These societies with atheist majorities—some of the most cooperative, peaceful, and prosperous in the world—climbed religion's ladder, and then kicked it away.

Natural Religion

The idea that religions are shapers of human societies is of course not new. There is a short but illustrious history of thought in the social sciences, notably Emile Durkheim, Victor Turner, and Roy Rappaport. Durkheim, Rappaport, and others recognized the fundamentally cooperative functions of religion. But they focused on the social bonding functions of rituals, and downplayed belief in gods as tangential to religion's capacity to cement communal life and create *organic solidarity*. More recently in *Darwin's Cathedral*, evolutionary biologist D. S. Wilson placed religion's social functions in a modern Darwinian framework. My thinking in this book draws from these contributions, as well as from theorists of religion who see the study of religion firmly in the cognitive sciences. The cognitive perspective, whose intellectual origins go as far back as Hume, sees religious belief as an accidental side-effect of human cognitive architecture. It has provided the basis of a compelling account of how human minds conceive of gods. But this perspective has been mostly silent about the prosocial effects of religion. The argument in this book is an attempt at integrating these two perspectives—the social and the cognitive—which are currently seen as competing accounts.[28]

I argue instead for a third way, which nevertheless retains key insights of these distinct views. Belief in certain kinds of supernatural watchers—Big Gods—is an essential ingredient that, along with rituals and other interlocking sets of social commitment devices, glued together total strangers into ever-larger moral communities as cultural evolution gained pace in the past twelve millennia. Thus, we do not have to choose between Hume and Durkheim. On the contrary, believing and belonging come together in religion as an integrated whole.[29]

Drawing together evidence from across the evolutionary, cognitive, and social sciences, the argument in this book offers this third path that locates the origins of prosocial religions in a powerful combination of genetic and cultural evolution. This alternative has three foundations. First, it builds directly on the cognitive approach, which provides important clues about how certain intuitions and cognitive biases push human minds toward some recurrent templates that support supernatural beliefs. Second, it combines cognitive tendencies with cultural evolution to explain how some cultural mutants of these beliefs spread in populations at the expense of rival mutants. Third, understanding the forces of cultural competition[30] between groups helps us explain why groups that stumbled on such successful mutants spread and expanded. Therefore, one virtue of this "third way" is that it reconciles and consolidates important insights and observations from both social and cognitive approaches.

The Organization of This Book

Chapters 2 through 6 explore the psychology that explains the rise of prosocial religions. As the saying goes, "watched people are nice people." In chapter 2, I explore how our basic social intuitions to monitor others' reputations, and care about our own, makes people nice to each other. This lays the foundation to discuss how these social intuitions give rise to supernatural watchers. Chapters 2 and 3 explain the process by which people play nice when they think God is watching. If so, it follows that belief in supernatural watchers encourages nice behavior even if no one else is watching, enabling stranger-to-stranger cooperation.

Chapter 4 delves into this connection between prosocial religions and trust. If thoughts of a watchful God make people cooperate with each other, then outward signs of commitment to God induce greater levels of mutual trust among religious believers. Where does this leave nonbelievers, who do not think that they are being watched by a supernatural police? Why are atheists distrusted in societies with religious majorities, even though they are not a cohesive or even a visible group? Chapters 4 and 5 build on the argument in this book and bring to light an overlooked but widespread prejudice tied to religion. In chapter 6, I ask, why are many religious behaviors and rituals so extravagant (from an evolutionary perspective), and how do they work to build trust and transmit passionate faith?

Chapters 7 through 9 explore the historical trends that have shaped the mutual rise of prosocial religions and large-scale cooperative communities over the last twelve millenia. By working upward from the mutually reinforcing sets of psychological mechanisms discussed in chapters 2 through 6, it becomes clear why such prosocial religious groups, by outsourcing social monitoring duties to supernatural watchers, built trust among religiously committed strangers and expanded and spread throughout the globe at the expense of rival groups. In chapter 7, I explore the connection between Big God prosocial religion and the puzzle of how large cooperative communities arose in the last 12,000 years. Chapter 8 explores how the forces of intergroup competition, including warfare, shaped prosocial religions. In chapter 9, I ask, what happens when people fall out of the moral community defined by religion? How does religion, by fostering sacred values, create intractable conflict? When does religious prosociality translate into intergroup hostility and violence? Can religion be co-opted for resolving conflict?

In the popular imagination, religion is the antithesis of secularism, yet history and psychology reveal unexpected continuities. The final great surprise of the argument in this book is the religious origins of secular societies, which is the topic of chapter 10. How did Big Groups manage to emerge and thrive without Big Gods in the last few hundred years? Largely atheist social welfare states in Scandinavia give us striking clues as to the particular kinds of institutions, practices, and social conditions that can displace religion and build godless but cooperative societies.

Moving Forward

After a long period of stagnation, scientific progress in explaining religion has picked up pace. To be sure, the scope of our knowledge is very limited, and there are many missing pieces to the puzzle. Nevertheless, tantalizing clues are emerging from a variety of fields. But because of disciplinary specialization and academic fragmentation, these insights are considered in isolation and their connections often go unrecognized.

I am a fan of what biologist E. O. Wilson calls *consilience*, or the ultimate unity of all knowledge.[31] In an age of knowing more and more about less and less, what is sorely lacking are efforts that help us see the forest for the trees. It is perhaps fitting that making sense of religion—the wellspring of the oldest, deepest yearnings of human beings—demand consilience. This book is a modest attempt, pulling together some of the key advances from these different fields to tell a unifying story. Undoubtedly, like other explanations, this account of religion will also be shown to contain flaws. If it has value beyond what is currently known, it is due to its ability to reconcile a wide range of observations about religious beliefs and behaviors derived from a variety of disciplines. The basic outline of an argument is emerging that simultaneously answers two of the biggest scientific enigmas about humanity: (1) Exactly how and why have some religious beliefs and practices galvanized the large-scale cooperative societies of the last ten millennia? (2) How did these processes in turn lead to the cultural spread of prosocial religions and colonize the minds of the majority of the world?

Chapter 2

Supernatural Watchers

Nothing in all creation is hidden from God's sight. Everything is uncovered and laid bare before the eyes of him to whom we must give account.

—Hebrews 4:13, New International Version

If there were no God, it would be necessary to invent him.

—Voltaire

If we were to travel back in time and visit medieval Europe between the ninth and thirteenth centuries—a mere twenty to thirty generations ago—we would encounter many institutions and practices that would seem bewildering to our modern sensibilities. But no institution would be stranger to a secular person than the trial by ordeal.

This was a time, of course, without DNA testing, phone records, security cameras, or even reliable eyewitness testimony. Judges had few mechanisms at their disposal to examine evidence or establish motive or opportunity. Therefore, in difficult cases, they ordered a trial by ordeal. A cauldron of water was boiled, and a piece of red-hot iron rod or burning stone thrown into it. The accused was then commanded to prepare to insert her hand and arm into the boiling water and retrieve it. If her flesh was unscathed, she was declared innocent. Otherwise, she was guilty. In another variant, the naked, bound defendant was thrown into a deep pool of holy water. If the defendant sank, he was condemned. If he floated, he was a free man.

For us moderns, the trial by ordeal seems like the epitome of medieval inefficacy and backwardness. Economic historian Peter Leeson disagrees. He points out that the practice of ordeal worked surprisingly well. It was, in fact, a far superior technique than extracting confessions under torture, a surviving practice that is as unreliable as it is cruel. Ordeals might have cleverly determined who was guilty and who was innocent with reasonable accuracy, without need for actual divine intervention. How did ordeals work?

The prevailing belief was that God would save innocent defendants from harm and would allow guilty ones to perish. Leeson explains, "the key insight is that ordeals weren't just widely practiced. They were widely believed in. It's this belief literally, the fear of God that could have allowed the ordeals to function effectively." In other words, the mere threat of conducting a trial by ordeal was what was needed to separate the true criminals from the wrongly accused. This genuine belief in divine intervention allowed the ordeals to function effectively. Those who knew they had something to hide expected God to reveal their guilt by harming them in the ordeal. Innocents, meanwhile, were convinced that God would save them. The only defendants, therefore, who would have any enthusiasm to go through with the ordeal, were the innocent ones. Guilty defendants confessed their crimes, settled with their accusers, or disappeared. Knowing this, priests and judges seemed to have exercised wide latitude to manipulate the process, and made judgment calls of guilt or innocence that were proportional to the degree to which the accused were willing to undergo the ordeal.[1]

Of course, no one knows for sure how effective ordeals were in separating the guilty from the innocent. But to the extent that this piece of cultural technology worked, it did because, and only because, the faithful sincerely believed in the presence of a powerful supernatural watcher who sees everything and directly intervenes in matters of human morality. While the trial by ordeal may appear to be a strange vestige of the medieval past, a critical feature that made it work continues to affect the lives of billions of people around the world. This feature is rooted in an evolutionarily ancient mechanism that reliably generates prosocial behavior: social surveillance keeps people in line.

What kinds of mental capacities are recruited to conceive of gods? How did some gods come to be supernatural monitors who watch people and intervene in their lives? What's the psychology behind belief in such gods, and how did the feeling of being under social monitoring cause a sea change in cooperative behavior?

To get some answers, I will occasionally turn to religious texts, and to shamans, priests, and preachers. But more importantly, religion's imprints on human nature are not so much found in dogmas in texts and teachings, but in *natural religion*—the thoughts and behaviors of believers. When teachings matter (they exist only in some religious groups and only in recent history), they matter only as lived interpretations and understandings by believers. Therefore the bulk of my attention will be on recent empirical studies from psychology, economics, sociology, and anthropology, where the actual behavior of people can be carefully observed in everyday life or under controlled conditions.

How Mind Perception Prepares Minds for "God Perception"

How do beliefs about gods and spirits arise in the first place? To get some answers, we'll take a moment to talk about a suite of cognitive faculties that reliably develop in children, and regularly reoccur across cultures and historical periods. There are several such faculties, which appear to incline human minds toward religious belief.[2]

Let's start with the *mentalizing*, or the *Theory of Mind* faculty, which helps people make sense of others as intentional agents with minds.[3] Consider someone who sees Mary hug Bob. A mind-blind Martian might interpret the hug as merely a mechanical event where two physical bodies come together for an instant and then part again. A mind reader, in contrast, might infer that Mary *desires* Bob, perhaps that Mary *intends* to win Bob's heart, or that she *believes* Bob desires her in return. There is a cartoon depicting an alarmed husband telling his visibly upset wife, "Of course I care about how you imagined I thought you perceived I wanted you to feel." While most mind-reading tasks are thankfully not as convoluted, daily social interactions would not be possible without understanding others' beliefs, goals, and desires.

Mind reading gives us important clues about how beliefs in gods and ghosts come about. Pascal Boyer notes that when believers talk about their interactions with spirits and gods, their reasoning betrays inferences about the mental states of supernatural agents. When people pray to God, they want to know what God *thinks* and *wishes*. When people want to appease ancestor spirits, they worry that the spirits might get *angry* and *vengeful* if proper ritual sacrifices are not conducted to honor them. In Hindu mythology, the rocky relationship between Lord Shiva and his divine consort Shakti includes enough mind-twisting gossip to challenge even the most sophisticated mind reader.

Paul Bloom takes this insight a step further, and argues that these types of mind reading supply the cognitive basis for *mind-body dualism*—the intuition that "mind stuff" is distinct from "physical stuff." You are an intuitive dualist if you feel that there is an "I" in you who has a relationship with your brain, but that the "I" is not your brain. Mind-body dualism is a naturally developing intuition that supports many religious beliefs. It is this intuition that gives rise to the pervasive belief in disembodied supernatural agents such as gods, souls, and spirits, who are believed to possess human-like mind stuff—beliefs, desires, emotions—allowing believers to have a personal relationship with God or other supernatural beings.[4]

Mind-body dualism, once in place, in turn prepares our minds to accept another intuition that turns out to be a very important foundation for many religious beliefs. If minds are an immaterial substance autonomous and separate from physical bodies, they may continue on even after the demise of the physical body. The idea of the *immortal soul* is ready to take root, or what psychologist Jesse Bering calls "psychological immortality."[5]

Finally, another related and widespread intuition that appears to play a critical role in religious thinking is *teleology*—or the sense that natural events and objects exist for a purpose. Teleological intuitions appear early in children's thinking, and seem untutored. As early as five years of age, children have the intuition that lions exist so that we can visit them at the zoo, clouds are for raining, and mountains are for climbing. Adults hold them too, sometimes overtly, other times more clandestinely. There is evidence that science education, far from rooting out these intuitions, merely suppresses them. For example, even professional scientists slip into teleological thinking when under time pressure. Many of these insights come from the work of psychologist Deborah Kelemen, who has studied teleological thinking in adults and children. She calls this phenomenon "intuitive theism," because it seems to prepare our minds for creationist thinking: if all things were designed for a purpose, doesn't it make sense that there is a creator who designed them?[6]

The intensity of these intuitions vary from person to person; so does belief in God. Aiyana Willard and I used statistical techniques to find out if the same people who have these intuitions are the ones who are believers in the supernatural. First, we looked at the degree to which individuals mentalize, endorse mind-body dualism, and see the world in teleological terms. Then we looked at the degree to which these same people believed in God. Do these intuitions prepare our minds to accept God? We found that they do indeed. Having these intuitions in abundance makes people more receptive to the idea of God. We also found that these intuitions increase the odds of believing in paranormal events, such as believing in UFOs and in extrasensory perception. Mentalizing tendencies encouraged more dualism and more teleology; in turn, these two intuitions increased the odds of believing in God and believing paranormal events.[7] Of course, intuitive biases increase receptivity to religious beliefs, but they do not wholly determine them. As we shall see later, several other factors are crucial for religious belief to take root. Among these, cultural exposure to displays of religious fervor is important. So are conditions of life that make belief in deities emotionally comforting.[8]

Returning to mentalizing tendencies, it becomes clear why they are so central in believing in, and committing to, divine beings. Without them, believers could not discern what God desires or dislikes, and therefore could not pray, ask for favors, or seek forgiveness. Without mind reading, believers could not meaningfully interact with God—after all, God and other supernatural agents are intuitively understood to be immaterial minds. God could not deploy supernatural powers to do what many gods are busy doing: respond to existential concerns like death or uncertainty, avert a misfortune or cause one to someone else, and of course, monitor and police social behavior.

"Perceiving" gods, therefore, is an act that is fundamentally tied to our ability to perceive other minds. There are several sources of evidence that point to this hypothesis about the cognitive origins of belief in gods. First, believers spontaneously reason about God as if God had humanlike mental states. Explicitly omniscient gods should be implicitly represented as having limited, humanlike (and ungodlike) mental abilities. In a now classic study, psychologists Justin Barrett and Frank Keil presented participants with a story of God performing various actions. For example, God could perform multiple mental activities simultaneously, and could perceive events without sensory inputs. Later, the participants were asked to recall the story. Overwhelmingly, participants, including believers who explicitly told the researchers that they believe God is omniscient, mentally recast the omniscient God as having humanlike mental limitations—this recast God needed to finish one task before embarking on another, and needed to see events to know that they occurred.[9]

People "see human" in all kinds of things and beings, from natural formations, to artifacts, to pets and gods. Anthropologist Stewart Guthrie gives many examples of this in his book *Faces in the Clouds*. Gods are no exception. Closely tied to Barret and Keil's original findings are studies showing that, despite scriptural prohibitions, God is believed to possess humanlike mental attributes such as beliefs, emotions, and intentions. Psychologists Adam Waytz, Nicholas Epley, and John Cacioppo tested everyday intuitions about the extent to which various entities had mental states, such as consciousness, awareness, and emotional experiences. They asked participants about four commonly anthropomorphized entities: nonhuman animals, natural entities such as rocks and mountains, technological devices such as computers and car engines, and God and other supernatural agents. Peoples' tendency to attribute humanlike minds to God was so tied up with their belief in God that it made no sense to separate anthropomorphizing God from believing in God. My own studies independently confirm this finding: the intuition that God is a personlike being with mental states and *believing in* God are highly related. An abstract, impersonal God is theologically possible, but psychologically not compelling.[10]

A third class of evidence more directly probes the brain networks that are recruited when people are thinking about God. If mental representations of God are rooted in ordinary mind perception, then the same brain networks that are involved when people think about the minds of other people should also become active when people think about the mind of God. Neuroimaging studies show exactly that: among Christian believers in the United States and in Denmark, thinking about or praying to God activates brain regions associated with ordinary mind perception.[11]

Fourth, the fact that mind perception abilities vary in the general population can give us clues about the origins of religious belief. Some people are much less versed in "mentalizing" than others. The extreme low end of this continuum overlaps with what is now understood as the autism spectrum. Autism spectrum disorders are complex and multifaceted. But one key characteristic is that individuals marked by this spectrum have more difficulty in *mind perception*—that is, recognizing emotions from faces, inferring beliefs and desires from overt actions, and telling the difference between the intended meaning of an utterance and its literal meaning.

If mind perception supports reasoning about God, then mind perception deficits should erode its cognitive foundations. Indeed, Kurt Gray and his colleagues showed that people who score high on the autism spectrum see God less as a personlike being with a mind of its own and more like an abstract, impersonal force. It is hard to be a devoted believer of God or other supernatural beings without having mentalizing capacities that enable one to interact with them. And it is hard to interact with gods without seeing them as agents with minds. In my own studies with Will Gervais and Kali Trzesniewski, this is exactly what we have found. Reduced mentalizing was associated with lower levels of belief in God, even after controlling for various factors that are related to religious belief. Mentalizing minds are prepared to be believing minds.[12]

These lines of evidence point to the same conclusion: contrary to some theological doctrines that cast God as an abstract universal force, *Ground of Being*,[13] or the totality of everything, in the everyday thinking of the faithful, God is perceived to be a personlike being with a mind. God "perception" piggybacks on mind perception. Mentalizing capacities enable believers to see God or gods as intentional agents with mental states, but these capacities do not fix the particular content matter of gods' minds. There is a great deal of room for cultural evolution to fill in this content, as long as the content doesn't stray too far from evolved human psychology. Historically and contemporarily, cultures differ in their conceptions of whether, and to what degree, gods know or care about human affairs, and importantly, if they do care, what particular domains of human activities they care about. As we shall see, one idea—Big, powerful, interventionist Gods—culturally spread at the expense of rival ideas because these types of gods could take on supernatural monitoring duties, allowing societies to expand their cooperative reach.

Under the Gaze of Watchful Eyes

We just saw that ordinary capacities for perceiving minds allow believers to make inferences about the mental states of supernatural beings. These inferences enable believers to respond and interact with their gods, and it is these mental capacities attributed to gods that make them potent supernatural monitors.

We are now ready to explore the first principle of Big Gods:

Watched people are nice people.

Our daily lives are replete with evidence of this basic principle. Drivers reduce their speed when they notice a police car in their rearview mirror.

When cameras and mirrors are installed in shopping malls, the temptation to steal is dampened. Politicians and corporations are less corrupt when they are held accountable to voters or to shareholders, respectively. There is less temptation to cheat the system when earnings and expense accounts of public servants and corporate bigwigs are made public. There is more generosity in the presence of others, prompting charities to raise money in public. When the donation box reaches you, and everyone is watching, what can you do?

This does not mean, of course, that people cannot be prosocial in the absence of such incentives. There is no shortage of acts of kindness in complete anonymity. In games of cooperation, contrary to economic predictions of purely self-interested actors, there is usually some residue of prosociality even when experimenters go to great pains to guarantee complete anonymity (this is sometimes called *strong reciprocity*).[14] While anonymity does not turn human beings into selfish psychopaths, there is also no question that social surveillance is a powerful and reliable mechanism to boost prosocial behavior.

A mountain of evidence in psychology and economics reveals how powerful social monitoring incentives are. Economic game experiments show that more people are prosocial and to a greater degree when the anonymity of the situation is undermined,[15] or when they expect repeated future interactions, than if future interactions are absent.[16] Experiments in social psychology have also shown that any cue that increases the feeling of being watched, such as exposure to cameras, mirrors, and audiences, increases prosocial tendencies, and those that encourage feelings of being hidden from view, such as ambient darkness or wearing dark glasses, license more selfishness and cheating.

In a series of clever experiments, Chenbo Zhong, Vanessa Bohns, and Francesca Gino created what they call "illusory anonymity," the false feeling of being hidden from view. Under the guise of testing a new product, they randomly assigned University of Toronto student participants to either wear dark sunglasses or clear eyeglasses. Then, in what appeared to be an unrelated task, participants were given $6 dollars and the opportunity to share any of that amount with an anonymous stranger. (This is the well-known one-shot Dictator Game, which I will describe in more detail later.) Results showed that clear eyeglass–wearing participants gave on average $2.71, whereas dark sunglass–wearing participants gave on average $1.81. This is a sizable difference, but this effect is interesting not because of its size. Wearing dark glasses did not merely reduce donations—it changed the norm for how to behave in this situation. That is, wearing clear glasses led to an *equal sharing* norm ($2.71 is statistically identical to $3—that is, splitting the amount evenly), whereas dark glasses induced a more selfish norm. Other experiments by Zhong and his colleagues found that being in a dim room led to greater rates of cheating than being in a well-lit room. As they put it, "a good lamp is the best police."[17]

Perhaps no social monitoring mechanism is as effective as a pair of eyes gazing at you. We use our eyes to monitor others; we are also wary of others' eyes monitoring us. In fact, detecting faces is so central to social life that there are functionally specialized brain networks, known as the *fusiform areas*, dedicated for this purpose.[18] The temptation to pay attention to eyes gazing at us is so rapid and automatic that people are unable to inhibit their responses to eyes even when instructed to do so.[19] Sensitivity to eyes appears to be an ancient evolutionary adaptation: it is found even in some birds and fish.[20] In group-living cultural species such as us humans, it has been exploited to its full extent for reputation monitoring, and conversely, for reputation protection. Does being watched by a pair of eyes make people nicer?

Kevin Haley and Dan Fessler put this idea to a strong test. They wanted to go beyond previous experiments on lack of anonymity and repeated interactions and show that even subtle cues of being watched are enough to elicit nice behavior. It should be possible to "trick" the powerful and automatic gaze detection mechanism by exposing people to drawings that mimic the presence of human gaze. In the first stage of their experiment, they covertly exposed some US participants to drawings of human eyes masquerading as an ordinary computer screensaver, while others in the control group saw a screensaver with no stimuli or irrelevant stimuli unrelated to eyes. Then in the second stage, which participants thought was an unrelated experiment, they played a version of the one-shot Dictator Game (similar to the one used by Zhong and colleagues, discussed earlier). In this game, everyone was given a certain amount of money and had the opportunity to transfer any portion of the money to a stranger who was unable to retaliate, and was kept anonymous from the participant. There was a 55 percent increase in generosity after exposure to human eyes.[21]

People are so sensitive to social monitoring that even schematic representations of eyes can change behavior in a more prosocial direction. This hypervigilance can be seen even when people are merely looking at three black dots arranged to look like a schematic face with eyes (in the form of an upside-down triangle standing on its pointed tip). Psychologist Mary Rigdon and her colleagues took advantage of the fact that such a configuration is known to weakly but consistently activate the face-recognition (or fusiform) area of the brain. They randomly assigned some of their US participants to look at this configuration, while other participants were randomly assigned to a control condition, where they also saw identical three black dots, but in a triangular configuration, which does not suggest a face or gazing eyes. All participants then played the Dictator Game. Despite being a very subtle social cue, exposure to a watching-eyes configuration tempered selfishness. Only 25 percent of participants who saw dots configured to look like a face gave nothing (the selfish strategy), whereas 40 percent of the control participants chose this strategy. This pattern was particularly pronounced among men, who sometimes play more selfishly than women.[22]

It is remarkable that in these experimental findings, people are merely exposed to eyes. There is no promise of reward, no threat of punishment. Just knowing that we are under surveillance is enough to motivate us to put our best foot forward. Thomas Jefferson was on to something when he said, "Whenever you do a thing, act as if all the world were watching."

Are people therefore less likely to cheat the system when they sense that someone is watching them? In one field study, researchers placed a self-service coffee stand in the hallway of a university building and an "honesty box." Passersby could avail themselves of some coffee, and leave money in the box. On some randomly assigned weeks, a poster with watchful human eyes was hanging above the stand; on other days, the poster showed various types of flowers. Despite the fact that consumption rates were similar across the two conditions, significantly more money was left on weeks when the poster with eyes was hanging on the wall. On average, people left 2.76 times as much money in the weeks with eyes. The feeling of being watched, even as subtle as posters of eyes on a wall, curbed cheating when no one was present to make sure the system works. Eyes on the wall did the job.[23]

If the most subtle of monitoring cues—such as dots arranged to look like schematic faces—can change social behavior, it is no surprise that the presence of actual human observers affects prosocial tendencies. The evidence is clear that various forms of social monitoring are a key factor in encouraging nice behavior among strangers. As we have seen earlier, people mentally represent supernatural monitors—gods and other supernatural beings—in ways that are strikingly similar (though certainly not identical) to the ways they think about monitoring human beings. Social monitoring is the precursor of supernatural monitoring, one of the key features of pro-social religions.

From Social to Supernatural Monitoring

We saw that social monitoring is a powerful motivator in prosocial interactions. But it can go only so far. It depends on the actual or implied presence of others; it also depends on keeping track of others' reputations, which is severely limited by group size. As the number of interactions increase, anonymity creeps back into the situation and reputational mechanisms break down. This is the key problem of large groups plagued by anonymity, and this is precisely why these large groups are always vulnerable to splintering or collapse unless additional processes arise to restore and maintain high levels of cooperation in these ever-larger groups. While social monitoring has ancient evolutionary roots and by all accounts predated religion, it came to serve as the basis of a supernatural solution to the problem of anonymity.

The trial-and-error processes of cultural evolution stumbled on *supernatural monitoring*, a principle that piggybacks on preexisting capacities for social monitoring. If watched people are nice people, watchful deities—Big Eyes in the Sky—could encourage cooperation, even when no one is watching. Being watched by morally involved agents—whether human or superhuman—is therefore one key reason why religion encourages cooperation. No need to postulate, then, a "God part of the brain." The same social intuitions that enable human social control also serve to realize supernatural surveillance. Recent social psychology experiments, discussed in the next chapter, support the idea that when God is on peoples' minds, there are greater levels of generosity, cooperation, and lower levels of cheating in anonymous contexts. Thoughts of God also make people feel monitored, precisely as one would expect if supernatural monitoring was at play.[24]

Big Eyes in the Sky

The supernatural agents of large societies around the world do double-duty as supernatural watchers, literally. Consider the following selection (see figure 2.1):

- The God of Abraham is endowed with extraordinary powers of observation. Everywhere in the Hebrew Bible, the New Testament, and the Koran, it is asserted that God sees everything, even and especially when no one is watching. A hallmark of devotion in these religious traditions is the belief that God is watching 24/7, and therefore no act, no matter how small or clandestine, can be hidden from Him.[25]
- Along with ubiquitous prayer flags, displayed everywhere in Buddhist villages in Tibet and Nepal are "Buddha Eyes" (see figure 2.1, panel b). They can also be found etched on *stupas*, sacred objects shaped like a column at the center of a circle, often found in monastic complexes, or at the center of towns and villages. Lord Buddha, also known as the "Eye of the World" in Buddhist scriptures, observes the comings and goings from high up. The eyes are believed to look in all four directions and reflect the omniscience of the Buddha.[26]
- One of the oldest and most significant deities in ancient Egypt was Horus, the sky god, also known as "Horus of Two Eyes." His head was often depicted as a falcon with sharp eyes, one representing the sun, the other, the moon. Some scholars think that the right eye was also known as the "Eye of Ra," although these could also have been separate deities. Horus or Ra watched over people in the towns and villages of Egypt, where intense cooperation was needed in one of the earliest agricultural civilizations.[27]
- One of the central and unifying deities of the Inca Empire was Viracocha (see figure 2.1, panel c). He was seen as the creator of mankind and civilization. Depicted as a tall man with a big bearded face and a

▶

Figure 2.1. (*facing page*) The God of Abrahamic religions is well known as a potent supernatural monitor, but watchful gods are widespread in prosocial religions. *Panel a*: Eye of Horus from ancient Egypt, late sixth to fourth centuries BCE (courtesy of Marie-Lan Nguyen). *Panel b*: Buddha Eyes on a stupa in Swayambhunath temple, Kathmandu, Nepal (courtesy of the author). *Panel c*: Stone carving of Viracocha, the chief God of the Inca Empire, from Tiahuanaco, Bolivia (Martin Gray/National Geographic Stock). *Panel d*: Eye in the Sky, an alchemical woodcut attributed to a European text from the sixteenth century. It is often depicted with the motto *Quo Modo Deum*, Latin for "This is the way of God" (courtesy of Rare Books Division, Department of Rare Books and Special Collection, Princeton University Library).

(a)

(b)

(c)

(d)

perceptive pair of eyes, he wore the sun for a crown, had thunderbolts in his hands, and had tears descending from his eyes as rain. Although the record of his abilities is fragmentary at best (he was supplanted by the Big God of the Catholic Spaniards, Dios), Viracocha was himself a Big God with powerful monitoring capacities.[28]

- The Kwaio people of the Solomon islands are preoccupied daily with the *adalo*, ancestor spirits who see and know what is going on in the villages, even events that are hidden from view. Anthropologist Roger Keesing reports that the Kwaio believe that the *adalo* want sacrifices, help those who follow social norms, and punish transgressors. Divination is typically used to know which spirits are angry and what could be done to appease them.[29]

It is easy to see how the idea of supernatural monitoring is rooted in the more ancient and mundane human preoccupation with social monitoring. If the notion of powerful and perceptive people watching is something people already intuitively accept, it is not a giant step from that notion to powerful and perceptive gods who see when no one else can. Nevertheless, omniscience that transcends physical, biological, and psychological limitations is a somewhat counterintuitive thought.

We saw earlier that experimental studies show that believers who say that God is omniscient nevertheless in their spontaneous retellings of God's various actions treat Him as if His powers of observations are subject to human limitations. Experimental studies also show that, despite scriptural prohibitions, the most devoted believers see God possessing human-like mental attributes such as beliefs, emotions, and intentions.[30] Like other counterintuitive ideas, this one too has to filter through evolved human psychology, sustained by repeated reminders that are reproduced by cultural practices and institutions. One such filter is the notion that God or gods are personlike beings—they transcend human mental and physical limitations, but only partly.[31]

Where does this leave Newton's or Einstein's God—an abstract, impersonal universal force? This abstract God is theologically correct and philosophically more palatable to educated tastes. But alas, this God has little psychological meaning or emotional power for most believers. Personlike supernatural beings are compelling as agents who monitor, respond, punish, and reward. People want a "personal" God who is involved in their lives, who can hear prayers, and who can offer forgiveness and mercy or dispense favors. It is no surprise that such a personal God attracts more passionate devotion than an abstract, impersonal God. Official theological doctrine in some religions like Judaism, Islam, and some branches of Protestantism prohibit any humanlike representations of God; nevertheless, in practice, the most passionate believers are the ones who are the most likely to personify God.[32]

Yet, a fully human god is no god either. Without some degree of omniscience and omnipotence, gods could not be potent supernatural monitors. The very point of supernatural monitoring is the outsourcing of social monitoring duties to gods so that moral concern can be extended writ large—to watch even when no one is watching, to care when no one cares, to threaten when no one can threaten. The more culturally successful Big Gods are, therefore, the ultimate balancing act between two competing psychological imperatives: one, these gods must exercise supernatural powers by transcending limitations that otherwise constrain human abilities to observe and morally intervene; two, these gods must also share enough properties of human mind perception to make them intuitively graspable and emotionally potent.

To be potent social monitors, supernatural watchers must satisfy another psychological imperative—the imperative of moral concern. As the anthropologist Pascal Boyer notes, although theologically speaking these beings are said to know and see anything and everything (hence "omniscient"), believers intuitively treat these gods as beings who are more likely to know some things than others—to use Pascal Boyer's term, these beings are "full access social strategic agents" who have privileged access specifically to behaviors that have moral consequences.[33] Believers seem to intuitively infer that gods know less about other, nonsocial facts that are morally irrelevant. In principle, God knows everything about Bill, but in the minds of believers, God knows more about whether Bill cheated on his wife than about what color socks Bill chose to put on this morning before going to work.

Benjamin Purzycki and his colleagues ran a clever experiment that demonstrates this. They had religious American students read a series of questions about God, one at a time, on a computer screen, and answer yes or no to the questions. Some questions had no moral relevance:

Does God know the recipe for Alice's cake?
Does God know how many carrots Barry ate?

Others had clear moral information about *good* deeds:

> Does God know that Ann gives to the homeless?
> Does God know that Frank is kind to children?

And finally, a third batch had moral information about *bad* deeds:

> Does God know that John cheats on his taxes?
> Does God know that Jen lied to her mother?

Obviously, believers in the all-knowing Abrahamic God would answer yes to all questions—the "theologically correct" answer. The researchers were interested, however, in how intuitive it is to think that God knows moral facts relative to nonmoral facts about people, and for moral facts, how intuitive it is to think that God cares about bad moral deeds relative to good moral deeds. One telltale sign of intuitiveness is the speed of response to a certain piece of information. Intuitive mental representations come to mind faster than representations that require conscious reflection and deliberation. Purzycki and colleagues found that participants overall—including those who specifically claimed that God is all knowing and all powerful—responded more quickly to moral than nonmoral questions, and moreover, they were even faster to answer questions about negative rather than positive moral behavior. It appears that believers intuitively treat God as a powerful and omniscient agent who is particularly interested in negative behaviors that have moral consequences for others, precisely what we would expect if God were a supernatural monitor who oversees cooperative and honest interactions among humans.[34]

God appears to be interested in misdeeds more than anything else, but does God care about thoughts about misdeeds? For example, does God judge you if you think about committing adultery, even if you don't act on the thought? In a now famous interview with *Playboy Magazine*, former US President Jimmy Carter said, "I've looked on a lot of women with lust. I've committed adultery in my heart many times."[35]

That, it turns out, depends on the type of your religious upbringing. Adam Cohen and Paul Rozin interviewed American Protestants and Jews about cases such as President Carter's, where individuals thought about committing a misdeed, such as adultery or neglecting one's elderly parents, but in the end didn't. They found Protestants were much harsher than Jews toward people thinking such thoughts. It seems that people raised in a Protestant culture are much more likely to moralize thoughts, and therefore more likely to assume that God judges not only acts, but thoughts as well.

Finally, a third feature of potent Big Gods is spatial position. These watchful, moralizing deities are more plausible and potent by being "high up," rather than "down below." Soaring cathedrals were built during the medieval Gothic era in Europe that encouraged the feeling of a powerful presence that descends from high up. When we talk about God, we say that God is watching us from above. Psalm 113:4 says, "The Lord is high over all nations, and his glory is higher than the heavens." Once again, this makes little theological sense. If God is omnipresent, which means He is everywhere, why would people think of God as being above us and not below?

Indeed, studies show that vertical position and thoughts of God go together in the minds of believers. In one study, psychologists showed participants words such as *God*, *Divine*, and *Lord*, either at the top or at the bottom of a computer screen. Participants recognized God faster when God was up, suggesting that believers intuitively see God as being high up. From the social engineering perspective of constructing cooperative societies, it is easy to see why gods who enjoy an elevated position are better cultural candidates to become supernatural watchers than "lower" gods who have obstructed views. From high up, they can more easily see what's going on "down below," in the realm of the mortals.[36]

The Origins of Supernatural Watchers in Cultural and Genetic Evolution

The scientific project of explaining religion can make great progress when we appreciate that the workings of human minds belong to cultural inheritance as much as to genetic inheritance. Belief in supernatural watchers is no exception. Devoted followers of prosocial religions rely on mental mechanisms that make gods an intuitive concept. But they also heavily lean on *cultural learning* mechanisms that enable particular cultural variants of religious beliefs and practices to rapidly propagate across minds.

Evolutionary explanations of religion have largely focused on universal building blocks, and certainly these re-occurring tendencies are extremely important. Yet, there is also vast cultural variability in religious beliefs and practices. This diversity is as important and consequential as the universal aspects.

In their landmark book *Not by Genes Alone*, Pete Richerson and Robert Boyd show how profoundly important the cultural inheritance system is for understanding the peculiarities of human evolution. As they explain, we human beings possess an evolved psychology that bundles together genetic adaptations with a sophisticated repertoire of genetically evolved cultural learning skills. These skills help us explain two key things: one, the fact that our species has managed to colonize the entire planet by adapting to radically different habitats in a timescale that is not even a mere second in evolutionary time; and two, the cultural features of these particular human groups that populated the globe favored the group's stability, survival, and expansion, at the expense of less successful rivals.[37] The story of how prosocial religious beliefs and practices got off the ground, and swiftly populated the earth, is part of this same logic, and is best understood as a joint product of both cultural and genetic evolution working in tandem.[38]

It is the iron law of Darwinian evolution that when there is variation and selective retention in any entity capable of some sort of replication (even if imperfect), traits that have fitness advantages will spread at the expense of their less fit rivals. This is the engine that drives genetic evolution. Analogously, in cultural evolution, there is variation in cultural traits, and there is selective retention (although typically there is transformation, rarely true replication).[39] Earlier, I explored how cognitive by-products of genetically evolved human brains encourage certain default intuitions, such as the feeling that minds can exist without bodies. Cultural evolution picks up on these default intuitions and works with them in a number of ways. Here, I briefly highlight how these cultural learning biases shape religious belief. These ideas are further elaborated throughout the book.

First, some variants of beliefs may spread at the expense of others if something about these beliefs has effects on human psychology that make them "contagious." Just as memorable or emotionally evocative ideas are more likely to spread, certain kinds of supernatural content are much more potent than others.[40] For example, research shows that supernatural concepts that mildly violate intuitive expectations we have about agents, life forms, and physical objects are more memorable in the long run than those that are wildly counterintuitive or completely intuitive. Surveying the kinds of gods and spirits one finds in the ethnographic record, Pascal Boyer observes that there is an infinitely large set of possible supernatural beliefs. Yet the actual supernatural beliefs we observe around the world are but a narrow subset of the possible set. (Boyer offers many amusing examples that are not good divine candidates, such as: There is only one God! He is omnipotent. But He exists only on Wednesdays!) Existing beliefs correspond to a few basic templates that are specific to how we intuitively think about agents, living things, and inert objects:

> There is only a rather short Catalogue of Supernatural Templates that more or less exhausts the range of culturally successful concepts in this domain. Persons can be represented as having counterintuitive physical properties (e.g., ghosts or gods), counterintuitive biology (many gods who neither grow or die), or counterintuitive psychological properties (unblocked perception or prescience). Animals too can have these properties. Tools and other artifacts can be represented as having biological properties (some statues bleed) or psychological ones (they hear what you say). Browsing through volumes of mythology, fantastic tales, anecdotes, cartoons, religious writings and science fiction, you will get an extraordinary variety of different concepts, but you will also find that the number of templates is very limited.[41]

Second, some variants of beliefs travel well not only because of their potent content but also because of the features of the cultural models who happen to endorse the beliefs. Setting aside the content of what to believe, when in doubt, people typically turn to the majority opinion ("when in Rome, do as the Romans do"). People also care deeply about what the prestigious or successful individuals in their local societies believe, and often selectively adopt beliefs or behaviors from these potent cultural models. Religious beliefs and behaviors are no exception to this general principle: supernatural watchers get a big boost in the cultural marketplace if they are already endorsed by (1) the majority opinion, and (2) the high-status opinion-makers in a group.[42]

A third reason why beliefs in supernatural watchers can be culturally contagious is when they are tied to extravagant behaviors that convince observers of the sincerity of the believer. The anthropologist Joseph Henrich has pointed out that cultural learners face a dilemma: on one hand, other people are a valuable source of fitness-enhancing information, which is why we are cultural animals in the first place; on the other hand, there is what psychologist Maciek Chudek calls the "evil teacher" problem—the possibility that cultural models would manipulate, mislead, or exploit learners by saying one thing but believing another. To avoid being duped, evolution has endowed cultural learners with a set of strategies that makes us pay attention to cues that a cultural model is actually committed to the beliefs he or she advertises. As Dan Sperber and his colleagues put it, there are strong reasons to suspect that *epistemic vigilance* is an important aspect of human psychology. One such strategy is for learners to pay attention to whether models engage in behaviors that would be costly if opposing beliefs were held. If so, learners can be more confident that the model actually holds the belief, and as a result they would be more likely to adopt the belief from the model. These credible displays address the problem of faking belief because "actions speak louder than words."[43] Related to, but distinct from this strategy, is the possibility that some religious behaviors serve as "costly signals." Anthropologist Richard Sosis and his colleagues explain that if religious groups are cooperative groups, and if religiosity serves as a signal for commitment to the group, then hard-to-fake costly rituals and restrictions on behavior may also ensure that freeriders could not undermine these cooperative communities. (I will discuss and critique these arguments in more detail in chapter 6.)[44]

There is no need, then, to postulate any special brain mechanisms exclusively dedicated to belief in gods. Nor is there any necessary partitioning between "cultural" and "religious" mental representations. The ordinary workings of human minds produce a constrained but diverse set of beliefs, some of which we may call "supernatural" because they rupture intuitive expectations about basic categories of existence. Cultural learning strategies shape, modify, and elaborate innate default intuitions. Both cultural learning and innate defaults are key to understanding how ideas of supernatural watchers are transmitted and stabilized, and each tells us something about which features of these beliefs are widespread, and which are culturally variable. How one such cultural variant—supernatural watchers, or the Big Gods of prosocial religions—create cooperation among strangers is the topic of the next chapter.

Chapter 3
Pressure from Above

How exactly do supernatural watchers encourage generosity, cooperation, and honesty? Under what conditions does supernatural monitoring work? And for whom does it work? In this chapter, I answer these
questions in three related parts.[1] First, does supernatural monitoring cause
generous and honest behavior? Second, are believers influenced by their
sense that they are under supernatural surveillance? Finally, how do nonbelievers respond to reminders of supernatural surveillance?

When people of varying religious conviction are surveyed, those who
frequently pray and attend religious services report doing more prosocial
acts—volunteering more and giving more to charity—than less religious
people. However, these findings should be taken with a grain of salt, because
they are vulnerable to myriad methodological problems.[2] A better way to
answer these questions would be to rely on the gold standard of the scientific method: we could get conclusive answers if we designed experiments in
which people are randomly assigned to "religion" or to a control condition,
and then measure actual prosocial behavior in controlled conditions. While
for obvious reasons we cannot randomly assign people to either believe in
God or believe in nothing, or join a religion versus join a tennis club, there
is a simpler strategy: we can prod people to temporarily think about God or
about something else that is unrelated to God or religion. Then we could look
at the effects of thinking about God on various behaviors of interest.

The logic of such experiments would be straightforward: if religious
thinking causes prosocial tendencies, then experimentally induced thoughts

of God should increase prosocial behavior in anonymous situations. Two kinds of evidence support this conclusion. First, religious reminders, or *primes*, decrease the temptation to cheat. Second, such religious primes also increase a host of prosocial tendencies, such as generosity, fairness, cooperation, and the willingness to punish noncooperators while incurring a cost to oneself. Later I explore the question as to whether these religious reminders have effects on nonbelievers.

In a typical cheating study, subjects are seated in front of a computer and given a typically tedious task such as difficult arithmetic problems or an obscure general knowledge test. Subjects could win a reward (typically money) for every correct answer or if they achieve a certain overall score. Cheating can be measured in one of several ways. In the "rigged computer" paradigm, subjects are told that they will occasionally see the correct answer to some of the problems due to a computer malfunction. They are instructed to press a certain button to avoid seeing the answer. Dishonesty is measured as the frequency of instances that participants fail to press this button. In another paradigm, participants take a paper-and-pencil test and are randomly assigned to one of two conditions: in the "cheating" condition, an honor system is implemented where participants turn in their answers after recording the percentage of correct responses. In the "no-cheating" condition, the experimenter verifies the number of correct answers in person. Cheating is thought to occur to the extent that the percentage of correct answers is reliably higher in the condition where subjects have an opportunity to cheat. In such experiments, opportunities are created to cheat; there are many reasons and motivations to refrain from cheating. The question is: all else being equal, do thoughts of supernatural monitors curb cheating?

In one experimental study of cheating, Jared Piazza, Jesse Bering, and Gordon Ingram instructed children not to look inside a box, and then left them alone in the room with it. Those who were previously told that a fictional supernatural agent, Princess Alice, was watching were significantly less likely to peek inside the forbidden box. Another related study found a similar effect among university students. Participants who were randomly assigned to a condition in which they were casually told that the ghost of a dead student had been spotted in the experimental room cheated less on a rigged computer task.[3]

A different study replicated this effect—but this time participants were subliminally reminded of God. In an experiment by psychologists Brandon Randolph-Seng and Michael Nielsen, participants saw words that are synonymous with God, or other neutral words, flashed in under 100 milliseconds—long enough to register in the mind, but too short for any conscious awareness. Then they were given a task where there was ample opportunity to cheat. In this task, participants are instructed to write specific numbers in small circles while alone in a room with their eyes closed. The temptation to cheat is high, as they can receive additional extra credit for high scores. Those who saw the God-related words prior to the task cheated less than those who were exposed to the neutral words. In the control condition of this study, religiosity as an individual difference measure did not predict levels of cheating.[4] In another study, researchers gave student participants at MIT a 50-item multiple-choice general knowledge test. Subjects could win money for every correct answer. Prior to this test, some participants were randomly assigned to have ample opportunity to cheat, whereas others were not given such opportunity. Some participants were randomly assigned to recall the Ten Commandments, and others (in the control condition) were asked to recall ten books they had read. When participants could cheat, cheating rates increased. However, this rate was completely eliminated in the religious reminder condition. Reminding MIT students of the Ten Commandments was as effective a deterrent as reminding them of MIT's honor code prior to the test (except that, unbeknownst to the students, MIT apparently has no honor code!).[5]

I argued in chapter 1 that the concept of Big Gods stabilized cooperation levels in large groups of anonymous individuals, where reputational and reciprocity incentives are insufficient. If so, then reminders of God may not only reduce cheating, but they may also curb selfish behavior and increase generosity toward strangers. Azim Shariff and I looked at this question by making use of economic games, one of the scientific "gold standards" for the study of generosity and cooperation. We recruited participants in Vancouver, Canada, and under the pretext of playing word games, we planted thoughts of God (*divine, God, spirit*) in some of them without their conscious awareness. Other participants played the same word game without religious content. A third group of participants were randomly assigned to play the exact same word game, but with words such as *civic, jury,* and *police*—thereby priming them with thoughts of secular moral authority. Then all participants took part in the so-called Dictator Game, in which each participant could act like a dictator and could choose to share any portion of $10 with an anonymous stranger. They were reassured that their decision would remain confidential, and they would not meet this anonymous stranger, minimizing any concerns about disapproval or retaliation. This widely used procedure ensures a "pure" measure of participants' generosity that is not influenced by any reciprocity incentives. It is as close to a situation as one can get, where "no one is watching." Do participants act differently if they think, unconsciously, "God is watching?" The results showed that they did:

- Givers with God on their minds offered nearly double the money compared to givers who saw neutral words prior to making their decision.
- The results showed not only a quantitative increase in generosity, but also a qualitative shift in norms. In the control group, the most common response was purely selfish: the typical player pocketed all ten dollars. In the God group, the norm shifted to fairness: a plurality of participants split the money evenly.
- The group that was primed with secular moral authority also showed greater generosity than the control group—in fact, as much as was found in the God group. As we shall explore elsewhere in this book, this is an important finding that shows that Big Gods are not the only source of prosocial behavior—secular mechanisms, if they are available and are trusted, can also make people prosocial.
- Participants' self-reports about their belief in God, or religiosity levels, were unrelated to how much they offered to the anonymous recipient. This nonresult has been found in most of the experiments reported here. Therefore, contrary to the sociological findings, there was little evidence of an intrinsic prosociality on the part of believers.

In another instructive study, Ryan McKay and his colleagues went further and probed whether thoughts of God, flashed subliminally, would affect another prosocial tendency that is an important feature of prosocial religious groups: the willingness to punish the unfair behavior of others even at a cost to oneself. Swiss participants played an economic game where they were offered a certain amount of money, which they could either keep or offer to others. They found that when religious participants were given the opportunity to punish others who were playing selfishly, religious reminders increased the willingness to punish these freeriders while incurring a monetary cost. This finding is important: it implies that members of prosocial religions are willing to pay a cost to punish noncooperators. This gives us one important mechanism by which fairness norms can be stabilized in large anonymous groups.[6]

The Sunday Effect

These experiments are important because they allow us to carefully isolate the variables of interest and measure their effects, holding other factors constant. They are, however, limited in the sense that they do not reflect, in a direct way, what occurs in the real world. It is important, therefore, to combine insights from the lab with field studies, despite the fact that field studies lack the rigor of the experiments. So are there real-life counterparts to these laboratory experiments? In the United States and other majority Christian countries, once a week on Sundays, many Christians naturally expose themselves to a high dose of religious priming. Do Christians behave better on Sundays?

In a field study, Deepak Malhotra looked at the willingness of people to respond to online appeals to bid for charitable causes over an eight-week period. (These were charities unrelated to religion or churches.) Participants received the following message: "We hope you will continue to support this charity by keeping the bidding alive. Every extra dollar you bid in the auction helps us accomplish our very important mission." The question was, would Christians respond to charity appeals more on Sundays than on other days of the week? The answer was a clear yes. On Sundays, appeals to charity were over 300 percent more effective for religious Christian individuals compared to nonreligious individuals. That's a whopping difference that should attract the attention of charitable organizations. But wait, on any other days of the week, religious and nonreligious individuals were absolutely no different—they responded to such appeals at similar levels. And it was clear that this Sunday Effect was specific to charitable giving. When the appeals were not to charitability, but to competitiveness—"The competition is heating up! If you hope to win, you will have to bid again. Are you up for the challenge?"—the Sunday Effect disappeared.

What about avoiding sin? One study by Benjamin Edelman compared Internet porn consumption rates in highly religious and not-so-religious

US states. One might expect that, availing oneself of adult entertainment—of all things—would clearly distinguish religious and nonreligious folks. It may come as a surprise that, once a number of demographic factors were statistically controlled, religious and nonreligious states did not differ. On average, states that teemed with regular churchgoers had no fewer porn subscribers than those with few churchgoers. However, what Edelman found next gives the age-old practice of sinning a new twist: porn consumption rates in religious states followed a particular ebb and flow: the rates went down on Sundays, only to go up again on other days of the week. On average, regular churchgoers consumed similar amounts of porn as others; however, they abstained more on Sundays and shifted their porn consumption to other days of the week.

On Sundays, then, religious folks are more charitable and less likely to indulge in sin. But why do Sundays evoke such good behavior? Will Gervais and I wondered whether these intriguing Sunday Effects are partly caused by greater levels of supernatural surveillance. We reasoned that Christians may be more charitable and less sinful on Sundays, because of all the days of the week, Sundays in particular are when thoughts of God are most likely to come to mind. This in turn would provoke greater feelings of being watched on Sundays, but not on other days. We asked Christian and nonreligious participants to complete a measure of "public self-awareness" throughout the week, over a period of several weeks. Participants had no clue that this was a study about religion. They completed an instrument that measures feelings of being under social surveillance. They expressed agreement with statements such as: "Right now I am self-conscious about the way I look," and "Right now I am concerned about what other people think of me." On average, Christians and nonbelievers did not differ in public self-awareness. On any day of the week except Sunday, there were no differences. However, on Sunday, and Sunday only, Christians expressed greater feelings of being watched compared to nonbelievers, and compared to other Christians who completed these questions on other days. This pattern of results mimics exactly the Sunday Effects found for charitability and for porn consumption. Importantly, this effect was not simply due to Christians attending church on Sundays. Even when we matched participants on frequency of church attendance, there was a greater tendency to feel watched on Sundays.[7]

At first glance, the idea that religious reminders decrease dishonesty and increase generosity, cooperation, and costly or altruistic punishment seems somewhat strange. Shouldn't believers *always* be more generous and cooperative than their nonbelieving counterparts? If Big Gods are omniscient and monitor people 24/7, why are religious people not acting according to their religious beliefs even without such reminders?

This question brings us to the second principle of Big Gods:

Religion is more in the situation than in the person.

The key to this puzzle can be found in the everyday workings (and failings) of the human mind. Even though God is omniscient and watches people 24/7, people aren't thinking of Him 24/7. Believers have to think of God and His omniscience at any given moment if that belief is to have an impact on their actions. From a psychological perspective, there is little reason to expect a wholesale, unconditional association between religion and prosociality. This is not an issue unique to religion; it is true for most other attitudes or values that people hold dear. For example, there is no reason to expect that individuals who are sincerely committed to protecting the environment will always recycle or pay a cost to avoid polluting the air.

One of the celebrated founders of social psychology, Kurt Lewin, famously argued that to understand human behavior, we must imagine that behavior is embedded in a social "field." There are multiple forces shaping this field and competing to influence an individual's mind. These forces, whether value, goal, motivation, or cultural norm, impact behavior in complex but predictable ways. Not all of these forces will be equally likely to influence behavior at any given moment, however. Which force takes precedence over others depends on many things, but one crucial factor is whether or not a given force has a *cognitive advantage* in that moment, trumping the others.[8] The question therefore is not whether people hold the belief that it is wrong to behave dishonestly or hold the conviction that it is normative to be generous, but rather whether they think of those social standards *at the moment* they are tempted to behave dishonestly or selfishly. This insight about human behavior clashes with deeply held everyday intuitions; people tend to think of these behaviors as a reliable reflection of personality dispositions. There is a term for this flawed intuition, of course—social psychologists call it the *fundamental attribution error*.[9]

Religiously motivated behavior is no exception. For believers, religious motivations have to compete with other goals and values at any given moment, and religion will have an impact on behavior only when it becomes a *salient norm*, coming into awareness at that moment at the expense of other priorities. In other words, unless a believer is thinking religious thoughts every moment of her waking life, awareness of a watchful God is merely one of many competing imperatives that might influence an action at any given moment. Something in the situation must prompt believers to act according to their religious beliefs.

Two notable field experiments, one done in a Muslim context in Morocco, the other among Hindus in Mauritius, illustrate how important the salience of religious situations is relative to religious dispositions. Erik Duhaime approached shopkeepers in Marrakech, Morocco, and asked them to choose one of the following three options: (1) I give you 20 dirhams (about $2.50); (2) I give charity 60 dirhams; or (3) I give you 10 dirhams and charity 30 dirhams. (This is yet another version of the Dictator Game, discussed earlier.) Critically, sometimes he approached them during the Muslim call to prayer, sometimes not. When the call to prayer was being sounded out from minarets throughout the city, 100 percent of the shopkeepers chose option 2, the most charitable option, compared to only around 60 percent of shopkeepers when he asked at times when the call to prayer was not audible.[10] In another field experiment, Dimitris Xygalatas went further and compared the relative effects of religious situations and religious dispositions on selfish behavior. He randomly assigned Hindu participants in Mauritius to play an economic game either in a religious setting (a temple) or in a comparable secular setting (a restaurant). Participants were given the opportunity to withdraw from a shared pool of money that otherwise would benefit the entire group. He found that participants who played the game in the temple withdrew 170 rupees, compared to 231 rupees on average when playing in the restaurant. Prior to the field experiment, participants had rated their intensity of religiosity. How religiously involved participants said they were had little bearing on how much money they withdrew from the shared pool—only the situation where they played mattered.[11]

When faced with the decision to be selfish or generous, one could be motivated by compassion, greed, need, or guilt. If awareness at the moment of temptation determines honesty and generosity, religious reminders should come to the mind's fore and reduce deception and selfishness. This is exactly what is consistently found across many studies, in the laboratory or in the field. And this is exactly why prosocial religious groups surround their members with constant religious reminders to induce honesty and cooperation within the group.

Findings from field studies, such as the Marrakech and Mauritius experiments, and the variety of Sunday Effects found in charitable donations, access to adult entertainment, and in reported feelings of being watched, are remarkably in agreement with the laboratory findings on religious priming. The temporary salience of religious norms is a key driver of prosocial behavior, often more important than "religiosity." This is a key insight to which I will return toward the end of this chapter, along with another question: are nonbelievers responsive to religious priming effects? But first, I explore in more depth the question of what psychological mechanisms link religion with prosocial behavior—in other words, why exactly do religious reminders increase prosocial behaviors, and how do we know that supernatural monitoring is a key part of this link?

Anatomy of Supernatural Monitoring

The experimental studies reviewed earlier, as well as the Sunday Effect studies, indicate that temporary reminders of God increase generosity, cooperation, and costly punishment of selfishness, and decrease the temptation to cheat. I have argued that supernatural monitoring is one critical explanation. To the extent that thoughts of watchful gods weigh on the mind, people feel monitored, and as a result, behave more nicely toward strangers even when the situation is objectively anonymous. However, there is a different explanation that must be dealt with: the *ideomotor* account. These two accounts are not incompatible (both could be true), but they are distinguishable accounts. Here, I discuss the evidence for the supernatural monitoring explanation and compare it to the ideomotor account.

According to ideomotor explanations of behavior, unconsciously primed concepts or stereotypes increase the likelihood of behaviors that correspond to these concepts. Thinking a thought makes us more likely to do something consistent with it, and indeed, there are hundreds of studies in psychology that demonstrate such ideomotor effects. In one classic study, for example, young participants were unconsciously primed with an "elderly" stereotype (words such as *Bingo, Florida, retirement*). Then researchers covertly observed the participants leaving the lab. Participants who thought of the elderly stereotype walked more slowly than those who were exposed to neutral words! In another study, priming "rudeness" (*rude, impolite, impatient*), again without conscious awareness, increased the likelihood that participants would interrupt a conversation. This account therefore says that perhaps nonconscious altruistic thoughts increase prosocial behavior because thoughts of God are associated with notions of benevolence, charity, and honesty, and therefore activating these thoughts automatically activates behaviors consistent with these prosocial thoughts.

So how can we distinguish the supernatural watcher account from ideomotor processes? There are several test cases. First, if God primes disentangle the felt presence of supernatural watchers from their alleged prosocial consequences, then these effects could not be solely the result of ideomotor processes. For example, if the supernatural watcher explanation is at play, religious primes should arouse feelings of external authorship, as well as perceptions of being under social surveillance, independent of any prosocial behavior. Second, if religious priming effects are weaker or nonexistent for nonbelievers, then the effect could not be solely due to ideomotor processes, which are typically insensitive to prior explicit beliefs or attitudes. (For example, the elderly stereotype prime slows down walking speed regardless of the age of the participants; rudeness primes increase rude behavior irrespective of how high or low participants score on politeness as a personality trait.) And third, and most importantly, these two types of explanations diverge about their predictions about what kinds of deities most strongly evoke prosocial tendencies. Ideomotor explanations predict that benevolent and kind Gods more clearly fit the prosocial stereotype that presumably causes greater prosocial behavior. In contrast, supernatural monitoring explanations predict that vengeful and punishing Gods make more potent supernatural monitors, and are therefore more likely to encourage nice behavior.

Now, let us look at evidence for each of these three possibilities. First, several experiments clearly separate the felt presence of a watchful supernatural agent from prosocial outcomes. The study by Ap Dijksterhuis and his colleagues, discussed earlier, found that after being subliminally primed with the word *God*, believers (but not nonbelievers) were more likely to ascribe an outcome to an external source of agency, rather than their own actions. Similarly, in a series of experiments I conducted with Will Gervais, we found that the same religious priming instrument that increases generosity in economic games also increased feelings of being watched or monitored, but again primarily for believers. (This is the same measure discussed earlier, that showed a Sunday Effect.)[12]

Second, while we ponder the question of whether atheism can penetrate deep into the human psyche,[13] it will become clear that, as described later in some detail, at least *some* atheists are unresponsive to nonconscious religious primes. This speaks against an ideomotor account, because everyone, including nonbelievers, is aware of (though does not necessarily endorse) the association between religious concepts and benevolence. Therefore, if ideomotor processes are all that is needed to get these effects, awareness should be sufficient to trigger priming effects. Yet some nonbelievers are impervious to priming effects. Other factors must be operating, and the most likely alternative possibility, as we have seen, is supernatural monitoring.

Supernatural Carrots and Sticks

The third piece of evidence supporting supernatural monitoring deserves deeper discussion, because it has wide-ranging implications for human behavior and society. This evidence takes into account the fact that believers have different, and often fluctuating, opinions about supernatural punishment and rewards. This is also reflected in conflicting scriptural claims about God's temperament. Consider, for example, this excerpt from James 3:17:

> But the wisdom that comes from heaven is first of all pure; then peace-loving, considerate, submissive, full of mercy and good fruit, impartial and sincere.

Contrast that kind, compassionate God with Deuteronomy 29:20:

> The Lord will never be willing to forgive him; his wrath and zeal will burn against that man. All the curses written in this book will fall upon him and then the Lord will blot out his name under heaven.

The critical question, then, is, does the notion of a kind, forgiving, God make people kind, forgiving, honest, and cooperative, as ideomotor explanations would suggest? Or is a wrathful, punishing God a more effective deterrent of bad behavior, as a supernatural monitoring account would predict?

This question brings us to the third principle of Big Gods:

Hell is stronger than heaven.

In a pair of studies, Azim Shariff and I set out to find the answer. We first measured the degree to which University of British Columbia students believe God is kind, compassionate, and forgiving or mean, wrathful, and punishing. It turns out that these two perceptions are moderately inversely related, meaning that the more one believes God is mean, the less one also believes God is kind. (This contradicts theological teachings that may prescribe both kinds of attributes to God simultaneously, but we have seen again and again that people are not theologians.) Days after participants rated God on these characteristics, we invited them to take part in an apparently unrelated study, in which the same participants took a rigged math test on a computer, where they had opportunities to cheat while alone in a room. In reality, the computer covertly recorded the amount of cheating. While religious belief itself was unrelated to cheating—believers and non-believers were equally likely to cheat or not cheat—among believers, mean-God supporters were much less likely to cheat than nice-God supporters. In short, we found in the lab what cultural evolution stumbled on and exploited for thousands of years: mean gods make good people.[14]

Amber DeBono, Azim Shariff, and Mark Muraven took a further step, and temporarily altered how positively or negatively people view God, then measured their willingness to steal when no one was looking. Some Christian participants were randomly assigned to read and write about how forgiving God is. Other Christian participants were randomly assigned to read and write about how punishing God is. Those in the Forgiving God condition read the preceding excerpt from James 3:17, then answered questions about it. In the Punishing God condition, participants read and answered questions about the excerpt from Deuteronomy 29:20 described earlier. Subsequently, participants were invited to take part in a seemingly different study, in which they were given anagrams to solve and told that they could pay themselves $1 for each solved anagram. Unbeknownst to the participants, however, only five of the ten anagrams had solutions. The experimenter then left the room, telling the participant that he or she could leave when the 15-minute timer rang, and keep all the money that was earned. How much participants paid themselves for unsolvable anagrams served as the critical measure of cheating. While the number of (genuinely solvable) anagrams solved did not significantly differ between conditions, and even though participants, when asked explicitly, denied stealing, the Punishing God group stole on average less than the Forgiving God group. Apparently, a punishing God keeps people in line. A kind and forgiving God, arguably, may have the opposite effect—it might encourage moral licensing to behave badly. (After all, why resist temptation if one would be forgiven by the kind and compassionate Almighty?)

There is more evidence that the action is in the fear of supernatural punishment. The promise of supernatural benevolence, if anything, backfires as a tool to curb antisocial behavior. Kristin Laurin, Azim Shariff, Joseph Henrich, and Aaron Kay looked at the effects of temporary religious reminders as well as religious belief on the tendency to punish freeloaders at a personal cost. When people witness someone violate a cooperative norm, do reminders of God make them more willing to pay a cost to punish a freeloader? Or do these reminders have the opposite effect? Their results are noteworthy in several respects. First, they found that the effects of reminders of God were specific to believers only, once again suggesting that many nonbelievers are immune to religious priming. Second, they found, like Ryan McKay and his colleagues in another study, that believers in God were indeed more likely to punish, especially when they were reminded of their religious belief. So far, so good, but what about those believers who are convinced that God is punitive? Contrary to an ideomotor interpretation, those believers in a punitive God punished *less*. In essence, those participants saw an opportunity to offload punishing duties to God. They who thought God, not people, is responsible for punishing norm-violators, punished less. In short, it appears that belief in divine punishment diminished the motivation for earthly forms of costly punishment.[15]

Mean gods also appear to make people kinder neighbors. Given these experimental findings, Azim Shariff and Mijke Rhemtulla wondered whether belief in hell (supernatural punishment) and belief in heaven (supernatural benevolence) have different consequences for a nation's crime rates. They compared national rates of various crimes, such as burglary, homicide, rape, and human trafficking across countries. They then looked at the percentage of the population that believes in heaven, hell, and God. They found that, all else being equal, countries with high percentage of believers in God had lower crime rates. But what kind of God people believe in was ultimately more consequential than whether or not they believed in God. Nations with the highest levels of belief in hell and the lowest levels of belief in heaven had the lowest crime rates. In contrast, nations that privileged heaven over hell were champions of crime. These patterns persisted across nearly all major religious faiths, including various Christian, Hindu, and syncretic religions that are a blend of several belief systems.

So why heaven, then? Azim Shariff explains:

> Because though Hell might be better at getting people to be good, Heaven is much better at making them feel good. So long as societies can find other ways of getting people to stay in line, then religions no longer have to shoulder that burden and they are free to drift towards the luxury of giving the individuals what they want. And if you're looking to gain converts, it's much easier to sell a religion that promises a divine paradise after death than one that threatens believers with fire and brimstone.[16]

Now, these are correlational findings, so one must be careful with inferring causation. However, Shariff and Rhemtulla were careful to consider and rule out a number of obvious alternative explanations. Their results held after statistically eliminating socioeconomic variables known to be related to criminal behavior or religiosity, such as a nation's gross domestic product, the level of economic inequality, and a nation's predominant religious denomination.[17] These findings, together with the experimental results described earlier, are difficult to reconcile with an account that is solely driven by ideomotor processes, which presumably would lead to the opposite expectation. A benevolent and kind God would more clearly fit the prosocial stereotype that should cause greater prosocial behavior and less antisocial behavior, and that reminders of a benevolent God would reduce punishing behavior. Yet we find the exact opposite pattern, which is more consistent with a supernatural punishment explanation.

Finally, these results speak to the more basic question of the origins of the relationship between religion and cooperation. Whereas the ideomotor hypothesis posits that the link between religion and prosociality is the *consequence* of a cultural association, the supernatural monitoring hypothesis speaks to the more basic question of why religion might *cause* large-scale anonymous prosociality in the first place. If people are less prone to selfishly cheat the system when they feel watched, then beliefs in moralizing gods, who can monitor social interactions even when no humans are watching, may have been instrumental in promoting large-scale human cooperation. Once these supernatural monitors culturally spread in human populations, and practices and institutions were built to promote them, repeated activation of thoughts related to them would have led to the habitual and unconscious cognitive associations between these thoughts and prosocial behaviors, exactly as predicted by the ideomotor hypothesis. Therefore, it is more plausible that ideomotor associations between God and prosociality were the consequence of belief in supernatural monitoring, rather than being a cause. The association of "God" with "charity" and "benevolence" makes sense primarily in light of God or gods as supernatural monitors who are morally involved in human affairs.[18]

Are Atheists Responsive to Reminders of Supernatural Monitoring?

Thus far, I have said little about religiosity defined as a person's self-reported involvement in religion. When I did consider it, it was to allude to two facts: (1) that at least some atheists (people who report having no belief in God) do not respond to nonconscious religious primes; and (2) what people say about their religious involvement is much less relevant in predicting social behavior than religious priming or religious salience is. It is now time to explore these two issues in more depth.

Are atheists and nonbelievers in general responsive to religious priming? The answer to this question gives us one important clue in helping us understand the psychological roots of atheism. Although it is a simple question, the answer is complex. To answer this question, we need to consult studies that satisfy three criteria. First, religious priming must bypass conscious awareness. Otherwise, atheists, who by definition do not consciously believe in gods, would be unresponsive to reminders of such belief. Second, research participants' religious beliefs or lack thereof should be measured independent of the priming procedure. This seems obvious, but regrettably, in several studies researchers have failed to establish the prevalence of nonbelief in their samples. Third, measures that are known to be responsive to religious priming (such as cooperativeness, or feelings of being watched) should be used.

Using these three criteria, we find that nonconscious religious primes have reliable effects on believers. Interestingly, the results are mixed when it comes to nonbelievers. Some studies find priming effects for nonbelievers, while others do not. However, close examination of the findings betrays a revealing pattern. Most, but not all, studies that satisfy the preceding criteria recruited student samples, which can be problematic since beliefs, attitudes, and social identity among students can be unstable, raising questions about the reliability of measures of religious belief and identity for students who are still in transition to adulthood. In short, student atheists might be "soft atheists." This is especially true for student participants in North America, where being a nonbeliever is counternormative. It is important to distinguish between such "soft atheists" or nonbelievers, and "hard atheists," who are strongly committed to nonbelief. However, studies often fail to distinguish between these two variants of nonbelief.

Therefore, using more stringent criteria for atheism, it appears that nonconscious religious priming does not have effects on at least some atheists. For example, in the priming study discussed earlier, we have found that adult nonstudent nonbelievers in Canada, who were much more certain about their disbelief than typical student samples, did not show the priming effect on generosity in the Dictator Game, although believers did. Dijksterhuis, Preston, Wegner, and Aarts conducted a religious priming study in the Netherlands, which, unlike the United States or Canada, is one of the world's least religious societies. They found that after being subliminally primed with the word *God*, Dutch student believers were more likely to see external agency behind an outcome that could have been the result of their own actions. Critically, they found no such effects for the Dutch atheists. In my own work with Will Gervais, we have found that implicit priming of God concepts increased the feeling of being under social surveillance for Canadian believers in Vancouver. However, the effect was unreliable for nonbelievers. Notably, Vancouver, like the Netherlands, has one of the least religious populations in North America. The findings of Kristin Laurin and her colleagues, discussed earlier, also showed a similar pattern. Working in Canada, they also found no effect of religious priming on altruistic punishment for nonbelievers. While this question currently remains open to debate, there is a growing number of hints pointing to the possibility that there might be different psychological profiles of nonbelievers. What distinguishes between "soft" and "hard" atheists? And are there distinct psychological origins to atheism, as there are to religion? I will return to these questions later, and offer some answers when I explore the rise of secular societies in chapter 10.

Does "Religiosity" Matter?

I now turn to another big question—whether or not religious belief as a reflection of an individual's self-description helps us predict prosocial behavior. While self-reported theism or atheism seems to affect who responds to religious reminders, this same variable produces mixed results in predicting prosocial behavior more generally. Most of the religious priming experiments reported earlier failed to find any effects of self-reported belief in God. These null results are not new. In the classic "Good Samaritan" study, for example, social psychologists John Darley and Dan Batson staged an anonymous situation modeled after the biblical parable—a man was lying on a sidewalk appearing sick and in need of assistance. Participants were students at the Princeton Theological Seminary who were in religious training, but nevertheless scored differently on several distinct dimensions of religious commitment. They were led past this victim (actually a research confederate) on their way to complete their participation in a study. Their likelihood of offering help to the victim was unobtrusively recorded. Results showed no relationship between dimension or degree of religiosity and helping in this anonymous context. Only a situational variable—whether participants were told to rush or take their time—led to reliable differences in helping rates.[19] In other experiments, Batson and his colleagues found that religiosity did not make people nicer in general; religious people acted more kindly toward strangers only when there was an opportunity to look good.[20]

Other studies, however, have found reliable associations between various indicators of religiosity and prosociality, albeit under limited conditions. In one study led by Richard Sosis, participants played a "public goods" game, which allowed researchers to compare levels of cooperation between secular and religious kibbutzim in Israel. In this cooperation game, two members of the same kibbutz who remained anonymous to each other were given access to a public good—an envelope with a certain amount of money. Each participant simultaneously decided how much money to withdraw from the envelope and keep for themselves. If the sum of the withdrawals was equal to or below the total amount in the envelope, players got to keep the money they requested. If the sum of the withdrawals exceeded this total, the players received nothing. The results showed that, controlling for relevant variables, systematically less money was withdrawn in the religious kibbutzim than in the secular ones. The difference between religious and secular kibbutzim was driven by highly religious men who engaged in daily and communal prayer. They were the ones who took the least amount of money from the common pool. Two other studies found similar results. Among the Candomble, an Afro-Brazilian religious group, more devoted individuals contributed more to a public goods game. And in rural India, devout Muslim students in a madrassah contributed more to a public goods game compared to a matched group of students in a secular school.[21]

Thus, unlike the Good Samaritan study and ones like it, religious involvement predicted greater contributions to the public good, and greater likelihood of cooperation. One key difference is that reminders of God are likely to be more chronically present in religious kibbutz, madrassahs, and Candomble communities, where religious prayer and attendance are a daily part of life. Another is that prosociality in these communities clearly benefited ingroup members (despite being anonymous), whereas in the Good Samaritan study, the victim was a total stranger. It is also possible that regular, communal prayer involves public ritual participation, which, independent of devotion to a morally concerned deity, might also encourage more prosociality.

Moreover, what kind of religion people practice may be more important than how religious people are. In a study spanning fifteen societies of pastoralists and horticulturalists, Joseph Henrich and colleagues measured the link between types of religious commitment and prosocial behavior in three well-known economic games. Unlike previous studies, this one specifically tested the idea that participation in prosocial religions with Big Gods engenders more prosocial behavior compared to participation in local religions whose gods typically are not powerful, all-knowing, and concerned about morality. In the previously discussed Dictator Game, two anonymous players are allotted a sum of real money (a day's wage in the local culture) in a one-shot interaction. Player 1 must decide how to divide this sum between herself and

Player 2. Player 2 then receives the allocation from Player 1, and the game ends. Player 1's allocation (the offer) to Player 2 provides a measure of generosity or fairness in this context. The Ultimatum Game is identical to the Dictator Game, except that Player 2 can accept or reject the offer. If Player 2 specifies that he would accept the amount of the actual offer, then he receives the amount of the offer and Player 1 receives the rest. If Player 2 specifies that he would reject the amount offered, both players receive zero. Player 1's offer measures a combination of intrinsic motivation toward fairness in this context and an assessment of the likelihood of rejection.

There was wide variability in the degree of prosociality across the fifteen societies. In some groups, people offered little, and receivers accepted any offers, however puny. These people acted "rationally," the way economists say people should. In other groups, people offered half the allocation, and the receivers rejected anything less than a fair offer. What explains this variability? Henrich found that the more people in that group were accustomed to dealing with strangers to make a living, the greater their prosocial tendencies. The other significant factor was religion: after controlling for various demographic and economic variables, participation in a world religion with a Big God (defined as Christian or Muslim) increased offers in the Dictator Game by 6 and in the Ultimatum Game by 10 percentile points (when the stake was standardized at 100).[22]

Now, you might have noticed a glaring inconsistency in the pattern of results. In virtually all of these priming studies, reported religious involvement was unrelated to prosocial tendenies, while religious priming made a substantial difference. In addition, religious involvement was unrelated to helping rates in the Good Samaritan study and similar ones conducted in the United States, Canada, and Europe. Yet several other studies conducted outside North America and Europe, including a fifteen-society comparative investigation, have indeed found a clear link between religious involvement and prosociality. How can we explain this apparent puzzle?

One answer jumps out of Henrich's comparative study: what makes a difference is adherence to prosocial religions with Big Gods—not any type of religious involvement. But why is that degree of religious involvement in cultures influenced by prosocial religions does not matter? Another possible answer is that the psychological studies that have failed to find any effects of religious involvement did not recruit people who are that religious. Many (but not all) of these studies sample from university student populations. Perhaps these samples have not internalized religious sensibilities deeply enough. Perhaps the most devout, who are especially likely to respond prosocially without any religious prompting, are not likely to be picked to be in psychology studies. This is a methodological issue that we cannot dismiss easily, especially in light of findings from more deeply religious societies that demonstrate a link between religious involvement and prosocial behavior. However, there is yet another explanation for these null effects that gives us clues about how some secular societies manage high levels of cooperation without religion. To solve this puzzle, and shed light on this clue, it is time to take a quick detour into an issue that plagues most of psychology research: this issue is not found in *what* psychologists study, but *who* they study. The choices they make about samples affect inferences they make about human behavior.

WEIRD Brains and Worldly Institutions

If you are reading this book, written in English, on the esoteric topic of the evolution of religion, chances are, you are WEIRD. No, I do not mean that you are strange or abnormal—most likely you are not—but I suspect you are Western, Educated, Industrialized, Rich, and Democratic. Even if you are not a Westerner (that is, someone who grew up in Europe, North America, or any of the English-influenced countries of the world), I venture to guess that you are literate, have a university degree, live in an industrialized society with social and economic institutions, and are relatively affluent by world standards. The issue is that the vast majority of research participants in psychology are also WEIRD, just like you. The psychologist Jeffrey Arnett estimated that 96 percent of all research participants come from Western industrialized countries, which represent a mere 12 percent of the worlds' population. Moreover, two out of three participants are undergraduate university students, who are themselves unusual with respect to their own societies. Joseph Henrich, Steve Heine, and I have calculated that an American undergraduate student is 4,000 times more likely to be selected to be in a psychology study than a random person outside the West.

Most minds studied by psychologists are WEIRD minds. But why is this an issue? This would not be a big problem if human brains were all the same. But brains, unlike, say, chemical interactions or physical laws, can operate differently in different places. From the moment of birth, and even before, human brains are immersed in richly structured cultural experiences that vary quite a bit from place to place and from one historical period to another. There is, therefore, considerable population variability in many aspects of human behavior, thinking, feelings, and motivations. For most psychological characteristics, there is a spectrum that reflects the human species. What is more striking is that, in survey after survey, my colleagues and I have found that WEIRD people occupy the extreme end of this spectrum. The WEIRDer people are, the more likely they are psychological outliers in the context of the world. WEIRD psychology, to name a few key features, means literate, living in large anonymous groups, participating in markets with money, and internalizing norms for cooperation with strangers. For the subset of those who are Westerners, it also means hyperanalytical thinking, experiencing the self as being autonomous and independent, emphasizing choice and personal control, and having a narrow conception of morality that revolves around caring/not harming, fairness, and justice. WEIRD populations are atypical of other human populations, and results obtained with these samples may reflect somewhat different psychological tendencies.[23]

Coming back to our puzzle, here is how the WEIRD problem may explain the seemingly confusing results regarding religious involvement and prosocial behavior. It turns out that virtually all the studies that have found weak or no reliable associations between religiosity and prosociality have been conducted in WEIRD societies. On the other hand, all the studies that have found reliable associations between religiosity and prosocial behavior have been conducted in non-WEIRD samples. Here is a key feature of WEIRD groups: these are societies characterized by strong secular institutions and rule of law, high levels of public trust, and low levels of corruption. We know that this is precisely the package of societal traits that encourages prosocial norms for everyone. This can also be demonstrated experimentally. In one experiment I conducted with Azim Shariff, secular reminders were as effective as reminders of God to increase prosocial behavior in the Dictator Game. In other words, there are strong secular incentives that promote high levels of prosociality for everyone, religious or not, leaving less room for religion to exert its effects. Therefore, experimental primes or situational salience brings out the effects of religion more than religious involvement in these WEIRD contexts. In non-WEIRD societies, in contrast, secular institutions (police, courts, juries, contracts) are either nonexistent, or if they exist at all, are unreliable and corrupt. People have little faith in them. Instead, they have faith in religion. For most of humanity, like in most of human history in most cultures, religion is, and has been, the main game in town—the primary motivator of prosociality among strangers. Therefore, the effect of religious involvement is muted in WEIRD societies. This insight helps us reconcile the findings on religious involvement and prosocial acts. It also gives us clues about the origins of secular societies. When secular institutions succeed in increasing trust and cooperation in a society, they encroach on religion's job and precipitate its decline. I explore this dynamic in chapter 10.

Chapter 2 explored the simple but powerful principle that *watched people are nice people*. Prosocial religions, by harnessing regular exposure to their powerful supernatural watchers, promote a sense of being watched. Such supernatural monitoring made possible cultural innovations like medieval ordeals. If the presence of human watchers is enough to encourage nice behavior, we begin to see why sincere belief in Big Gods encourages cooperation even when situations are seemingly anonymous. Moreover, believers can then selectively trust and cooperate with those who also credibly demonstrate belief in such supernatural watchers. This would partly solve one of the key problems that has always plagued large anonymous groups— the problem of knowing which strangers to trust. In the next chapter, I explore this connection between religion, trust, and social solidarity, another building block of prosocial religions.

Chapter 4
In Big Gods We Trust

The Maa Tarini Temple in the Indian state of Orissa attracts millions of followers from all over India. In a devoutly religious country, there is nothing remarkable about swarms of Hindu pilgrims flocking to such temples. What is interesting about Maa Tarini, however, is that this Goddess is especially partial to coconuts. In fact, She has an insatiable appetite for them, which creates an enormous daily demand for the delicious nuts. According to BBC journalist Sanjaya Jena, the coconuts are offered to the gods, used in various rituals and ceremonies, distributed and sold cheaply around town, feeding a local sweets industry. Every day, thousands of coconuts, about 15,000 of them, must be collected and transported to the main temple. In a country like India with very poor infrastructure, this is a massive logistical headache. How do the priests of Maa Tarini manage to rely on a daily delivery of thousands and thousands of coconuts?

They depend, it appears, on a remarkable religious courier system supported by the wider Hindu population. Devotees around the larger region drop off their offerings of coconuts in a network of collection boxes, or give them to bus drivers, who deliver them as far as they can, and then pass them on to the next courier heading toward the temple. Like batons in a relay race, the thousands of coconuts change hand after hand, until they reach their divine destination. Sanjaya Jena explains:

> The drivers' faith in the goddess Maa Tarini is complete—it is common to find the space behind their seats stacked with coco-

nuts. Even if the bus is on a different route, the driver will make
sure to drop the coconuts in a collection box en route or pass them
on to a bus headed for Ghatgaon.

Why wouldn't these mostly poor folks refuse to transport the nuts, or simply stash them? A clue is found in an interview with one bus driver, who
says, "If I refuse to carry coconuts to the goddess, I may face various odds
on my way."[1]

The coconut temple courier service is a modern surviving example of
something that goes back thousands of years: it is the pivotal place prosocial religions have occupied in the establishment of social networks of trade
and cooperation with high degrees of trust and social solidarity. These networks have often been the impetus for the creation of large-scale societies
of cooperators, resulting, in turn, in the further spread of religious beliefs
and practices. In the absence of modern cultural institutions such as courts,
contract-enforcing laws, and police, Big Gods have been, for most people
in the world, for most of history, a major ingredient of the social glue that
bound anonymous people together.

The Gods of Long-Distance Commerce

Long-distance commerce is an ideal case study of large-scale cooperation
because it requires that merchant communities engaged in it be able to
solve collective action problems related to anonymity and lack of ac-
countability, travel through long geographic stretches and across cultural
boundaries, and exchanges of precious goods that create ample opportunities for exploitation and cheating. Therefore, such networks (and the
global communities supporting them) would not survive and prosper
unless they were able to find ways to secure high levels of social solidarity. In *The Sacred Bonds of Commerce*, Nicholas Rauh analyzes archeological evidence to reconstruct economic and social life in Delos, which
between the second and first centuries BCE was an epicenter of Roman
maritime trade in slaves and precious goods. What did these Roman merchants rely on to establish relationships of trust that made long-distance
trade possible and profitable? They assembled themselves into religious
fraternities, and they invoked watchful gods, in particular Mercury and

Hercules, to enforce oaths and bind people into contractual agreements. Rauh explains:

> Not only was the presence of gods mandatory for an agora [marketplace], but they somehow facilitated the agoras' commercial activities. What was the necessary link between the gods and commercial activity? The answer to this question lies in the use of the gods as witnesses to the promissory oaths businessmen swore to bind their commercial agreements. This divine function, more than anything else, provides the common denominator for the features encountered in both Greek and Roman marketplaces.[2]

Consider two more recent historical examples that point to religion's role in the creation of large-scale cooperation and trust in the form of long-distance commerce. One is the emergence in the early seventeenth century of an extensive network of trade operated by Armenian silk merchants who originated from the town of New Julfa in Isfahan, located in the then Persian Empire (in present-day Iran). At its peak, this network stretched from major European cities such as Amsterdam and London all the way to India and as far east as Tibet and the Philippines. The New Julfa Armenian merchants ran a sophisticated trade network operating simultaneously in all the major empires of the time for almost 300 years. Manufacturing and trading a precious commodity like silk, and transporting it through vast distances across various continents and empires, requires a very high degree of trust and cooperation, and the presence of credible mechanisms for punishing transgressors. They accomplished this feat without the benefits of an Armenian state or military-political establishment to support their activities. How did they do it? The Armenian merchant families spread around the world depended on an intricate network for communication and social monitoring that intertwined with the Armenian Apostolic Church. Historian Sebouh Aslanian explains:

> Merchants were not the only ones to depend on the intelligence network connecting communities in India and the East with the nodal center in Julfa. The church also depended on this system to send information to its diocesan sees in India. General encyclicals, pontifical bulls from Etchmiadzin [the seat of the Church], letters of blessing, alms donations, payment of church taxes, correspon-

dence between priests overseeing a parish in India and the primate in in New Julfa, and, in rare cases, letters of excommunication all circulated between the diocesan center of the All Saviors Monastery in Julfa and its daughter churches in India and farther east by means of the same courier system. The ability of this system to circulate information from one end of the Julfan network to another was thus just as crucial for merchants as it was for the clergy, one of whose functions was to maintain the integrity of the commercial network by ensuring that its members stayed firm in their ethnoreligious identity and, therefore, continued making generous donations to the church.[3]

Being an ethnoreligious diasporan community spread around the world, the Armenian traders were committed to the cultural survival of their communities, but were uninterested in attracting converts. Not unlike Jewish Maghrebi merchants who established their trade networks all around the Mediterranean between the eleventh and twelfth centuries, ethnic and religious solidarity jointly cemented the tight bonds of trust.[4] Such trust was necessary for these trade networks to function in the face of constant social threats.

Where religion transcends ethnicity, however, trade networks have brought religious conversion with them. The best known such case is how Islam made inroads into Africa, as well as in Southeast Asia, as far east as Malaysia and Indonesia. Stunningly, Indonesia is now the most populous Muslim country in the world today, far ahead of Saudi Arabia, the cradle of Islam, or even Egypt, the most populous Arab country in the world. Unlike the spread of Islam in the Middle East, Asia Minor, and the Balkans, Islam's spread in these parts of the world owed more to networks of highly disciplined Muslim merchants, rather than to highly disciplined Muslim armies (although the two often went together, and no doubt, military power played a role even there). Focusing on Africa, Jean Ensminger argues that Arab Muslim merchants, with their high levels of religious commitment, trust, and cooperation, offered economic benefits that attracted converts. By establishing long-distance trade networks in Africa, these merchants in turn facilitated the spread of Islamic beliefs and practices in the societies where they established their outposts. She writes:

> The fact that Islam was also a religion and not merely a set of secular institutions further reduced the transaction costs of exchange.

Islam was a powerful ideology with built-in sanctions which contributed to considerable self-enforcement of contracts. True believers had a non-material interest in holding to the terms of contracts even if the opportunity presented itself to shirk. All of this resulted in lower transaction costs associated with doing business among fellow Muslims, despite the enormous transportation and in- formation costs involved, given the incredibly long distances and cultural barriers to be traversed across the Sahara and the rest of the continent.[5]

Ensminger's analysis highlights the fact that these networks of trust, by having contracts that were self-enforcing, lowered transaction costs, making it economically attractive to join them. But why, we may ask, would economic contracts be self-enforcing in religious communities engaged in long-distance trade? One powerful tool (although certainly not the only one), no doubt, was a credible fear of a God, a God who knows and monitors moral behavior, and doles out rewards and punishments. Sincere belief in a Supernatural Monitor is like agreeing to be followed by a powerful judge, 24/7, 365 days a week! In addition, while human judges are prone to error and costly to the system, a supernatural judge is failsafe and comes for free. Strangers who showed sincere belief in being monitored were, therefore, more likely to be invited to join these networks and were trusted more. If people trust each other even when no one is monitoring them, then human monitoring mechanisms, which are costly and difficult to enforce, can be supplemented and reinforced with supernatural monitoring.

This brings us to the fourth principle of Big Gods:

Trust people who trust in God.

The logic of trusting those who fear God is simple, and follows elegantly from the first principle of supernatural monitoring, that *watched people are nice people.* We have seen that consistent with this principle, reminders of watchful supernatural monitors encourage cooperative behavior among strangers. Because cooperators seek other cooperators, it follows that, all else being equal, believers would be more likely to trust other believers who also sincerely believe themselves to be under supernatural monitoring. Therefore, signals of sincere belief in Big Gods would be a reliable indicator of who to cooperate with. Prosocial religious groups would not cohere if it weren't for the fact that people are quite discriminating about their cooperation partners. Genuine devotion to the same supernatural deity may have therefore lowered monitoring costs and fostered cooperation, especially in communities spread across geographic and ethnic boundaries.

This chapter answers three intriguing questions that arise when we ponder the coconut temple courier service of Maa Tarini, the Armenian trade networks stretching from Europe to India, the spread of Islam in Africa and Southeast Asia, "sacred bonds" of commerce in Delos, as well as the many other cases of religiously inspired cooperative networks of trust and solidarity. First, how could people trust their valuables to complete strangers, who in turn do the same with other strangers? Second, why do people devote precious time and resources to their deities at a significant cost to themselves? Third, how far does the religious circle of trust extend, where does it collapse, and what can this tell us about prejudice against atheists? Bringing these three interrelated questions together, we may ask, how are people transformed from random strangers into a community of true believers? Why are prosocial religions with Big Gods reliable builders of trust? Why are these beliefs connected to displays of extravagant behaviors that are often costly to the self, and how do these displays encourage community spirit? History presents us with the puzzle, but the answers come to us through the recent work of anthropologists, behavioral economists, and social psychologists.

The argument in this and the following chapters is that several psychological tricks were packaged together over time to galvanize trust among strangers. As I will explore in detail in chapter 7, this foundation of trust led to the mutually reinforcing rise of large prosocial religions and modern large cooperative societies. For this to happen, two conditions must be met. First, believers ought to cooperate with others who show evidence of *belief* in supernatural monitors—the Big Gods of prosocial religions. This, I argue, explains the intense antipathy toward disbelief in prosocial religious groups. However, belief is easy to fake—opening the door to impostors who masquerade as believers who receive group benefits but do not contribute, and worse, exploit the system. Cooperative groups that are invaded by impostors would collapse quickly. This is why one of the most pressing threats that any religious group must combat is the threat of religious hypocrisy (discussed in chapter 6). Prosocial religious groups therefore are in constant vigilance to identify and weed out impostors who masquerade under a cloak of devoutness to reap benefits from the group. The second condition, then, is that belief ought to be *credible*, backed up by displays that would be hard to fake. When these two conditions are met—that is, when individuals display *credible belief in Big Gods*— greater numbers of true believers are able to trust each other in ever larger social networks, even when no one is capable of monitoring social interactions.

The Dilemma of the Traveling Salesman

In 1904, on a long railroad journey throughout America, the German sociologist Max Weber was sitting next to a traveling salesman when the conversation turned to religion. In a now famous quote, the man said: "Sir for my part everybody may believe or not believe as he pleases; but if I saw a farmer or a businessman not belonging to any church at all, I wouldn't trust him with fifty cents. Why pay me, if he doesn't believe in anything?"[6]

This often-quoted statement attracted Weber's curiosity. It has generated much discussion about religion and trust in America, but what is remarkable is that the salesman is not saying that he would only trust someone who belongs to his own church. After all, that kind of rule, while useful for someone who has no compelling incentive to interact with strangers, would be rather meaningless for a *traveling* salesman. The dilemma of the traveling salesman is that earning his living depends on trading with strangers, but the challenge is to sort out the trustworthy ones among the countless new faces he will meet every day. Believing in something, even if that something is different from what I believe in, can be taken as an indication that this person can be trusted, as long as that "something" places the individual under some kind of moral constraint. It is this kind of trust that pervaded business relationships among unrelated businessmen in early America.

The dilemma of the traveling salesman is essentially the main problem of large, anonymous societies, where strangers have opportunities to interact with each other; mutual trust is beneficial to everyone, as they all reap the rewards of cooperation. Not trusting at all is worse, but not as costly as trusting the freerider or the cheater. This dilemma is behind the cultural selection pressures that have led people to calibrate their psychology to particular culturally learned cues that reliably discriminate cooperators from freeriders and cheats. One such powerful cue is whether or not a stranger believes herself to be under supernatural surveillance.

Supernatural Origins of Trust

There is ample survey data showing that in societies with religious majorities—that is, in most of the world—believers are trusted more (and conversely, disbelievers are distrusted; more on distrust of atheists in the next chapter). In the words of conservative religious commentator and media guru Laura Schlessinger, "it's impossible for people to be moral without a belief in God. The fear of God is what keeps people on the straight and narrow."[7] This is not just the opinion of the religious fringe or fundamentalist preachers and televangelists. In the United States, survey after survey finds that Schlessinger's intuition is widely shared. Most people express more trust toward religious people,[8] and endorse the belief that religion is necessary for morality. In a 1998 US national survey, for example, only 15 percent of American respondents agreed that the United States "would be a better country if religion had less influence." The Pew Research Center found that among Americans, "being a Christian" ranked second on the list of traits that they found most appealing in a presidential candidate, out of a list of 23.[9]

These kinds of attitudes are not unique to American society—they can also be found in varying degrees in much of the world where there are religious majorities. In a worldwide survey of 81 countries representing 85 percent of the world's population, conducted between 1999 and 2002, overall, almost two-thirds of all participants said they trust religion, compared to only half who trust their government, and only about one-third who trust political parties.[10]

As insightful as survey findings are, they have to be taken with a grain of salt. For one thing, we can never be sure whether survey respondents mean what they say. (People often behave in a manner inconsistent with their stated attitudes, or often manufacture attitudes to justify their behaviors.) Moreover, survey results are often affected by the wording of the questions. However we do not need to rely on opinion surveys to see evidence of worldwide intolerance of atheists. A recent global report by the International Humanist and Ethical Union (IHEU) found that laws and public practices that discriminate against atheists and religious skeptics are widespread in many countries with religious majorities.[11] Yet these kinds of analyses, as important as they are, cannot tell us if religious conviction is the key elicitor of distrust or hostility toward atheism, rather than something else that is tied up with a country's level of religiosity (such as low levels of human development, or traditionalism). Experiments are needed where peoples' actual social behavior or attitudes could be observed in controlled conditions. While such experiments are in very short supply, the available evidence lends support to the survey findings and cross-national analyses of laws, and points to a link between religious conviction and trust.

In one early study, a team of economists led by John Orbell examined cooperative behavior in the Prisoner's Dilemma Game toward strangers in two American cities with vastly different levels of religious diversity. They found that individuals in a religiously homogenous Mormon society (Logan, Utah), where one could be confident that the stranger shared one's religious beliefs, were far more willing to engage in cooperative behavior toward each other than those in a religiously heterogenous society (Eugene, Oregon). Furthermore, while greater levels of religious attendance was associated with more cooperative behavior in the homogenous Logan sample, no such correlation was observed in Eugene. This lends some support to the idea that religious markers elicit prosociality, and shows the bounded nature of religious trust. However, in this study it is hard to know if participants were responding to religious cues or other cues such as ethnicity. Moreover, trust levels were inferred from cooperative behavior, but not directly measured.[12]

Trust can be defined and measured in a variety of ways. Broadly, it could refer to *an attitude of confidence in the reliability of another person or institution*; when we say Sally trusts Mary, or that Bob trusts the police, this is what we typically mean. But it is useful to add to our definition of trust the willingness to behave according to such an attitude. Going further, a behavioral commitment in the reliability of another agent may not fully capture trust, especially in situations when it matters the most. Trust happens in a context where a mutually cooperative relationship is possible but not guaranteed. Therefore, we also need to include beliefs about the other agent's willingness to cooperate, to act honestly, and so on. Therefore, one common definition of trust is that it is a costly and risky investment in a person or entity, with the future expectation of cooperation. Several economic games have been designed to elicit and measure trust defined in this way. Economists Jonathan Tan and Claudia Vogel went beyond surveys of attitudes, and assessed whether religiosity can be linked to trust under controlled laboratory conditions where many confounding factors that plague survey reports and historical examples are reduced.

In one well-established laboratory game, participants are randomly assigned to be a proposer (truster) or a responder (trustee). In the first step, the proposer decides how much money to forward to the responder, which gets tripled. In the second step, the responder decides how much money, if at all, to send back to the proposer. By transferring money to the responder, the proposer stands to gain, but only if the responder can be trusted to reciprocate. For example, a fully trusting proposer who starts with $10 would transfer the entire sum to the responder, which then accrues to $30. A trustworthy and fair-playing responder would then split the sum evenly and send back $15. Thus both players are rewarded with a healthy profit. In a variation of this trust experiment, Tan and Vogel measured individual differences in the religiosity of the proposer and the responder in a German sample. In addition, in some trials, proposers knew about the level of religiosity of the responder but nothing else. Results indicated that:

- More money was forwarded to responders perceived to be religious, indicating that believers are trusted more than nonbelievers.
- The tendency to trust believing responders was especially strong among believing proposers; thus, the strongest circle of trust was observed when both parties were believers.
- There was an interesting asymmetry in religiously motivated trust. While believers strongly trusted their own kind, nonbelievers were either indifferent or, if anything, mildly trusting of believers.
- Finally, religious responders, who were the recipient of greater trust, in fact were more likely to reciprocate the proposer's offer than less religious responders.

Beliefs in supernatural monitors are a potent motivator of prosocial behavior. Under a range of contexts, they are also potent signals of prosocial intention. It makes sense that believers of a faith trust other believers of the same faith, but how far does this trust extend beyond the confines of the group? For example, would religious believers rather trust members of other, perhaps competing, faiths than those who show no faith at all? This brings us to another key question: are there any groups of people who are systematically excluded from even the widest circle of religious trust?

No doubt, believers would be expected to be most trusting of those who worship the same deities as them. However, the logic of religiously motivated prosociality predicts that trust can be extended beyond the immediate religious community as long as these outsiders adhere to some kind of supernatural sanctioning that constrains their behavior. Thus, Muslims might be able to trust Christians, who also believe in an all-powerful, morally involved God. Christians might trust Hindus, who believe in the law of karma, and an entire pantheon of supernatural monitors. Trust can be extended to potential cooperation partners if the latter adhere to some kind of supernatural monitoring that induces greater cooperativeness.

The claim that members of one religious group will also trust members of other religious groups is admittedly speculative, and may sound counterintuitive to some. But there is anecdotal and other evidence to support it. In surveys done in the United States, Christian Americans express the most trust toward fellow Christians, but express a considerable degree of trust toward other faith groups as well, such as Jews and Hindus. Anthropologist Richard Sosis argues that, under some conditions, religious signals of trustworthiness can be coopted by members of other religious groups. When the choice is between two religious strangers with unknown credibility, the one who truly fears God is trusted more.[13] Supporting this, the economist Robert Frank observes that many wealthy nonreligious New Yorkers place their ads for nannies in Salt Lake City newspapers, apparently believing that Mormons are particularly trustworthy nannies.[14] Similarly, Sikhs are viewed by non-Sikhs as trustworthy economic partners.[15] Although sincere belief in the same supernatural monitor is the best elicitor of trust, there is a sliding scale of religious trust that could extend to religious outgroups.

In at least some situations, then, and in the absence of other cues, believers appear to use commitment to even rival gods as signals of trustworthiness. But what about those who do not believe in any god? This question brings us to distrust of atheists, one of the most puzzling and least studied prejudices tied to religion.

In Atheists We Distrust

Those are not at all to be tolerated who deny the being of a God.
Promises, covenants, and oaths, which are the bonds of human
society, can have no hold upon an atheist. The taking away of
God, though but even in thought, dissolves all.

—John Locke, *Letter Concerning Toleration* (1689 [1983])[16]

On March 12, 2007, long-time congressman Pete Stark, Democrat from California, made history. He did not author a far-reaching legislation that created jobs, cleaned the air, or shaped foreign policy. He made American history by openly declaring that he does not believe in a God or gods. He thus became the first member of the US Congress to "come out" as an atheist. In 2012, Stark lost to fellow Democrat Eric Swalwell Jr., who publicly attacked Stark's atheism. According to the *Secular Coalition of America*, in a country of more than 300 million, he has been the first, and possibly the only member of Congress who was on record as an atheist. The organization claims there are 26 other members of Congress who are closet atheists or agnostics.[17]

The 2008 presidential election in the United States offered the most diverse group of viable candidates in American history. In the Democratic camp, there was Hillary Clinton, a woman, and Barack Obama, an African American. On the Republican side, there was the mainstream candidate, John McCain, but also Sarah Palin, another woman, and Mitt Romney, a Mormon. A February 2007 Gallup poll revealed a remarkable degree of social acceptance of this diversity vying for the highest political office in the country. Majorities of Americans reported a willingness to vote for a candidate who is Catholic (95 percent), African American (94 percent), Jewish (92 percent), female (88 percent), Hispanic (87 percent), Mormon (72 percent), twice divorced but currently married (67 percent), elderly (57 percent), or gay (55 percent). Of the provided list of possible candidates, only one—the atheist candidate (45 percent) — could not garner a majority vote.

Another survey conducted in 2008 by the Pew Forum asked Americans if other religions could lead to eternal life. A majority of Americans (80 percent of whom describe themselves as Christian) said that Judaism (74 percent), Islam (52 percent), and Hinduism (53 percent) can lead to eternal life. These numbers were somewhat lower when only white Evangelicals were considered, although, remarkably, a sizable percentage of them also said that other religions can lead to eternal life. But once again, atheists (42 percent) were the only group that could not garner a simple majority, and were again at the very bottom of the list of all the groups that survey respondents were asked about.[18] It appears that believing in the "wrong" god is far better than believing in no god at all.

Historical trends in the United States also show that distrust of atheists is remarkably resilient. One standard question that sociologists ask is, "Would you be willing to vote for a presidential candidate of your own political preference, who is _____," offering respondents various options, such as African American, Catholic, female, Jewish, Muslim, atheist, and so on. Over time, we see an encouraging pattern of increasing social acceptance of almost all groups that have been historically marginalized. In 1948, only 48 percent of Americans said they would be willing to vote for an African American presidential candidate. By 1999, that number had almost doubled, to over 90 percent. True to these numbers, Americans elected in 2008 the first African American president. Catholics, Jews, women—in fact, every single group polled, including gays, who only a few decades ago were excluded by the majority of Americans—have crossed the critical 50 percent mark already by 1999—except atheists, who even today, cannot garner the approval of a simple majority. This singling out of atheists is something that is found repeatedly by pollsters surveying American social attitudes.[19]

Are these numbers an artifact of survey methodologies? Perhaps Americans and other believers may say to pollsters that they reject atheists, but in fact in real life they do not? There are several reasons to doubt this. For one thing, the problem with survey research of this type is not inflated social rejection, but quite the opposite. Respondents, concerned about appearing bigoted, may exaggerate their acceptance of marginalized groups. But if anything, this should lead to *high* levels of acceptance of atheists, and therefore would not explain why atheists trail almost any other group in social acceptance surveys. Perhaps believers, who may avoid expressing negative attitudes toward other ethnic or racial outgroups, have less concern when it comes to atheists. Anti-atheist prejudice, unlike prejudice against racial or religious minorities, could be a socially accepted prejudice in America. But that would push the question further back—why would this prejudice be socially acceptable? Moreover, these polls predict voting behavior with a reasonably high degree of accuracy. Voters in the United States have never elected an openly atheist president. Judging from the rarity of self-declared atheists holding political office in America, the polls might, if anything, underestimate how widespread the rejection of atheists is. Finally, in our own experimental research, we find that believers in the United States and Canada distrust atheists even when we use subtle and indirect measures of distrust and prejudice that sidestep some of the problems of survey research.

It may not come as a surprise that in religious countries that lack civil liberties, atheists are persecuted. In many majority-Muslim countries such as Egypt, Saudi Arabia, Indonesia, and Iran, open declaration of atheism is a punishable crime under Islamic "apostasy" laws, although these laws are seldom applied, given how exceedingly rarely atheists in those countries go public. What is less commonly known, however, is that antipathy toward atheists has deep historical roots even in Western democracies that inherited Enlightenment ideals of social tolerance. The quote that opens this section comes from the *Letter Concerning Toleration*, an essay instrumental in establishing America's separation of church and state. In it, Locke preaches religious tolerance, then ironically singles out atheists as the only group that does not deserve tolerance or legal protection. The same theme can be found in none other than one of the founding fathers of America, Benjamin Franklin. In a 1757 letter attempting to dissuade an atheist from attacking religion, Franklin argues that while a select few people might be able to lead moral lives without the influence of religion, most of humanity needs religion to be good. He explains:

> Think how great a Proportion of Mankind consists of weak and ignorant Men and Women, and of inexperienced and inconsiderate Youth of both Sexes, who have need of the Motives of Religion to restrain them from Vice.

He then goes on to worry: "If Men are so wicked as we now see them *with Religion* what would they be if *without it*?"[20]

The moral exclusion of atheists is not unique to the political domain, and the sentiments expressed by Locke and Franklin—pragmatic intellectuals who were hardly religious zealots—continue to resonate today and extend to a wide range of other domains that are seen to have a moral dimension. In an in-depth analysis of Americans' prejudice toward atheists, a team of sociologists found in an extensive 2006 survey that respondents who were asked about their attitudes about a variety of perceived outgroups rated atheists as the group that least shares their own vision of America, and rated an atheist as the individual that they would most disapprove of as a marriage partner for their child. This pattern is striking. As these authors note:

> Americans are less accepting of atheists than of any of the other groups we asked about, and by a wide margin. The next-closest category on both measures is Muslims. We expected Muslims to be a lightning-rod group, and they clearly were. This makes the response to atheists all the more striking. For many, Muslims represent a large and mostly external threat, dramatized by the loss of life in the World Trade Center attacks and the war in Iraq. By contrast, atheists are a small and largely silent internal minority.[21]

Indeed, in the context of the September 11, 2001, attacks on the World Trade Center and the Pentagon, and recent American involvement in conflicts in the Middle East and Central Asia, it comes as no surprise that Communism and the Soviet Union have been replaced in the minds of many Americans by a new external threat: Islam and Muslims. But why is it that atheists are seen as *even more* of a threat than even Muslims?

The fact that atheists rouse more antagonism among Americans than even Muslims post 9-11 brings us to another intriguing observation: American attitudes toward atheists are only modestly related to their attitudes toward other stigmatized groups, such as gays and African Americans. This is surprising if anti-atheist feelings were merely the result of generalized prejudice, xenophobia, or an intolerant personality.

One might think that anti-atheist prejudice is peculiar to America—a religious country with a history founded on puritanical zeal. And indeed, international surveys do show that there is considerable variability in the prevalence of this prejudice across nations. For example, there is virtually no rejection of atheists in Scandinavian societies such as Denmark and Sweden (more on this later). But these same international surveys also show that wherever there are religious majorities—that is, most of the world—there is also strong anti-atheist prejudice (although there are mitigating factors, which I discuss later). In Arabic, for example, calling someone "lacking religion" is a grave insult. Worldwide trust toward religion and toward people who are religious is quite high. The flipside is that worldwide trust toward atheists tends to be quite low.

Anti-atheist prejudice is also noteworthy given the sheer number of atheists across the globe. Although we live in a world where most people are religious, the number of atheists worldwide is not trivial. Sociologist Phil Zuckerman illustrates this fact vividly: if we counted atheists all over the world, and considered them a "religious" group, they would be the fourth largest one in the world, trailing only Christians, Muslims, and Hindus. In his estimate, people who do not believe in God or gods are 58 times more numerous than Mormons, 41 times more numerous than Jews, and twice as numerous as Buddhists.

Admittedly, counting atheists is notoriously difficult. In deeply religious societies, the numbers are likely underestimates, as atheists are unwilling to reveal their lack of belief. Conversely, in officially atheistic societies such as China, they may be overestimated, as cultural norms push people to mask their religiosity and falsely claim to be atheists. There are also issues of semantics—what does it mean to be an atheist? Should we count those who say they are agnostics and nonbelievers? Should we include in our definition people who do not believe in God but nevertheless attend religious services, such as many secular Jews? Should we include people who say they do not believe in God but are "cultural Christians," such as many Danes and Swedes? Is opposition to religion an important part of the definition? Nevertheless, using conservative methods that exclude government statistics in officially atheistic societies, and focusing on a straightforward definition of atheism as absence of belief in God or gods, Zuckerman's estimates place the number of atheists worldwide on par with many major world religions.[22]

The puzzle of anti-atheist prejudice deepens as we think about atheists themselves. Despite their considerable worldwide numbers, atheists are not a particularly cohesive group, nor are they visible, or powerful. Unlike religious or ethnic groups who imagine themselves in communities united in faith and destiny, most atheists do not see themselves as a community at all. What they share in common is absence of a particular belief. As the comedian and atheist Ricky Gervais jokes, "Atheism is a worldview like not skiing is a hobby."[23]

Finally, at first glance, prejudice against atheists might seem to be the result of perceived dissimilarity. Maybe, religious people dislike atheists because they seem different or unfamiliar. Yet this doesn't seem to capture the quality of the antagonism either. In fact, if we trust the surveys, believers would rather have their child marry an ethnically and linguistically different person from the other side of the globe practicing a different religion rather than a culturally similar atheist from the same neighborhood. Why then, are atheists the least trusted group in societies with religious majorities around the world? Does religion's role in building trust explain anti-atheist prejudice? Aside from decline of religiosity, are there any circumstances, or psychological tendencies, that can reduce this prejudice even among believers? These are the questions that are addressed in the next chapter.

The key insight in explaining the puzzle of anti-atheist prejudice lies in understanding religion's role in trust and cooperation. Atheists might think of their lack of belief as a private matter about a metaphysical issue; believers, on the other hand, see atheism as a public matter, a threat to cooperation and trust. If sincere belief in a morally concerned deity serves as a reliable cooperative signal, it follows that those who explicitly deny the existence of God are inadvertently sending the wrong signal: they are being perceived as subversive noncooperators by the religious. Hence, John Locke's sentiment in *Letter Concerning Toleration* can be captured by the fallacious but intuitively compelling idea in the religious public's imagination that freethinkers are de facto freeriders. In other words, prejudice against atheists is a direct consequence of the fourth principle of supernatural monitoring, discussed earlier. It essentially says, *don't trust people who don't trust in God*.

Nonbelievers are often puzzled about why believers find them threatening. Religious people are devoted to their beliefs, fine. But why feel threatened by the absence of these beliefs? Why not simply ignore atheism? Antagonism toward atheism becomes intelligible in light of what we have learned about the prosocial effects of religions. The psychology behind believers' antagonism toward atheists is that believers infer that atheists pose a very specific threat to cooperation in large prosocial groups. I explore this idea in detail in the next chapter.

Can Atheists Really Be Trusted?

But before doing so, it is worth explaining why antipathy toward atheists qualifies as a form of prejudice. One may wonder, if religion has been a galvanizing force for cooperation, isn't distrust of atheists less the result of prejudice and more the result of rational expectations? And given the connection between religion and prosocial behavior, shouldn't believers distrust atheists as a matter of principle?

This objection is flawed on at least two counts. First, believers who intuitively link religion with morality fail to understand that there are multiple motivations and reasons to be nice and to do good. We have seen that religion, by harnessing supernatural monitoring and the bonds of community, is one such source of prosociality. But it is far from the only one. Feelings of being under social surveillance, for example, encourage nice behavior regardless of religiosity. Expectations of mutual gain push people to be nice with each other, even in situations devoid of religious meanings. Moral emotions such as feelings of empathy and compassion can also motivate profound acts of kindness. Empathy and compassion are viscerally easier to apply to one's kin and to ingroup members, but children and adults can be socialized to extend these emotions as virtues to be cultivated and applied to a broader range of humanity.[24] In such an expanding moral circle, we feel connected to complete strangers. Perceptions of shared fate or similarity can also be applied to wider and wider circles of strangers. The broadening of the moral compass in turn may recruit the moral emotions in a virtuous cycle of including more and more people into the moral circle. This is what the philosopher Peter Singer means when he argues for expanding the moral circle.[25]

This line of reasoning leads to an interesting possibility: since nonbelievers do not rely on supernatural monitoring, is it the case that they, more than the religious, act prosocially out of compassion? Several studies by Laura Saslow and her colleagues looked exactly at this idea. In one study, participants reported their current feelings of compassion, then played several economic games with strangers where several prosocial tendencies were measured. Would they share a windfall with a stranger? How much would they trust a stranger? How much would they contribute to a common pool that would benefit everyone? (Prior to participating in the study, participants reported their levels of religiosity, and were matched on gender, socioeconomic class, and political orientation, factors that might independently influence their behavior.) The results showed that among nonbelievers, the greater the feelings of compassion were, the more prosocial their behavior was. Among believers, feelings of compassion were unrelated to prosocial behavior. In another study, believers and nonbelievers were induced to experience compassion by watching a video about child poverty. (Comparison groups watched a neutral video about two men talking.) Then, in a seemingly unrelated task, all participants played the anonymous Dictator Game, where they had the opportunity to share any portion of the equivalent of $10 with a total stranger. The compassion video made nonbelievers more generous, but it had no effect on believers. Thus, it appears that the absence of supernatural monitoring is compensated for by stronger compassion.[26]

Moreover, there is another, *secular* route toward nice behavior: effective institutions that encourage cooperation and high levels of trust. Atheists as well as theists who are socialized in such secular societies have powerful incentives to be prosocial that are not immediately motivated by religion.[27] Where there are strong institutions that govern public life—that is, where people are reassured that contracts are enforced, competition is fair, and cheaters will be punished—levels of trust and cooperation are high for everyone, believers and nonbelievers alike. And it appears that believers who do live in such secular societies with strong rule of law (see chapter 5) are influenced by this fact, and for them the idea that religion is necessary for morality is not as compelling. As a result, they are not as driven to distrust atheists.

Second, an equally important reason why atheist distrust is ill-founded is the second principle of supernatural monitoring. This principle says that religious situations are more powerful than religious dispositions. In chapter 3, I discussed results from laboratory experiments and field studies in which religious reminders and situations increased actual prosocial behavior. In those same studies, however, the effect of self-reported religious devotion or lack thereof was null. Recall also the Sunday Effect in charitability, that Christians were no more charitable than non-Christians Monday through Saturday, only to become generous once they were reminded of their religious duties on Sundays.[28] These new findings nicely complement a long line of studies from decades of research by psychologist Daniel Batson and colleagues, showing that in situations devoid of the opportunity to leave a good impression on others, religious and nonreligious individuals do not differ in their levels of altruism.[29] Nowhere is this lack of difference illustrated better than in in the famous Good Samaritan experiment, discussed in chapter 3. In that study, only a situational variable—whether participants were told to rush or take their time—produced differences in helping rates.[30] In other studies, religious involvement predicted greater altruism only when there was the opportunity to leave a good impression on others.

This suggests that religious situations are a more reasonable trust cue than religious persons. It makes more sense to trust that believers who are in church will be less likely to cheat and steal than believers who are at an anonymous intersection. Or as a field study showed (discussed in chapter 3) in Morocco, it would be reasonable to "trust" the Muslim call to prayers as an institution that elicits prosocial acts among the devout.[31] Recognizing this, prosocial religions sprinkle religious reminders at regular time intervals and key places—like call to prayers in Muslim communities, Buddha Eyes in Tibet and Nepal, or church bells or ubiquitous signs of the cross in Christianity. But these religious situations are not unique elicitors of trust—it would be also reasonable to trust secular institutions that encourage nice behavior toward others. However, before the advent of the relatively recent secular institutions, religious cues reflected the wisdom of cultural evolution to harness the power of the situation, rather than rely on internalized chronic awareness of supernatural monitoring, a feat that is difficult to obtain.

The one possible exception where religious devotion—as long as it reflects sincere commitment to deep faith—matters, is in societies where strangers must interact with each other, but policing institutions are corrupt, weak, or largely absent. In study after study done in North America and Europe, where there is strong rule of law, there is little evidence that religiosity as a personality characteristic makes people act more prosocially. However, as discussed in chapter 3, the few studies conducted in countries with corrupt or weak institutions, such as India and Brazil, have found reliable effects of religiosity on prosocial behavior in economic games.[32] Similarly, Joseph Henrich and his colleagues have found that among several nonindustrialized societies, there are greater levels of generosity by participants who belong to religions with Big Gods, compared to those who endorse local gods who are not as omniscient and typically are indifferent toward human morality.[33]

In a society where the rule of law is weak, and overall levels of trust and cooperation among strangers are quite low (that's indeed most people for most of history), credible signals of fearing a god are, and have been, the only game in town, and in those societies, it would be reasonable to rely on such religious badges as a trust cue. I say "religious badges," to borrow a term from Richard Sosis,[34] because in these societies, atheism is largely absent, and therefore the only available cue is the degree of credible religious commitment. In contrast, in modern societies with strong institutions, where there are strong incentives that maintain high levels of overall trust and prosocial behavior, and which is where the vast majority of atheists live, there is little justification for distrusting atheists. In *Society without God*, Phil Zuckerman points out that Denmark and Sweden, the world's least religious societies, where overwhelming majorities do not believe in God, are also the ones topping international rankings of rule of law, low levels of corruption, high levels of cooperation and trust, and generally high levels of societal well-being.[35]

To be clear, just as religion is not the only source of prosociality, supernatural monitoring is not the only source of prosociality in religion. No doubt, the moral emotions such as deep feelings of empathy and compassion are at play in religions for at least some believers some of the time. These moral emotions are found among exceptional spiritual exemplars, such as Mahatma Gandhi or Martin Luther King, in the universal compassion of the Buddha, the ecstatic union with the divine found among Christian saints, Sufi mystics, or Hindu sages. But they are also found in secular societies and nonreligious examplars as well (such as in secular humanism). Moreover, prosocial religions could not have assembled together vast communities of cooperators just by exploiting the moral emotions. The gazing eyes of divine watchers, fear of being judged by the gods, eternal damnation, hell, karma, fate—in short, a variety of beliefs that hinge on supernatural monitoring and policing—are a powerful set of mechanisms harnessed by prosocial religions that mobilize believers. It was these forces of supernatural monitoring and related processes that pushed human groups to rapidly scale up, from hunter-gatherer origins to the vast societies of millions today. I explore these processes in detail in chapter 7. But first, in the next two chapters I investigate in closer psychological detail the making and unmaking of prejudice against atheists, and of another perceived threat—the one coming from religious hypocrites.

Chapter 5

Freethinkers as Freeriders

But, I asked, how will man be after that? Without God and
the future life? It means everything is permitted now, one can
do anything? "Didn't you know?" he said. And he laughed.
"Everything is permitted to the intelligent man," he said.

—Fyodor Dostoevsky, *Brothers Karamazov*
(as declared by Ivan Karamazov)[1]

What is the threat that atheists are seen to pose? The survey numbers discussed in the previous chapter, as well as countless other observations, begin to tell us an intriguing story about the origins of anti-atheist antipathy. This antipathy cannot just be a reflection of rampant xenophobia, or a general distrust of people seen as the "outgroup." For one thing, we see in the poll numbers a general decline of prejudice over time, but this decline doesn't seem to have affected atheists all that much. Moreover, prejudice against atheists is much broader and only weakly related to prejudice toward other groups. And most instructive, people following other religions are as much outsiders, and often more so, than atheists. Yet surveys, and our own experimental research, show that atheists who are culturally similar are trusted less than even members of outgroups who are religiously, linguistically, and ethnically different. These observations, taken together, suggest that the origin of anti-atheism cannot be found in familiar explanations such as imagined dissimilarity, xenophobia, or general fear of otherness.

It is time now to bring together two insights that, in combination, demystify atheist distrust in religious societies. First, to fully understand prejudice toward a specific group of individuals, we must appreciate the specific threat that this group is perceived to pose. Second, we have seen that supernatural agents capable of monitoring human behavior are potent motivators of prosocial behavior. Religious commitment in turn serves as a signal of trust, as long as believers walk the walk, not just talk the talk. No doubt, believers are most trusting of those who worship the same deities as themselves. However, as the dilemma of the traveling salesman illustrates, trust can also be extended beyond the immediate religious community as long as outsiders are perceived to adhere to some kind of supernatural sanctioning that keeps them accountable. The logic underlying anti-atheist prejudice therefore becomes clear if we combine (1) belief in supernatural monitoring in prosocial religions, and (2) the belief that atheists do not see themselves to be accountable to such supernatural monitors.

This line of reasoning brings us to a number of specific hypotheses about the psychological roots of prejudice against atheists. Will Gervais, Azim Shariff, and I explored these hypotheses in some detail. Much of the psychological research that I describe in this chapter is the result of their leading efforts. These hypotheses go beyond the survey findings and paint a more detailed picture of the origins and contours of this prejudice. To start with, let's consider a few key expectations:

- Different prejudices are characterized by different reactions to distinct perceived threats. Atheists, who do not believe in punishing supernatural agents and who do not adopt conspicuous signals of religious commitment, should be viewed as untrustworthy rather than "merely" unpleasant. This might not be the case for other groups, who might have different prejudice profiles.
- If atheists are seen as threatening to religious groups because of their perceived unreliability as cooperators, then belief in God should be more strongly related to specific *distrust* of atheists rather than to general *dislike* of atheists.
- Following the same logic, belief in supernatural monitoring, or the belief that "people behave better if they feel God is watching them," should be at the heart of why religious believers distrust atheists.
- Exclusion of atheists should be most pronounced in social contexts where trust is a particularly valued characteristic. Conversely, exclusion of atheists should be less of an issue, and may disappear entirely, in social contexts where other characteristics, such as intelligence, are more valued.

We tested these and other specific ideas using a variety of experimental methods. In the studies I describe later, we compared anti-atheist prejudice with prejudice against other groups. This turned out to be crucial, since the crux of the argument rests on the idea that antagonism toward atheists has a peculiar psychological profile tied to supernatural monitoring, a fact that makes it distinguishable from other prejudices. We compared anti-atheist prejudice to prejudice against a variety of other groups, including gays, Jews, feminists, Muslims, and Christians.

We were particularly curious about how anti-atheist prejudice compares to prejudice based on sexual orientation. Anti-gay prejudice is an instructive comparison because both atheists and gays are often described as threatening to majority religious values and morality. After all, atheists and gays routinely score at the bottom on large-scale cultural acceptance polls in America and other religious societies, and have for decades. Like atheists, gays are frequently targeted and excluded by strong religious believers and many religious organizations. This is typified by the Boy Scouts of America, who as of current writing, continue to explicitly deny membership to both atheists and gay males. (Interestingly, public pressure on the Boy Scouts of America has focused far more on lifting the anti-gay ban than on lifting the anti-atheist ban.) Nevertheless, despite surface similarities, our theory predicts that these two different prejudices are rooted in different psychological sentiments.

We relied on national samples of Americans, as well as more secularized samples of university students in Vancouver, Canada. We knew from the previous survey findings that atheists are not going to be popular for most Americans. While Americans distrusted atheists to a greater extent than Canadians, we were not prepared to find strong tendencies to distrust atheists even among mildly religious and largely secularized Canadians!

First, consider the first prediction. If different prejudices are characterized by different reactions to distinct perceived threats, then the case against atheists should have a markedly different profile from other prejudices. Our team investigated this very question by drawing a large and broadly representative sample of American adults. In addition to assessing demographic information and individual religious beliefs, we asked participants to rate the degree to which they viewed both atheists and gays with either distrust or with disgust. As hypothesized, attitude profiles toward atheists and gays clearly diverged. Atheists were viewed as less trustworthy than gays, but gays were viewed as more disgusting. In other words, anti-atheist prejudice was derived from a distrust reaction, whereas anti-gay prejudice was derived from a disgust reaction. Another clue was how belief in God was related to these patterns. While greater belief in God was related to greater expressed antipathy toward both atheists and gays, we found that belief was more strongly related to *distrust* of atheists than to disgust toward atheists, whereas it was more strongly related to *disgust* toward gays than distrust of gays.[2]

This study was significant because it went beyond the general finding that atheists are one of the most disliked groups among believers, and revealed a more nuanced picture that gives us clues as to where this dislike comes from. However, the findings in this study were susceptible to a few counterexplanations. First, the distrust measure we used was quite overt. It is possible that, for whatever reason, people may have felt similarly toward both atheists and gays, but felt more comfortable openly voicing distrust of atheists than of gays. In addition, our sample consisted of American adults, overall a quite religious group. To address these concerns, we performed additional studies in a population with considerable variability in religious involvement, but overall far less religious on the whole than most Americans. We studied the attitudes of university students in Vancouver, Canada. To circumvent any possible artifacts that result from overtly asking people about their prejudices, we designed studies that included more covert ways of measuring distrust. We capitalized on a classic judgment task that has been widely used by researchers.

For many judgments, people rely on quick intuitive reactions, rather than on more deliberative reasoning. These intuitive responses often tend to be suboptimal, leading people to logically incorrect choices. For instance, consider the famous "Linda problem" from Amos Tversky and Daniel Kahneman:

> Linda is 31 years old, single, outspoken, and very bright. She majored in philosophy. As a student, she was deeply concerned with issues of discrimination and social justice, and also participated in anti-nuclear demonstrations.
> Which is more probable?
> 1. Linda is a bank teller.
> 2. Linda is a bank teller and is active in the feminist movement.

Most participants given this question choose option 2. However, the second option is necessarily less probable than the first. This problem works only because, at an intuitive level, the description of Linda just *sounds like* a description of an active feminist. This is termed the *representativeness heuristic*—judging the probability of events based on perceived representativeness to a description, rather than based on consideration of probabilities. Crucially, this effect works only if the description of the target (liberal and focused on issues of discrimination) matches the potential group membership of the target (feminist). If option 2 instead read "Linda is a bank teller and is an active supporter of tax cuts for the wealthy and looser gun control laws," there would be considerably less intuitive pull to select option 2.[3]

Will Gervais conceived of the idea that this classic task can be used as an indirect measure of implicit stereotypes of various groups. We modified the description to include an archetypical freerider:

> Richard is 31 years old. On his way to work one day, he accidentally backed his car into a parked van. Because pedestrians were watching, he got out of his car. He pretended to write down his insurance information. He then tucked the blank note into the van's window before getting back into his car and driving away. Later the same day, Richard found a wallet on the sidewalk. Nobody was looking, so he took all of the money out of the wallet. He then threw the wallet in a trash can.

Next, participants chose whether it is more probable that Richard is (1) a teacher or (2) a teacher who is also an atheist. In this task, the proportion of participants who succumbed to the intuitive pull of the second option provides an indirect and subtle measure of stereotyping of atheists as criminally untrustworthy. For other participants, *atheist* was replaced with another comparison group, such as gay, feminist, Christian, Muslim, Jewish, and so on. The question was, would believers make more logical errors when a criminally untrustworthy individual was paired with atheist than with other comparison groups?

In several studies using this design, we found that by and large participants did not intuitively judge the description representative of Christians, gays, Muslims, Jewish people, or feminists. But they did intuitively judge that a description of a criminally untrustworthy individual was representative of atheists. The magnitude of atheist distrust in these studies was especially remarkable, and shockingly, the only group we found that was distrusted to the same degree as atheists were people with a known criminal track record: rapists.

At the same time, not all participants reacted in the same way to this task. Intuitive distrust of atheists was significantly weaker among those who expressed low levels of belief in God, and significantly more prevalent among those who expressed strong belief in God. And then we found the smoking gun: the religious intuition that people behave better when they feel like God is watching. That is, religious (and perhaps even some nonreligious) people who equate religiosity with moral conduct and cooperative behavior are the ones who are especially prone to distrust atheists. And this is why belief in God is a powerful predictor of whether or not someone distrusts atheists.

Subsequent studies provided additional evidence that prejudice against atheists is driven specifically by distrust, rather than by other more general negative appraisals. In one study, we constructed a description of a person who was judged by our participants to be just as unpleasant as the criminally untrustworthy individual. However, this person was unpleasant in a way that was unrelated to trustworthiness:

> Richard is 31 years old. He has a rare inherited medical condition. This leads him to have dry, flaky skin and produce excess mucus. His skin often flakes off at embarrassing times, and he almost always has a dripping nose and phlegm in his throat. On his way to work one day, Richard was scratching his itchy shoulder. Some of the dry skin that flaked off caused him to sneeze, and some snot ended up on his tie. He failed to notice that the phlegm got on his tie. He wore this dirty tie through an entire work day.

When given this description, almost no participants thought it likely that Richard was both a teacher and an atheist. Of course, not associating atheists with poor hygiene does not prove that atheists are stigmatized only as freeriders—there could be other anxieties and stereotypes at play that we did not measure. However, at the very least we know that while believers tend to think that a description of an untrustworthy individual is representative of atheists, they do not find that a description of a merely unpleasant fellow is representative of atheists.

Associating atheists with criminal untrustworthiness in a decision task that is ostensibly unrelated to religion is a much more subtle way to gauge atheist distrust than asking survey respondents point-blank if they distrust atheists. Nevertheless, one could still argue that this method leaves open the possibility that participants could see through the decision task. Maybe they responded based not on what they truly believed about atheists, but based on expectations of what they thought would be appropriate. (This is quite unlikely, especially given the secular culture of a West Coast Canadian university.) Nevertheless, to rule out this remote possibility, in another study, we used a computer task known as the Implicit Association Test (IAT), which allows researchers to see how strongly participants associate members of a given group with particular attributes. The IAT measures these associations implicitly, rather than relying on overt, explicitly voiced attitudes.[4] It measured participants' reaction times when an atheist target was paired with distrust words like *lying* and *dishonest*, as opposed to dislike words like *hostile* and *hate*. In this study as well, we found that belief in God was a better predictor of associating atheists with *distrust* than with *dislike*.

Finally, the logic of supernatural monitoring in prosocial religions predicts that anti-atheist prejudice should be exaggerated when trust is especially important, and minimized when trust in not a factor. We investigated this possibility using a job selection survey in which participants varying on religious involvement chose candidates for two jobs varying in the degree to which they require trustworthy candidates using only limited demographic information, which included whether the candidate was religious or was an atheist. We compared simulated hiring decisions for two jobs that were similar in terms of required pleasant or friendly personality, but differed on required trustworthiness (for example, day-care worker versus waitress). This way, we could assess the impact of trust, holding constant pleasantness. As expected, participants significantly excluded the atheist when hiring a day-care worker, and once again believers showed this tendency to a greater extent than nonbelievers. However, participants showed no such preference when hiring someone for a job for which trust is less essential, and belief in God was unrelated to the hiring decision in this low-trust context.

In all of our studies, we found repeatedly a strong trend such that believers distrusted atheists. What about the opposite? Do atheists distrust believers? Distrust of believers was something that we of course looked for in our data, but found none. What we, and others, found instead among nonbelievers was attitudes ranging from total indifference to mild trust *toward believers.*[5] No one doubts that disdain of religious believers exists. There is no shortage of historical examples in the last 100 years of persecution of religion in the name of atheism—for example, in the Soviet Union and in Communist China. If we had gone to officially atheistic totalitarian states, we might have found atheists who are also anti-theists who would fit this mold. However, it is noteworthy that our results are consistent with the observations of sociologist Phil Zuckerman, who, in his ethnographic interviews with atheists in Denmark and Sweden—perhaps the most atheistic societies on earth—found little hostility or distrust toward the religious. Mostly, he found widespread apathy toward the issue of religion, which is also what we found.[6] In contrast, we find consistent and strong distrust of atheists even among moderate believers even in largely secular subcultures in Canada.

This asymmetry—believers distrust disbelievers but not the other way around—at first glance may come as a surprise, especially in light of recent public attacks on religion by some atheist intellectuals. But this asymmetry is exactly what we would expect if this is not an ingroup–outgroup antagonism analogous to ethnic divides or clashes between different religious denominations. Most atheists do not see themselves as a "group," nor do they see themselves having a "worldview" in opposition to religious groups. (Matters might be different when it comes to liking or admiring individual believers.) In fact, some atheists appear to endorse Benjamin Franklin's intuition that belief in supernatural monitoring, even if false, is a good thing that keeps people in line. And this might be the basis of what philosopher Daniel Dennett laments as "believing in belief." This is the attitude, held among some nonbelievers and atheists, which says that belief is a good thing worth preserving, because it keeps some people moral, or gives some people a sense of meaning, and so on.[7]

These experimental studies, together with the survey findings, begin to paint a picture of the origins of one of the least appreciated or understood prejudices in the modern world—prejudice against atheists. We found repeatedly, using a variety of methods, that there is a specific threat that atheists are perceived to pose. That threat is moral distrust. It is not fear or disgust, and not general feelings of dislike. In short, freethinkers are seen as freeriders. Moreover, we found that the single most powerful predictor of atheist distrust is religious belief. In contrast, when it comes to ethnic or racial prejudice, belief in God is not a reliable predictor and may under some conditions be associated with less prejudice (if more coalitional aspects of religious involvement, such as religious attendance or fundamentalist beliefs, which are related to more prejudice, are controlled for).[8] These findings once again reinforce the point that atheist distrust is both deep and narrow: it is deeply rooted in involvement in prosocial religions, and at the same time is narrowly context-specific.

What about Other Explanations of Anti-Atheist Prejudice?

The evidence I just reviewed closely matches the predictions of the cultural evolutionary theory presented here, which places the origins of distrust of atheists in the logic of religiously motivated prosociality. But what about other explanations? Most psychological research on prejudice and stereotyping focuses on general processes, and often overlooks the content of what people believe about various groups. One promising exception to this general trend is a theory advocated by psychologists Susan Fiske, Amy Cuddy, and Peter Glick. This approach partitions prejudice into two separate dimensions: perceived warmth (for example, friendliness, pleasantness) and perceived competence (for example, intelligence, capability). This perspective helps highlight the textured reactions that characterize some prejudices. For example, people tend to pity individuals seen as high in warmth but low in competence—such as individuals with mental disabilities—but envy people seen as high in competence but low in warmth—such as rich folks.[9]

Might this approach explain the variety of evidence I have presented on prejudice toward atheists? The argument would go like this: The content of many stereotypes is influenced by the degree to which people from other groups are perceived as either warm or competent. It is possible that it is not religious prosociality, per se, that causes distrust of atheists, but rather a general process by which low-warmth (or perhaps low-warmth and high-competence) groups are distrusted. If this is the case, then untrustworthiness should be viewed as representative of any outgroup seen as competent but not warm. On the other hand, our model predicts that untrustworthiness should be viewed as more representative of atheists than of other groups—even groups viewed as comparably competent and comparably lacking in warmth.

So, does competence and warmth explain anti-atheist prejudice? We tested this idea by comparing peoples' stereotypes of atheists to their stereotypes of feminists and Jewish people. Canadian participants perceived all three groups as having similar profiles of competence and warmth. Nevertheless, we found that untrustworthiness was still viewed as more typical of atheists than of either feminists or Jews.

This theory is a step in the right direction, and helps us appreciate that the content of stereotypes matters a great deal, and that the diversity of different prejudices is part of the explanation. However, it does not go far enough to explain the peculiar nature of atheist distrust, and because it is not a cultural evolutionary theory, it is silent about the religious origins of large-scale cooperation. Aside from failing to distinguish stereotypes of atheists from those of feminists and Jewish people—who despite their identical warmth/competence profiles are trusted much more than atheists—it does not clearly delineate between trust and pleasantness, which would likely be classified together under the umbrella of "warmth." Trust and pleasantness, however are different things, and in fact in our studies they led to very different moral reactions. More significantly, however, we have found many indications that antipathy toward atheists has religious origins: (1) it is specifically about distrust rather than disgust, fear, or general dislike; (2) it is strongly and consistently predicted by religious belief; and (3) to be even more precise, it is driven by the religious intuition that people lacking belief in supernatural surveillance cannot act morally.

It is also worth considering another perspective, which says that maybe atheists are distrusted because they are seen as a threat to ingroup morality. Social psychologists have known for a long time that people tend to view their ingroups in moralistic terms. This may lead to distrust of outgroups to the extent that outgroups are perceived to threaten the basis of this ingroup morality. For participants with a prominent religious ingroup identification (for example, Christians), atheists might be distrusted because they threaten the moral basis of the ingroup. This perspective also predicts that, as we have found, distrust of atheists is related to religiosity. However, this approach does not obviously predict that atheists should be more distrusted than other groups often viewed as opposed to traditional Christian morality, such as Muslims and gay men. Perhaps atheists' denial of God is seen as more directly antithetical to religious ingroup values than the beliefs and lifestyles of Muslims and gay men, leading to more distrust of atheists.[10]

Although this possibility has some merit, there are two key findings predicted by the theory discussed here, but not a framework based on threats to ingroup morality. First, we have found that people who believe in God, but report having no religious affiliation (and therefore no religious ingroup to defend against moral threats), still distrust atheists. And even in this group of nonaffiliated individuals, greater belief in God still predicts greater distrust of atheists. Second, we have found that concerns about supernatural monitoring explain why believers distrust atheists. These concerns are basic to our explanations focusing on supernatural monitoring, but wholly absent from an approach that emphasizes threats to group morality.

Finally, there is a third perspective that is also informed by a cultural evolutionary approach. In this view, religiously transmitted and enforced prosocial norms may also contribute to distrust of atheists. This could happen because religious similarity is, among other things, a potent cue that another individual shares one's norms and beliefs, and thus can be trusted. In this view, ethnic outgroups, gays, and atheists may differ in the particular norms to which they are perceived to adhere, and perceptions of atheist norms (or the lack thereof) might lead religious individuals to distrust atheists.

The perceived norms of atheists might simply be more threatening to religious individuals than those of other groups. This is likely because although religious people might infer that ethnic outgroup members or gays hold norms that differ from their own, atheists might be seen as holding norms that are directly antithetical to their own. Or, it could be that atheists may be distrusted because people are unsure what exactly atheists believe. A Christian or a Hindu, for example, might be able to infer some of the norms of a Muslim, but an atheist might be viewed as a wildcard; religious people might distrust atheists not only for the norms they are perceived to follow, but also for their perceived lack of norms.[11]

This possibility is not a counterexplanation to the account I presented here. In fact, it complements it rather nicely because, even if atheists are believed to share one's social norms, one might nonetheless be doubtful of the atheist's commitment to uphold those norms given that atheists do not think they are being watched by gods. The perceived belief in supernatural monitoring, and the threat of supernatural punishment that comes with monitoring, may ensure the belief that a person of faith adheres to prosocial norms, but this motivation is seen to be lacking in an atheist.

From Watchful Gods to Watchful Governments

So far, I have painted a picture that may seem quite bleak. Religion with Big Gods is the key reason why there is prejudice toward atheists. Most people in the world are religious in this sense. Not surprisingly, most people who share these cultural traditions distrust atheists. Not only that, but they seem to be deeply distrusted even as tolerance of other stigmatized groups has improved markedly. Since trust is an essential ingredient of social life, atheists who live in deeply religious societies and openly express their beliefs risk being targeted and excluded.

However, things are not as bleak for atheists after all. There is one critical condition that, when present, markedly reduces atheist distrust. And by this I do not mean secularization per se. Of course, since the roots of this prejudice can be found in the beliefs of prosocial religions, one place to look would be the factors that weaken religion's grip on society. (I discuss this issue in chapter 10.) We know that distrust of atheists declines significantly as religious currents themselves wane. After all, international comparisons show that atheist distrust is miniscule to nonexistent in highly secularized countries such as the ones in Scandinavia and Northern Europe. However, this is hardly newsworthy. For one thing, it boils down to saying that atheists are less likely to distrust themselves! Moreover, despite secularization in some parts of the world such as Europe, levels of religiosity in the world have remained largely unchanged.[12] Therefore, banking on the decline of religion to combat prejudice against atheists is not going to be very successful for the time being.

What I have in mind is something much more interesting and important. It is interesting because it is an unlikely source of prejudice reduction that flows directly from the logic of the analysis presented here, but does not easily flow from other perspectives; and it is important because it leads to the decline of atheist distrust *among believers*—the very group that is most likely to hold exclusionary attitudes toward atheists in the first place.

That unlikely source is *effective secular institutions*. What I mean by this is cultural exposure to institutions and mechanisms such as courts, contracts, and police that have emerged in some modern societies and that are designed to monitor human behavior and make people accountable. The logic of the argument is as follows: if atheists are seen as untrustworthy because they do not believe in *supernatural* monitoring, then perhaps exposure to *secular* monitoring might erode the root cause of atheist distrust—the religious anxiety that atheists are moral wildcards because they are unconstrained by any kind of social monitoring.

We know that supernatural monitoring is far from the only source of prosociality in the world. Secular authorities have joined (and perhaps supplanted) watchful gods as guarantors of cooperation in some places, with interesting psychological consequences that I discuss in more detail in chapter 10. There is extensive evidence for this claim from the field, and preliminary evidence from the lab. In the field, economists and sociologists consistently find that people living in societies with strong secular institutions, compared to those living in societies with weak institutions, are far more trusting of other citizens, more prosocial, and more likely to punish freeriders.[13] In the laboratory, we have seen in chapter 3 that reminders of secular concepts (for example, civic, jury, police) are as effective as reminders of a watchful God in promoting generous behavior among Canadians.[14] This suggests an intriguing dynamic, that when it comes to enforcing cooperation and trust, gods and governments may be interchangeable.

This dynamic has direct implications for distrust of atheists. The view that atheists are untrustworthy because they do not believe that their behavior is monitored by a divine power may erode to the extent that people are aware of effective monitoring by other "higher"—though not supernatural—powers. If true, then we should expect two things: First, believers who live in societies with strong secular institutions should express less distrust of atheists than believers in societies having weak secular institutions. This suggests a straightforward hypothesis: across nations, strength of secular rule of law should be associated with lower distrust of atheists holding constant religiosity levels and other relevant factors. Second, this analysis suggests that exposure to secular authority *causes* reduced distrust of atheists. In cross-national analyses, we cannot show conclusively that rule of law is the causal factor, but what we can do is conduct laboratory experiments in which we could make people temporarily think about secular institutions before asking them about their attitudes about atheists. This suggests another straightforward hypothesis: reminders of secular authorities that enforce prosocial behavior should reduce distrust of atheists. Furthermore, this effect should be specific to atheist distrust, and not a general feature of prejudice. Will Gervais and I tested these ideas, combining a cross-cultural analysis with laboratory studies.

In a study spanning 54 countries across the globe, we took advantage of cross-cultural variability in atheist distrust to evaluate the first hypothesis. First, we measured average levels of distrust of atheists for each country, relying on a standard measure that assesses how willing people are to vote for atheist political candidates. We then borrowed a per country measure of "rule of law" developed by the World Bank, which assesses a government's ability to establish effective institutions. Rule of law directly measures the degree to which secular authorities create and enforce laws that help guarantee several aspects of individual coordination and cooperation. It includes factors such as quality of contract enforcement, firmness of property rights, low perceptions of corruption in the police, and high levels of trust in the courts. There is also wide variability in the world on this measure, with countries in Northern Europe, Canada, Australia, Chile, Japan, and the United States scoring very high, whereas most developing countries score low. Finally, we included only believers in our samples (excluding self-described atheists), and took into account a host of other variables that served as controls. We found that, all else being equal, believers from countries with a firmly established secular rule of law showed markedly reduced distrust of atheists compared to believers from countries with weak secular rule of law. In other words, this finding says that two equally fervent believers express different levels of distrust toward atheists depending on whether they live in a society with strong or weak rule of law.[15]

There are two important insights to appreciate about this finding. First, rule of law was associated with less atheist distrust not just because people in countries with strong rule of law trust people in general. We know this because this finding did not change even after we included levels of trust toward people in general in our statistical models. We found that rule of law specifically reduced atheist distrust, above and beyond contributing to general levels of trust. Second, rule of law reduced atheist distrust even after controlling for individuals' demographic characteristics, such as age, sex, education, and income. More importantly, we found that rule of law remained a significant source of reduced atheist distrust even after we removed the contributions of two known country-level factors that are associated with diminished atheist distrust: human development as measured by the United Nations (combined measure of economic wealth, longevity, and education levels) and individualism. What this means is that believers in countries with strong rule of law distrust atheists less not simply because these countries happen to have high levels of human welfare, and not simply because these countries value the autonomy of individuals and their rights to freely express themselves. Matching countries on human development, individualism, and religiosity levels, those with stronger institutions have believers who are markedly less likely to distrust atheists.

At this point, you the reader might be wondering, what about the United States, which is characterized with both high levels of rule of law but also high levels of atheist distrust? Interestingly, the United States is an outlier. At the dawn of the twenty-first century, 39 percent percent of Americans strongly agree or agree that politicians who do not believe in God are unfit for public office. This high number is lower than other highly religious but much poorer countries such as Pakistan (95 percent), but comparable to its very religious southern neighbor Mexico (39 percent). In America's northern neighbor and close cultural cousin Canada, this distrust is much less pronounced (21 percent). But Canada's atheist distrust is higher than comparably developed nations with high human development and strong rule of law, but much less religious, such as the UK (11 percent), Denmark (8 percent), and Sweden (4 percent), where distrust of atheists is virtually nonexistent. Why is it that the United States has levels of atheist distrust that are so out of step with other wealthy advanced democracies? This is a complex issue, but there is at least one answer to this puzzle that has to do with two oddities about the United States: for interesting reasons, America, despite being an economic power-house, has anomalously high religiosity levels, and we have seen that religiosity is the single most important determinant of atheist distrust.

Despite the American exception, as a rule, and with the usual caveat "all-else-being-equal," strong secular institutions significantly dampen believers' distrust of atheists. Nevertheless, cross-cultural studies such as this one, as insightful as they are, have one big weakness: they cannot tell us with certainty the causal direction of the effect. There is always the possibility that some other third variable that we did not think of causes societies to develop strong institutions and causes people who live in these societies to trust atheists. The gold standard for establishing causality is the experiment with random assignment and a control condition. In a series of such experiments led by Will Gervais, we wanted to know if mere reminders of secular authority would reduce distrust of atheists.

Gervais and I tested whether reminders of secular authority reduce distrust of atheists among believers. In addition, we tested three plausible alternative explanations. First, it is possible that a reduction in atheist distrust might just be one instantiation of a broader effect whereby reminders of secular authority reduce prejudice not just toward atheists, but toward any group. Second, as we have seen, evolutionary approaches to prejudice demonstrate that different prejudices are characterized by different perceived threats; secular authority may dampen these specific reactions across different forms of prejudice. Finally, it is possible that reminders of secular authority might simply make all outgroups seem more trustworthy.

In one study, we randomly assigned Canadian believing participants in Vancouver to watch a video that detailed the many successes of the Vancouver Police Department in 2010. (It was, in fact, a portion of the Vancouver Police Chief's year-end report, the same year that Vancouver hosted the Winter Olympics.) In the control condition, believing participants were randomly assigned to watch a traveler's impression of Vancouver as a tourist attraction ("the city lives outdoors," "bland architecture"). Following this treatment, all participants were asked how they felt toward a variety of groups, including atheists. We found that reminders of effective secular authority reduced distrust of atheists, but did not affect feelings toward three other groups—gay men, Muslims, and Jewish people. In a second study, we utilized a more subtle priming technique in which participants are not consciously aware that researchers are priming a given concept. This was, in fact, the same implicit secular authority prime (words such as *court, police, contract*) that was previously found to increase generosity in an economic game. We found that subtle reminders of secular authority reduced distrust of atheists, but did not reduce prejudice against gays. Finally, we found that implicit reminders of secular authority once again reduced distrust of atheists, but had no effect on distrust of other groups. These results nicely match the cross-cultural pattern and suggest that secular authority reduced atheist distrust among believers. But it is important to emphasize that these studies were conducted in Canada, a country with strong government and high levels of trust toward secular institutions. Had the present experiments been conducted in a country where people have little trust in their government, reminders of an inept or corrupt government might instead have *increased* atheist distrust. Having a watchful government that monitors every move of its citizens is not going to replace religion and reduce atheist distrust. Corrupt police states such as Pakistan, Syria, and Belarus, after all, have watchful governments but populations that have little trust in them, and therefore score quite low in rule of law.

Before ending this chapter, I'd like to mention one other mitigating factor that Will Gervais has identified. In his classic study of prejudice, the noted psychologist Gordon Allport observed that there are stronger feelings of prejudice toward groups that loom large. Subsequently, researchers have confirmed this pattern. For example, anti-black prejudice is stronger in regions of the United States where black people are a greater percentage of the local population. However, most research relating prejudice to outgroup size comes from investigations of anti-black prejudice in America, and we know that when it comes to this particular prejudice, fear is a prominent emotional reaction.[16] It is unsurprising that prejudice is positively associated with the relative size of a feared group that is seen as a threat to safety and property. However, prejudices based on different perceived threats might be differentially affected by outgroup prevalence.[17]

Although outgroup size elevates prejudice characterized by fear, it may have the opposite effect for prejudice characterized by distrust. To appreciate why this might be, note that there is some inherent tension between distrust of atheists and the latter's collective inconspicuousness. One would expect that such an untrustworthy group would be readily apparent, as their widespread immorality would leave obvious effects. These two facts could be reconciled if atheists were rare: even an untrustworthy group can escape notice if it is small enough. But atheist distrust may be undermined if atheists are both inconspicuous and believed to be numerous.

Gervais found converging evidence to support this prediction. First, across nations, anti-atheist prejudice among believers was reduced where atheists are more numerous, even after controlling for important individual and international differences, such as conservatism, human development, and individualism. Second, in a Canadian university sample, anti-atheist prejudice was reduced among believers who thought that atheists were more common, and this was the case especially among the *most* deeply religious participants. Last, it was found that experimentally induced reminders of how common atheists are statistically eliminated anti-atheist prejudice. These reminders did not affect perceptions of contact with atheists or other prejudice toward other groups.

These findings have important policy implications, and there may be lessons for atheists in the gay liberation movement. As Gervais observes:

Like atheism, homosexuality is concealable, and people may similarly be uncertain of how numerous atheists and homosexuals actually are. This similarity is strongly emphasized by Dawkins . . . who argues that anti-atheist prejudice might be overcome if atheists can find a way to "come out" and raise public awareness of atheism like the Gay Pride movement mobilized widespread support for the acceptance of homosexuality. These movements make plain how numerous atheists and homosexuals actually are.[18]

In summary, we know of three factors that can reliably reduce believers' prejudice of atheists: (1) exposure to or reminders of strong institutions that create prosocial norms; (2) exposure to or reminders of atheists' prevalence, and (3) of course, the decline of religiosity in a given society.[19] It is interesting to note that these three factors are likely to operate in tandem and could be mutually reinforcing. As societies increasingly rely on secular institutions to enforce cooperation, religiosity declines, and so does distrust of atheists. With more secularization and greater acceptance of atheists, atheism spreads, and as atheists become more prevalent and visible, distrust of atheists declines further, which in turn contributes to more secularization. This state of affairs appears to describe societies in Scandinavia, such as Denmark and Sweden, where one finds one of the world's top performers when it comes to rule of law, very high levels of social solidarity and trust, very low levels of religiosity, and virtually no distrust of atheists. It is a matter of debate as to why some modern societies such as Scandinavian ones succeeded in building strong government institutions but others still do not. But whatever the origins of these institutions, they likely unleashed a transforming process that has had wide-ranging effects. These processes will be discussed in more depth in chapter 10.

Chapter 6

True Believers

Why are major world religions so preoccupied with religious hypocrisy? Christian teachings, for example, seem almost resigned to the fact that, by virtue of being a cooperative community, the Church will always be vulnerable to "bad seeds" in its midst. In Matthew 13:24–30, Jesus says in the form of a parable:

> The kingdom of heaven may be compared to a man who sowed good seed in his field, but while his men were sleeping, his enemy came and sowed weeds among the wheat and went away. So when the plants came up and bore grain, then the weeds appeared also. And the servants of the master of the house came and said to him, "Master, did you not sow good seed in your field? How then does it have weeds?" He said to them, "An enemy has done this." So the servants said to him, "Then do you want us to go and gather them?" But he said, "No, lest in gathering the weeds you root up the wheat along with them. Let both grow together until the harvest, and at harvest time I will tell the reapers, Gather the weeds first and bind them in bundles to be burned, but gather the wheat into my barn."[1]

Religious hypocrisy makes for famously despised characters in literature as well. In Molière's celebrated play *Tartuffe*, Orgon, a wealthy family don, falls for Tartuffe, a con man who pretends to be a devout believer. Tartuffe manipulates Orgon into showering him with generous gifts and social privileges, at one point even influencing Orgon to offer his daughter in marriage. After repeatedly rebuffing warnings about Tartuffe, finally Orgon discovers Tartuffe's hypocrisy when he overhears Tartuffe's attempts to seduce his wife. Cléante, Orgon's brother-in-law, expresses his deep contempt of religious hypocrisy:

> And just as there is nothing I more revere
> Than a soul whose faith is steadfast and sincere,
> Nothing that I more cherish and admire
> Than honest zeal and true religious fire
> So there is nothing that I find more base
> Than specious piety's dishonest face.[2]

So far, I have argued that (1) watched people are nice people, and (2) people who sincerely believe that they are being watched, are, in turn, trusted more. Together, these two observations can go a long way in explaining how cooperation can evolve among genetic strangers. However, there is a missing piece in this explanation. If belief in supernatural monitoring elicits more trust and cooperation, what would prevent religious hypocrites from faking belief in supernatural monitors to get into the group and receive benefits without contributing? If there were no safeguards to keep these impostors in check, prosocial religious groups would be invaded by these selfish religious hypocrites, who would soon outnumber sincere believers. Group solidarity would soon fizzle out.[3]

The problem of religious hypocrisy brings us to the fifth principle of supernatural monitoring:

Religious actions speak louder than words.

To complete the picture, we must pay a visit to one of the most interesting—and puzzling—aspects of many religious practices and behaviors: their extravagance and apparent cost to the self.

For a historical example of an extreme form of extravagance, we have the charismatic priests of the Anatolian goddess Cybele who ritually castrated themselves, and subsequently took on female identities. These public self-castrations often led to waves of popular devotion to Cybele in the early Roman Empire, and Cybele religion attracted a large following, often competing with the inroads made by early Christianity. Ecstatic followers of Cybele were known to take part in nightly orgies involving music, song, dance, shouting, and drumming—practices that, no doubt, were popular among the following but most likely unpopular with their sleep-deprived, less devoted, neighbors.[4]

As extreme as self-castrating practices are, the followers of Cybele were not an isolated case. The nineteenth-century Russian Christian sect known as *Skoptsy* also practiced self-castration. Both men and women did away with their genitalia in an effort to achieve sexual purity and facilitate the second coming of Christ. Although persecuted by the Imperial Russian government, they attracted a sizable following from various social strata, including peasants, nobles, and civil servants. Many were deported to Siberia. Although reliable statistics about *Skoptsy* followers are hard to come by, judging from the number of arrested members, by the early twentieth century when their decline started, their numbers may have reached as high as 100,000 followers.[5]

The Thaipusam festival, among Tamil Hindu communities in Malaysia, Singapore, and elsewhere, is a yearly celebration in which devoted Hindus engage in various public acts of self-sacrifice, known as the Cavadee. It is believed that these acts will appease Lord Murugan, the Tamil God of War, or result in favors granted. These acts can range from the mild, such as shaving one's head and carrying a light load, to severe, such as days of fasting prior to the festival, walking on nails, and piercing the skin, tongue, and cheeks with skewers (figure 6.1). The greater the pain, the more divine credit earned with Lord Murugan, and the greater the social prestige achieved in the community.[6]

▶

Figure 6.1. (*facing page*) *Panel a*: Self-scarification known as the Cavadee, in the annual Thaipusam festival among Tamil Hindu devotees in Mauritius (courtesy of Dimitris Xygalatas). *Panel b*: Annual reenactment of the Crucifixion in the Philippines, where devout Roman Catholic volunteers are actually whipped and nailed to crosses (courtesy of Baptiste Marcel). *Panel c*: Annual hajj (Muslim pilgrimage) to Mecca involving an elaborate series of rituals including fasts, restrictions on clothing, and physical endurance (courtesy of Bluemango2zz). Such extravagant behaviors are commonly found in prosocial religions, convey credible devotion to members and potential converts, and are likely to be culturally contagious.

(a)

(b)

(c)

Why would religious devotees do such things that sabotage one's fitness? Evolutionary scientists have long puzzled over such extravagant practices and rituals, found in some religious groups, that demand sacrifices of time, effort, resources, and in some cases of life and limb. These displays—such as rites of terror, scarification, and various restrictions on behavior (sex, material belongings, giving away valuable animals), diet (long fasts and costly food taboos), and lifestyle (strict marriage rules, dress codes)—are endemic, though not unique, to prosocial religions. They are often costly, are emotionally loaded, and appear irrational to outsiders. However, just as the irrationality of falling in love tells us that there is a genuine commitment to a romantic relationship,[7] religious fervor may have its logic too: it communicates a hard-to-fake commitment to the beliefs of the religious group.

The anthropologist Joe Henrich offers an account of these extravagant performances that is based on cultural evolutionary logic. I dwell on this account in some detail, because it is a critical piece of the puzzle, and works with supernatural monitoring to explain the cultural spread of belief in Big Gods. I will also explore a "costly signaling" explanation of these religious behaviors. These two evolutionary explanations are not incompatible—in fact, they may work together to build solidarity. But they do have different implications that will become clear as we explore these behaviors in some detail and try to make sense of them.

As a cultural species, human beings are highly dependent on others for fitness-relevant information. Therefore, a powerful set of cultural learning mechanisms allows learners to acquire useful beliefs and behaviors from reliable cultural paragons—these include preferentially learning from the majority of ingroup members, and from prestigious or successful individuals who exercise disproportionate social influence on group members. However, cultural paragons have to be credible, and credibility does not come for free. Belief can be easily faked, which allows cultural opinion makers to manipulate cultural learners by believing one thing but convincing the latter of something else. One evolutionary solution to this dilemma, Henrich argues, is a cognitive bias toward accepting beliefs that are backed up by deeds that would otherwise not be performed unless they were genuinely believed by these opinion makers. In short, we want to see that people walk the walk and not just talk the talk. In this sense, extravagant religious behaviors are what Henrich calls "credibility-enhancing displays," or CREDs—behaviors that in religious groups are reliably associated with genuine belief in counterintuitive gods and can be used to infer sincere commitment to them.[8]

These kinds of extravagant displays are often seen in influential religious leaders, who then transmit these beliefs to their followers. For instance, the ritualized public self-castrations of the male priests of the goddess Cybele, discussed earlier, were followed by cultural epidemics of Cybele religious revival in the early Roman Empire. This suggests that these public acts of devotion were not only signals of reliability for other Cybele devotees, they were also tools for proselytizing: they led to the cultural propagation of these credible beliefs to nondevotees. A similar dynamic could be seen in early Christian saints. By their willing martyrdom, they became potent cultural exemplars and encouraged the cultural spread of Christian beliefs. What better way to prove one's sincerity than the willingness to die for these beliefs? And what better way to transmit these beliefs to others than to hold them with irrefutable sincerity?

There are three aspects to this dynamic that are relevant to understanding how these CREDs help build prosocial religions. First, when religious leaders' actions advertise underlying belief with sincerity, their actions energize witnesses and help their beliefs to spread in a group. If, on the other hand, they are not willing to make a significant demonstration of the sincerity of their belief, then observers—even children—may withhold their own commitment. Second, when people believe, they are more likely to perform similar displays themselves. This means that beliefs backed up by extravagant behaviors have the potential to cascade and spread in a population of minds. Third, extravagant displays often are altruistic acts toward other ingroup members. These acts of altruism further escalate the level of ingroup cooperation in prosocial religious groups. Therefore, the fifth principle of supernatural monitoring ensures that belief in supernatural monitors that are backed by credible displays will be more likely to influence witnesses (cultural learners), meaning that these belief-behavior complexes are more likely to enjoy a transmission advantage in the cultural marketplace. In turn, groups that adopt such practices would be expected to outcompete groups that fail to find alternative mechanisms to ensure trust and solidarity.

It is important to appreciate three clarifications about credible displays of devotion. First, people are not always willing to engage in these extravagant displays, and there is variability in the degree to which people want to do them. In fact, cultural demand for extravagant religious behaviors appears to wax and wane over time even within the same group. (Consider, for example, how strictly American Catholics followed religious doctrines and rituals in the past, compared to the lenient lifestyles of mainstream American Catholics today.) In their book *The Churching of America*, sociologists Roger Finke and Rodney Stark observe a common cyclical pattern seen in American Christian denominations between the eighteenth and twentieth centuries. Sects come into existence, gain adherents, and establish themselves, and as they get older and enter the mainstream, they soften their doctrine and demand less of their adherents. Dissatisfied with the laxness of what is now a mainline church, splinter groups emerge that once again attract adherents by offering a more strict and zealous version of the faith, only to once again expand and succumb to the effects of time, leading to further schisms, and so on.[9]

Second, although these displays are commonly found in many prosocial religions, they are not universally associated with religious belief. Many supernatural concepts found, for example, in folktales, do not seem to be attached to credible displays. As just discussed, Finke and Stark's observations show that mainline religious groups have much less of these extravagant displays, or none at all (self-castration for Unitarians, anyone?). Indeed, our task is precisely to explain why such displays get attached to some supernatural beliefs but not others—an issue I turn to later in this chapter.

Third, although endemic to prosocial religious groups, CREDs are not unique to them. It is hard to imagine atheists coming together and engaging in passionate displays of commitment to their absence of belief in a god. Nevertheless, we see CRED-like behaviors in a variety of nonreligious contexts, such as in political persuasion, education, sports, the military, and indeed any domain of life where cultural leaders exert an influence on cultural learners, and in contexts where cultural groups form and try to attract sincerely committed adherents. All three of these characteristics are compatible with a cultural evolutionary perspective, which, unlike genetic accounts, does not require that these practices be universal features of religions, nor be unique to them.

What about "costly signaling" theories of religion, which also deal with such extravagant displays? In fact, this approach precedes the CRED idea. Evolutionary anthropologists William Irons, Richard Sosis, Joseph Bulbulia, and their colleagues have argued that these displays are rooted in genetic evolution. Their starting point is the field of behavioral ecology. Behavioral ecologists have long been fascinated by the extravagance and costliness of animal signals—for example, the colorful and expansive peacock tail, birdsong, or dominance displays in primates (all of these traits are costly because they consume precious resources and may attract predators). Costly signaling theory says that these displays are hard-to-fake signals that reliably indicate an underlying trait to observers. For example, the extravagant male peacock tail was sexually selected to indicate to peahens the male's mating quality.[10]

Similar to these animal signals, some theorists see extravagant religious displays as costly signals of group commitment that was a naturally selected adaptation for life in cooperative groups. In this view, a signal is reliable only to the extent that it is costlier to fake by potential freeloaders than for cooperators. If religious groups are cooperative groups, what would prevent selfish imposters from faking prosocial intent, receiving cooperative benefits without reciprocating? Because mere professions of religious belief can be easily faked, evolutionary pressures have favored costly religious displays that are not subject to rational calculations of cost-benefit analysis. Thus, costly religious behaviors are seen as naturally selected honest signals that reliably advertise the unobservable trait of group commitment.[11]

Costly signaling and cultural evolutionary or CRED explanations are not incompatible approaches. On the contrary, they may be mutually complementary. They are, however, distinct accounts that could help us make sense of religious extravagance. There are, therefore, interesting differences between the two accounts. First is whether these behaviors are necessarily costly. When I described CREDs, I carefully avoided the term *costly*, and instead used *extravagance*, because CREDs, unlike costly signals, need not be costly. To see why, consider an example discussed by Henrich. Imagine you are foraging for mushrooms in the forest, but you are worried that some of them could be poisonous. Then you meet a stranger who tells you that it is fine to eat the flat yellow mushrooms. Should you trust this person's advice? Now imagine that this stranger not only says that the flat yellow mushrooms are safe and nutritious but actually picks one and eats it in front of your eyes. Now, in the second scenario, you just witnessed a CRED, and I suspect you agree that this CRED makes the stranger a much more persuasive cultural model: she just performed an action that she would be extremely unlikely to do if she held the opposite view. And importantly, the stranger's action was not costly at all. (There is no cost to eating a nutritious mushroom that one knows to be safe.) But it was nevertheless a *credible* signal to the observer. Actions speak louder than words, but they need not be costly to be credible.

A second difference between CREDs and costly signals is that costly signals are thought to be the product of genetic evolution, which suggests that costly behaviors should be a universal feature of religions. The CRED model, on the other hand, is a cultural transmission model and does not require, or predict, such universality. If many, or even some, religious behaviors are extravagant displays, that pattern would be consistent with a cultural evolutionary framework. Genetic accounts, on the other hand, although certainly not incompatible with cultural variability, are more consistent with the idea that these behaviors are universally shared by religions.

A third difference is that in signaling, the behavior is a reliable reflection of group commitment and/or cooperation, whereas in CRED, it reliably reflects an underlying culturally transmitted belief. One issue with signaling accounts of religious displays is that it is unclear why it is more costly for nonbelievers to perform the costly acts than for believers, since beliefs are culturally transmitted, and are quite unlike possessing a genetically fixed physical attribute (such as physical stamina, height or large body size, or a colorful tail). Therefore, it seems that explaining costly religious displays requires cultural transmission of beliefs underlying these behaviors, which brings us back to a cultural evolutionary consideration of how beliefs get transmitted in the first place.

As I discussed earlier, these two approaches overlap considerably, and are quite compatible. A key difference between them is that they tell a different tale about the origin of these displays—genetic versus cultural transmission. This divergence allows us to make different predictions from these two approaches about whether exposure to extravagant displays causes individuals to adopt religious beliefs that underlie the behaviors. The CRED framework predicts that witnessing extravagant religious displays *causes* cultural contagion of religious beliefs. For example, consider a situation where people observe someone perform an act of sacrifice to, say, Shiva. Observers who witness this act would increase the tendency to be persuaded by the potency of Shiva as a god, and as a result, they would feel greater commitment to Shiva. In short, CREDs have the power to induce greater belief and commitment among observers.

The costly signaling framework sees costly displays as reliable signals that elicit cooperation, but it does not clearly expect causal effects on levels of belief or commitment in observers. To continue with the previous example, if sacrificing for Shiva is a costly signal but not a CRED, then witnesses would be more cooperative toward the self-sacrificing Shiva-worshipper, but they would not become more dedicated Shiva-worshippers themselves. Therefore, if extravagant religious behaviors are costly signals evolved by natural selection and nothing more, exposure to these signals should induce more cooperation toward the signal-holder but should not cause greater cultural contagion. In contrast, if these behaviors are also CREDs, we would expect that exposure to them should lead to both greater cooperation and greater likelihood of adopting the beliefs that are associated with the behaviors. Historical examples suggest that extravagant religious behaviors, above and beyond any signaling, also act like CREDs, but careful experimental work is needed to tease apart these different possibilities.[12] In one such field experiment, a team of researchers led by Dimitris Xygalatas investigated prosocial behavior in a sample of Tamil Hindus in Mauritius, who had participated in, or witnessed, the Cavadee ritual in the yearly Thaipusam festival, discussed earlier. One interesting result was that both participation in and witnessing this intense ritual equally increased anonymous donations to the temple, and heightened identification with Mauritian culture. The fact that witnessing was as potent as participating suggests a CRED-like effect.[13]

Regardless of the precise mechanisms underlying extravagant religious displays, there is mounting evidence that they do contribute to group solidarity, further cementing prosociality in religious groups. For example, sociological analyses show that groups that impose more costly requirements have members who are more committed. For example, Lee Iannacone reports that, controlling for relevant sociodemographic variables, "strict" Protestant and Jewish denominations (Mormons, Orthodox) show higher levels of church and synagogue attendance, respectively, and make more monetary contributions to their religious communities (despite *lower* average income levels) than less strict ones (Methodist, Reform).[14] No wonder, denominational differences in religious commitment are the source of countless jokes: Orthodox Rabbi to Reform Rabbi, "This kid wants a Harley for his Bar Mitzvah, what's a Harley?" Reform Rabbi: "It's a motorcycle. What's a Bar Mitzvah?"

These findings are an important piece of the puzzle, as they show that extravagant behaviors are associated with greater levels of commitment to the group. But they do not demonstrate, by themselves, that strictness is associated with community survival and growth. For direct evidence on group solidarity, we turn to a groundbreaking study that was done by the anthropologist Richard Sosis. In chapter 1, I discussed Sosis's study regarding the survival rates of religious and secular communes in nineteenth-century America. One of Sosis's main findings was that religious communes were found to outlast those motivated by secular ideologies such as socialism. However, there is more. In a follow-up study, Sosis and his colleagues went further. In a more fine-grained analysis of 83 of these religious and secular communes for which more detailed records are available, they explained *why* religious communes outlasted secular ones. They turned their attention to costs imposed by religious and secular communes on their members. Two critical questions were posed: (1) Did religious groups outlast secular ones because religious groups imposed more costly requirements than secular ones? (2) Did religious groups with more costly requirements survive longer than religious groups with fewer costly requirements?

All in all, they counted 22 categories of costly requirements, which included food taboos, fasts, restrictions on material possessions, marriage, sex, and communication with the outside world. Their findings were striking:

- Religious communes imposed more than twice as many costly requirements than secular (mostly socialist) communes, and this difference emerged for each of the 22 categories of costly behaviors examined.
- Religious communes were about four times less likely than secular ones to dissolve at any given year as a result of internal conflict, economic hardship, or natural disaster. Importantly, the number of costly requirements predicted religious commune longevity, after controlling for population size and income and year the commune was founded (to control for fluctuations in historical events that might have independently influenced commune longevity).
- Religion was not a predictor of commune longevity once the number of costly requirements was statistically controlled, suggesting that the survival advantage of religious communes was due to the greater cost commitment of their members.

- Interestingly, the number of costly requirements did not predict longevity for secular communes. This means that there is something distinctive about religious groups that makes costly behaviors a potent source of social solidarity. There could be several reasons why religious but not secular communes benefit from imposition of costly behaviors, but supernatural monitoring ought to be one key factor that galvanizes and amplifies social solidarity if it is backed up by extravagant displays of faith.[15]

It is becoming clear that prosocial religious groups, by promoting trust among their members, attract adherents at greater rates than groups without mechanisms to enforce trust. Also, there is good reason to expect that groups with high trust are, all else being equal, politically and militarily more potent, and able to directly impose their beliefs on others through political coercion and warfare. Extravagant behaviors such as CREDs are a powerful mechanism for reducing religious hypocrisy and building trust, which, combined with supernatural monitoring, have given prosocial religious groups an edge over rival groups. Returning to Ensminger's analysis of the spread of Islam into Africa, it is apparent that belief in an all-powerful Allah who knows everything and cares about morality, supported by credible displays of sincere devotion that included charity, fasts, daily prayer, and restrictions on diet and sexual behavior, permitted greater trust, shared rules of economic exchange, and the use of credit institutions among newly converted Muslims. This facilitated more trade and greater economic success. Kenyan pastoralists, as well as other local African groups, began adopting the religious beliefs along with the associated institutions and rituals. Ensminger writes, "such groups [Islamic converts] may have attracted followers at a greater rate than other, thus increasing the ranks of the converted."[16]

Having explained how cultural evolution favored extravagant religious displays of commitment, I now turn to another riddle that has challenged cognitive scientists of religion: why do some supernatural agents attract passionate devotion (such as belief in Jesus or Allah), while others are merely the object of fantasy (fairies), fiction (Santa Claus for adults), or even amusement (Zeus who once was a powerful god who no longer is)? Any explanation of how people come to be "true believers" ought to help us understand not just how people think about supernatural agents, but how it is that these true believers come to passionately commit to some deities but not others.

To get answers, we must turn, once again, to the cultural learning biases that influence peoples' tendency to selectively acquire beliefs from some people but not others, even when the content of beliefs is similar.

Anatomy of Religious Belief

When I was a graduate student of psychology in the late 1990s, I came across a fascinating book by Pascal Boyer, titled *The Naturalness of Religious Ideas: A Cognitive Theory of Religion*. I was instantly captivated. You see, this was a time when psychology and cognitive science had little, if anything, to say about what is religion and what features of the human mind makes us religious. (Even today, religion is hardly on a psychology student's menu of readings. But there is now considerably more research than before.) For someone like me who grew up in the religious strife of Lebanon in the 1980s, this was shocking. Like many people, I was very curious and wanted to know: What is religion? What makes people religious? What predisposes people toward supernatural belief? Why are people willing to sacrifice or kill for some of these beliefs (but not for others)? I would flip through psychology textbook after textbook, searching, in vain, for the words *religion, belief, supernatural*, or *ritual*. I could not find a single entry, not even in social psychology, my own home field, where one would have expected a mountain of interest in one of the most enduring and deeply affecting aspects of social life around the world. Given this dearth, *The Naturalness of Religious Ideas* offered a bold new theory, a scientifically plausible account of how human minds give rise to religious ideas.

Boyer's perspective, along with work by other psychologists and anthropologists such as Robert McCauley and Tom Lawson, Justin Barrett, Scott Atran, and others came to be known in the evolutionary study of religion as the *cognitive by-product* perspective. In chapter 2, I discussed some of the key insights from this perspective that help us understand how Big Gods got off the ground by resonating with core intuitions that human minds are equipped with.

The basic idea of the cognitive by-product view is that mental content that is psychologically more evocative, or "contagious," propagates better. This makes religious belief not a naturally selected adaptation but a nonadaptive by-product of a suite of cognitive predispositions that originally evolved to serve other (nonreligious) functions.[17] We can be more specific about this basic insight. We pay attention to, remember, and transmit concepts that resonate with strong emotions, that help us understand and predict the world better, and that are moderately (but not totally) compatible with our intuitive understanding of the world.[18]

First, information that is emotionally evocative sparks more positive or negative emotional responses that our brains pay attention to, remember, and subsequently transmit. Research by psychologist Dan Gilbert and his colleagues suggests that when mental representations are initially encountered, they are spontaneously perceived to be true, resulting in immediate acceptance; however, when we have strong affective reactions such as disgust and fear, we devote more cognitive resources to the relevant information. This means our memories, and retellings of these memories, have more of this emotionally loaded content, which in turn leaves a stronger mark on what gets culturally transmitted.[19]

Chip Heath, Chris Bell, and Emily Sternberg demonstrated such emotional effects on cultural contagion by looking at urban legends. Remember the one about the rat in the soda bottle? Or the movie star and the gerbil extracted from, well, you know, the anus? Laboratory experiments showed that people are more likely to spread stories that are strongly emotional (evoking feelings such as disgust and anger), even after matching stories on their factual accuracy, as well as their practical and entertainment value. The story about the rat in a soda bottle has far more potential to spread if it ends with the man quenching his thirst and then seeing that there were pieces of dead rat inside the bottle, as opposed to discovering the dead rat in the bottle before taking a sip. A survey of legends on the Internet also revealed that more emotionally loaded urban legends travel farther than their more cool-headed counterparts. As they argued, "Truth doesn't always win out in the 'marketplace of ideas,' sometimes emotion does."[20] Speaking of emotions mattering more than truth, Marwan Sinaceur and Chip Heath showed that such emotional content is not confined to what people remember and transmit—it also affects what people do. They examined the panic over mad cow disease in France in the mid-2000s, and looked at whether or not emotional content influences buying habits. Now, the same disease can be named mad cow (a vividly emotional label) or referred to with an abstract, unemotional scientific name such as BSE or Creutzfeldt-Jacob disease. Not surprisingly, the label *mad cow* won handily—it was twice as common in newspapers and six times more common on the Internet. But more strikingly, the researchers showed that French consumers ate less beef when there was more media attention to *mad cow*, but beef consumption did not decline when the media covered the same disease under scientific labels.[21]

A second reason why concepts travel better is that they help brains do what brains are designed to do: understand and predict life's events. (Pascal Boyer calls this a concept's "inferential potential."[22]) Take for example, the idea that misfortune, such as getting struck by a debilitating illness, is random—it can happen to anyone, anytime, without logic or purpose. This is not a very memorable or popular idea, because it doesn't lead to useful or helpful inferences or actions. Even if true, knowing this fact wouldn't change what we do. In contrast, the folk notion that illnesses are caused by the curse or jealousy of others, or by the wrath of God, is a powerful piece of information that compels further thinking and action. It tells us to be careful about other people who might not have our best interests in their hearts, or to hide our successes from them, or to obey God's will without question, and so on. Ideas that compel action tend to be contagious.

The variety of intuitions that a person might have about how the world works is the third factor that determines how successfully ideas transmit. Beliefs rely heavily on reliably developing intuitions, including intuitions people have about inert physical objects, plants and animals, and intentional beings with consciousness. For example, modern quantum physics tells us that the same particle can exist in two locations simultaneously, which radically violates intuitive expectations from folk notions of physical causality; neuroscience tells us that mental experiences arise from brain activity, which radically violates folk notions of mind-body dualism. These notions don't go far in the cultural marketplace unless they are supported by a heavy dose of instruction and institutional support. Alternatively, according to Dan Sperber, these types of ideas spread only as placeholders. Much like obscure religious ideas like the Holy Trinity or reincarnation, they become popular shells but their content remains opaque and open to interpretation.[23]

Beliefs that radically depart from common sense don't readily transmit, but this does not imply that more intuitive ideas are always better candidates for cultural survival. In fact, the presence of mildly counterintuitive content in concepts or narratives can bias memory in a manner that appears to favor such concepts or narratives in cultural evolution. Counterintuitive concepts or events violate our core assumption about the nature of things in the world, usually about intentional beings, animals, inanimate objects, or events. By departing systematically, but mildly, from established cognitive rules we use to understand and organize information in our environment, these concepts achieve greater memorability. This might be one reason why, as Cristine Legare and her colleagues explain, when children and adults try to make sense of significant events such as illness and death, they seem to simultaneously draw on both supernatural and natural explanations. These are not incompatible ways of seeing the world, as some might think.[24]

Furthermore, the presence of a few counterintuitive concepts in a narrative, even when embedded in otherwise ordinary concepts, improves the transmission advantage of the entire narrative. Many counterintuitive concepts create complex mixtures of plausibility, applicability, and emotional evocativeness. Many religious beliefs, for example, would appear to be more applicable, more emotionally evocative, but less plausible than alternative nonreligious concepts or explanations. If counterintuitive concepts, by their very nature, make stories or beings seem less plausible (less believable), the optimal number of such violations should be small. In a study I did with Scott Atran, Mark Schaller, and Jason Faulkner, we compared a sampling of successful and unsuccessful fairy tales in the famous Brothers Grimm collection. Successful (widely known) fairy tales, such as *Cinderella* and *Little Red Riding Hood*, had just two or three counterintuitive violations. Unsuccessful ones (have you heard of the *Donkey Lettuce*?) had none, or in other cases, quite the opposite—they had far too many violations. Successful counterintuitive representations and stories were also likely to generate emotional responses, like fear, and encouraged additional inferences.[25]

These kinds of memory biases play an important role in religious belief.[26] The extraordinary agents endemic to religions appear to possess a particularly evocative set of abilities not shared by ordinary beings. They can be invisible; they can see things from afar; they can move through physical objects. This minimal counterintuitiveness is memorable, giving these concepts an advantage in cultural transmission. These departures from common sense are systematic but not radical enough to rupture meaning completely. As Sperber has put it, these minimal counterintuitions are *relevant mysteries*: they are closely connected to background knowledge, but do not admit to a final interpretation.[27] Because they arouse attention and are open-textured, people can think about these concepts and what they mean in different, endless ways. These features make them ideal candidates for cultural survival.

Why Mickey Mouse, Santa Claus, and Zeus Are Not Gods

The picture I have painted so far explains why religious concepts tend to have the peculiar cognitive structure that they do, and why such structure is memorable and contagious. However, here is the puzzle: memorability and cultural dispersal are not the same thing as sincere belief in and passionate commitment to religious concepts. There are many minimally counterintuitive agents people know about and think about, but only a subset of these many agents are worshipped. If these cognitive biases operating on belief content are sufficient to explain the persistence of religious beliefs, why do people come to believe in only one or a few supernatural agent concepts, when so many concepts share the same or similar content conducive to cultural success?

Put another way, we must explain one of the most critical features of religions, that of *faith* or *passionate commitment* to supernatural agents. There is a profound psychological difference between supernatural beliefs that are mentally represented but treated as fictional (fairies in folktales, the gods of other religions) and those that are mentally represented and worshipped (the gods of one's own group). Cultural learning biases can explain why some counterintuitive representations galvanize profound commitment, while others are treated merely as entertaining curiosities, despite their transmission advantage. The distinction between mental representation and belief-commitment is crucial to explain cultural differences in the degree of religious commitment around the world, the existence of disbelief, and how certain gods, like Zeus—despite having similar cognitive content throughout the ages—can move from a worshipped deity to the fictional character of myths and stories.

Once I read and digested Boyer's *Naturalness of Religious Ideas*, I went to see Scott Atran, who was at the time visiting the University of Michigan, where I did my doctorate. There was one thing that puzzled me about Boyer's account: if cognitive content was sufficient to explain religious beliefs, why was it that Tom and Jerry, the two beloved cartoon characters of my childhood, were not gods? After all, they seemed to have supernatural powers, such as defying gravity, surviving gruesome death, and telepathy. Where were the droves of devotees ready to sacrifice themselves for Tom the cat and Jerry the mouse? This came to be later known in cognitive science circles as the "Mickey Mouse problem." Here is a related one that Will Gervais and Joseph Henrich call the "Zeus problem": why can a supernatural agent with identical content and supported by exactly the same cognitive biases in one place or time be an idol of immense devotion, while in a different time or place be merely myth or fanciful tale? And then there is the "Santa Claus problem." As the old Santa Claus song says:

> He sees you when you're sleeping
> He knows when you're awake
> He knows if you've been bad or good
> So be good for goodness' sake.

By all accounts, Santa Claus is a powerful moralizing god for children. Yet, when children become adults, Santa is transformed from god to myth, although adults continue to be able to mentally represent, remember, and transmit the mythical idea of Santa Claus, mainly back to children![28]

The answer to these three interrelated puzzles brings us to the sixth principle of Big Gods:

Unworshipped Gods are impotent Gods.

In other words, gods lack power if potential converts see little evidence of social proof—passionate devotion to them by zealous followers. Our answer can be found, once again, in the cultural learning biases that direct people to selectively commit to certain supernatural agents but not others. If *religious actions speak louder than words* (the fifth principle of Big Gods), then it follows that witnessing actions that convey genuine commitment to a particular deity—painful or costly rituals, restrictions on behaviors, and sacrifice of time, effort, and wealth—will in turn lead to greater belief in and commitment to this god. Conversely, the absence of such public displays erodes commitment without necessarily disturbing the intuitive building blocks that allow people to conceive of a particular god.

Without such cultural exposure, there are strong reasons to suspect skepticism on behalf of cultural learners, even children. Psychologist Paul Harris and his colleagues have found that children show a sophisticated understanding of the difference between reality and fictional concepts. They often question counterintuitive concepts, unless they see that reliable or familiar adults show commitment to them.[29] By paying attention to the testimony of adults around them, they come to believe, for example, that angels are real, but Harry Potter isn't. Children and adults do not believe in *any* idea that is interesting and memorable. They adopt the interesting and memorable religious beliefs of their parents and peers. Of these culturally supported beliefs, they especially gravitate toward those that are backed up by credible displays of devotion—public prayer, painful rites, acts of sacrifice.

And what about the difference between *belief* in a god and *commitment* to a god? This might look like hair-splitting, but it is a psychologically important nuance. Commitment implies belief, but one could believe in the existence of a god without being committed to that god. In the Abrahamic tradition, belief and commitment are conflated, but that is just an odd consequence of monotheism, which, despite its spectacular cultural success in the last two millennia, was historically a rarity in the cultures of the world. I came to appreciate this distinction between belief and commitment while traveling in Nepal a few years ago.

There is a joke about Unitarians, that they believe that at most, there is one God. In Nepal, people believe in too many gods. A majority Hindu country, it has an intoxicating mixture of Hindu, Tibetan Buddhist, and animist traditions. These traditions often coexist side by side. When I would ask local villagers, "What is your religion?" I would often get a quizzical facial reaction. Many Nepalese are what religious scholars would call *syncretic* believers, comfortable in asserting the existence of a mixture of gods and spirits that cross boundaries of what people in the West would call different religious traditions, although typically they favor one particular god or gods over others. While traveling in the Himalayas, and visiting sacred temples and shrines in Kathmandu, I talked to *sadhus*, or wandering holy men who were devotees of one Hindu god or another, but they would not, of course, deny the existence of other gods. I quickly came to the realization that religion in Nepal is like soccer in Europe or hockey in Canada. One could be a passionate fan of Manchester United, but this devotee of Man U would not, of course, deny the existence of Barcelona. These observations led to two insights: (1) that commitment to a god does not imply denial of the existence of other gods (except in the peculiar Abrahamic tradition), and (2) that one can believe in the existence of a god without worshipping this god.

Once again, what explains passionate commitment to a particular god is influenced by what kind of cognitive content this god has, but not just—to get potent Big Gods, cultural exposure and the witnessing of credible displays of commitment to that particular god in one's group are also required.

Returning to our three interrelated puzzles, if the features of the belief itself are sufficient to explain the prevalence of belief, then how do people come to believe in, or commit to, the "right" gods (as usually judged by their community)? Why do Christians not worship Zeus or Shiva? Why are Hindus indifferent or hostile toward Allah or Jesus? Although this selective commitment is puzzling if we focus on the features of the belief (all of these deities have the right cognitive features to make them proper gods), it is easily explainable if cultural learning dictates the specific gods people commit to. Cultural learning also explains historical shifts in the status of deities. Gods, like Zeus and Thor, despite having stable cognitive features throughout the ages, can move from a worshipped deity to the fictional character of no longer believed myths and stories if their cultural support base is drained. Last, cultural learning biases explain bafflement at the gods of other cultures. These gods of other faiths, when they make their appearance in a new cultural environment, lack (at least initially) public displays of commitment to them. In the absence of such cultural support, they intuitively arouse skepticism, incredulity, or indifference, unless their introduction is accompanied with powerful displays of commitment by dedicated followers.

Finally, cultural learning biases also explain belief in some supernatural agents across the lifespan. Will Gervais and Joseph Henrich point out that for many children, Santa Claus is a real, morally concerned supernatural agent who wields the power to dispense either gifts or coal as just desserts for good and bad behavior. But as children who were taught the Santa Claus myth grow older, they gradually become skeptical, even though Santa's profile (the details of the idea) remains largely intact. Context changes, however, and as children age, they stop witnessing credible displays of others' faith in Santa. As a result, Santa Claus is a god to children, but an entertaining folktale for adults. Similarly, children who are entertained by Mickey Mouse, the Tooth Fairy, and SpongeBob do not witness passionate public commitment to these fictional characters—in other words, these are not worshipped beings, despite the fact that their cognitive content could make them, in principle, potential divine candidates.

Binding True Believers Together to Create Religious Solidarity

In this chapter, I started with the observation that prosocial religious groups have succeeded in fostering trust among their devoted members. Supernatural monitoring, together with credible displays of extravagant commitment to Big Gods, created and sustained communities of true believers, who were bound together with high levels of social solidarity within their group. One cornerstone of this social solidarity in prosocial religions entails passionate commitment to gods that goes beyond the mere ability to mentally represent and reason about them.

In the next chapters, I explain how prosocial religious groups spread around the world and came out on top in the intensifying intergroup struggle that has shaped human history. How this happened is a complex cultural evolutionary story. These successful religious groups—the cultural ancestors of most human beings alive today—pieced together a whole cluster of psychological mechanisms that, building on supernatural monitoring and credible displays of sincere faith, fostered and cemented social solidarity. Credible displays of commitment to Big Gods were the joint foundation of these prosocial religions, but additional social bonding mechanisms, drawn from innate psychology and culturally learned practices, fused true believers into moral communities of cooperators. Taken together, this potent package of beliefs and behaviors make up religious solidarity. I discuss three additional mechanisms briefly here, focusing on synchrony in ritual dance and music, cultivation of self-control, and fictive kinship. Be mindful, however, that the research is in its infancy, and our conclusions must be preliminary until there is more evidence.

First, let's look at synchrony. Observers of religions have noted the ubiquity of certain kinds of music and dance in religious rituals. Why would this be the case? There could be many reasons for why music is tied up with religion, but one key feature that music encourages is shared synchronous movement within the group. Singing in unison, moving or dancing together in a coordinated fashion, are the kinds of shared activities that motivated Emile Durkheim's famously termed "collective effervescence" that is often found in religious and cultural practice.[30] In one recent study of a fire-walking ritual in a Spanish town, Ivana Konvalinka, Dimitris Xygalatas, Joseph Bulbulia, and their colleagues found shared patterns of heart-rate dynamics among the participants and their friends and relatives, but not among random spectators.[31] Synchrony also improves self-regulation, which may in turn enhance team performance. One study by Emma Cohen and her colleagues found, for example, that rowing synchronously with team members (compared to rowing alone) led to higher levels of pain tolerance.[32]

Do synchronous activities encourage prosocial behavior toward group members? They do. Scott Wiltermuth and Chip Heath had participants play what is called a *common resource pool game*. In this game, participants could freeride, or they could contribute to the group by suppressing their self-interest. Before playing this group economic game, participants were randomly assigned to one experimental condition or several control conditions. In the experimental condition, they sang and moved in synchrony with other group members. In the various control conditions, they sang and moved at their own pace as individuals, or listened to music without singing or moving. Results showed that, relative to control conditions, synchrony produced greater trust and greater feelings of being on the same team, reduced levels of freeriding, and caused more willingness to cooperate with other group members.[33] It is not surprising, therefore, that prosocial religions have drawn upon the social bonding powers of rhythmic song and movement. Of course, as the preceding experiment illustrates, synchrony can have its effects without being in religious contexts—synchronous rituals, although endemic to prosocial religions, are not unique to them—they can also be found in armies, university fraternities, and sports teams, to name a few examples. In addition, not all religious rituals necessarily involve synchrony, as there are other reasons why rituals are important for religious and cultural life.[34] This is exactly what would be expected if these practices were cobbled together by cultural evolution over historical time, rather than the product of genetic adaptations unique to religion.

Aside from synchrony, prosocial religions also cultivate a self-regulation in a variety of ways. By self-regulation, I mean any tendency to adjust one's behavior in pursuit of a desired outcome or goal. These may include resisting temptation and suppressing unwanted behaviors (not eating that piece of chocolate cake), pursuing a goal (finishing a difficult task), and monitoring one's own behavior (doing the proper thing in a particular social situation). Of course, there are many cultural and individual practices that encourage self-control, but there is reason to suspect that religions have been, at least in some respects, one such source of greater reservoir of self-control capacities. This is because self-control processes are an important element of social cohesion. They contribute to religion's capacity for effective social coordination and suppression of selfishness in the interest of the group. After reviewing a large amount of research, Michael McCullough and Brian Willoughby concluded, "religion, self-control, and self-regulation are indeed intimately related."[35]

Recently, Kevin Rounding, Albert Lee, Lijun Ji, and Jill Jacobson showed this intimate relation in a series of experiments. They found that religious reminders toughened people, making them more willing to endure unpleasant experiences. For example, after nonconscious reminders of God, believers were more willing to drink a distasteful mix of juice with vinegar. Similar effects were found on delay gratification: religious reminders increased the tendency to agree to wait for one week to receive $6 instead of being paid $5 immediately. Also, religious reminders caused believers to persist longer at an unsolvable anagram task. On the other hand, there are reasons to think that religion can also be a burden on self-control. Michael McCullough and Brian Willoughby point out that ecstatic experiences such as speaking in tongues seem to reflect a loss of self-control. Clearly, not all aspects of religion encourage self-control. Kristin Laurin, Aaron Kay, and Grainne Fitzsimmons emphasize that many believers see God as a controlling force who constrains their lives. They have shown that to the extent that belief in a controlling God is prevalent, reminders of God increase temptation resistance, but *decrease* goal pursuit. Clearly, given the complexity of religion, we should not expect a straightforward link between religion and self-regulation. Nevertheless, there is reason to think that greater self-control is part of what prosocial religions do, at least under some contexts.[36]

Finally, it has been observed that members of prosocial religious groups treat each other as *fictive kin*, to use a term popularized by evolutionary scientist Randolph Nesse. Thus, "Among the Hebrews and Phoenicians ... the worshipper is called brother (that is, kinsman or sister of the god)." Christians and Muslims also describe themselves as belonging to a *brotherhood*, a common term that often applies today to the global fraternity of Islam (*ikhwan*).[37]

I see three different possibilities of how this could work. It could be just a manner of speech with no palpable consequence for how people treat each other. At the other extreme, invoking kinship in religious groups may cause believers to actually confuse their co-religionists with real brothers and sisters. Or, a third, more plausible possibility is that invoking kinship terminology, with its associated altruistic tendencies, reminds believers of the proper social norms to follow when treating others. "In this group," the norm says, "we treat each other as if we are brothers and sisters." I do not know of any psychological studies exploring the implications of these different possibilities, but there are good reasons to suspect that kinship psychology is a factor that binds people in prosocial religions.

This cluster of mechanisms—synchronous movement and music, self-regulation, and fictive kinship, together with credible displays of faith in Big Gods who monitor and intervene, can be seen as the ingredients of religious solidarity and the creation of prosocial religions as communities that extends the boundaries of moral concern beyond genetic relatives and reciprocating partners to complete strangers. In the next two chapters, I explain how this potent mix, packaged together by the rapid forces of cultural evolution, gave prosocial religious groups a competitive edge in the harsh race for cultural survival.

Chapter 7
Big Gods for Big Groups

First came the temple, then the city.
—Klaus Schmidt[1]

Göbekli Tepe is the world's oldest known religious structure. It's made of massive, humanlike, T-shaped stone pillars, arranged into a set of rings, and carved with images of various animals such as gazelles and scorpions (see figure 7.1). Long mistaken for a medieval cemetery, this ancient monumental architecture in present-day southeastern Turkey dates back to about 11,500 years, which makes it at least twice as old as Stonehenge (4,000 to 5,000 years old), the Great Pyramid of Giza (4,500 years old), and a few thousands of years older than Armenia's Karahunj, another ancient megalithic structure with religious significance. Göbekli Tepe's importance is magnified by the fact that no evidence of settled agriculture has been found so far. This could be explained by the fact that Göbekli Tepe is old enough to have been one of the world's earliest temples built by hunter-gatherers. If true, it may hold clues to one of the deepest puzzles of our time, the question of how the Neolithic Revolution got off the ground, and gave rise to the origins of human civilization itself.[2]

Who built these structures, and how did they do it? The sheer scale of the operation must have been unprecedented—the stones in the Göbekli site weigh between 7 and 10 tons each, located on a site far away from any other known settlements, at a time when sedentary life, and its benefits, was still nonexistent—there were as yet no writing, masonry, metal tools, and domesticated animals to carry loads. And for what purpose would these hunter-gatherers—if indeed they were that—have built these monuments, which must have incurred spectacular costs in calories, time, and effort?

Figure 7.1. Göbekli Tepe, in present-day Southeastern Turkey, is one of the world's oldest places of religious worship (Vincent J. Musi/National Geographic Stock).

There are many puzzles and unanswered questions about this ancient site that will wait for more evidence and will be debated for a long time. The current picture that this site paints is incomplete, and open to multiple interpretations. Perhaps these were agricultural peoples, and it will take time to find evidence of domesticated plants and animals in Göbekli. To add to the mystery, the reasons behind the transition from hunting game and gathering wild foods to domestication of grains and animals remain somewhat puzzling and are hotly debated by archeologists. Unlike the more reliable supply of daily calories from hunting and gathering, domestication is a long-term affair fraught with risk. The diet of early agricultural peoples was poorer in protein content than the diet of hunter-gatherers. Evidence from prehistoric human remains suggests that early farmers were less healthy and less well fed than were hunter-gatherers.[3] Despite negative

effects on health and diet, early agriculture had one advantage over hunting and gathering: in the long run it could feed more mouths and sustain
larger populations.

What we do know, with some confidence, is that in the cradle of agriculture that is the Middle East, not far from Göbekli Tepe, clear evidence
of this transition is found to be about 11,000 years old. We also know that
this transition coincided with population explosions. However, in more
than 15 years of careful excavation, archeologist Klaus Schmidt, who first
discovered these stone structures on top of a mound buried in earth, and
others who have worked there since then, have not found any in Göbekli.
If the builders and early worshippers of Göbekli Tepe were indeed hunter-
gatherers, then we face the intriguing possibility that early forms of organized religious activity predated the agricultural revolution and the massive
cultural transformations it ushered. This scenario, if confirmed, would turn
on its head the conventional wisdom that organized religion, with priesthood classes, elaborate rituals, and sacrifices to powerful Big Gods, was a
mere consequence of the transition to agricultural societies.

Göbekli Tepe suggests the idea that early stirrings to worship Big Gods
motivated people to take up early forms of farming, and not the other way
around.[4] An analysis of the blades made of volcanic ash found on the site
suggests that it attracted pilgrims from a wide range of locations. This raises
the possibility that the temple was an early cosmopolitan center.[5] Schmidt
argues that the initial religious impulse to periodically congregate and
worship among at least some hunter-gatherer groups in the Middle East
might have led to semipermanent settlements around the sacred area. People likely continued to lead a hunter-gatherer existence, possibly for a long
time. Eventually, however, settlements swelled. Hunting and gathering cannot feed large populations. This might have created the impetus for experimentation with an agricultural lifestyle in addition to hunting. Animal and
plant domestication, in turn, would have led to food surpluses, and larger
population sizes. In turn, this demographic growth, along with conquest or
absorption of smaller groups, would have facilitated the cultural spread of
these peculiar religious beliefs.

This hypothesis, which sees prosocial religions with Big Gods as a contributing factor (rather than merely as a side-effect of settled agriculture),
fits better with the other observations discussed in this book. It is consistent
with the psychological evidence that supernatural monitoring, and credible

displays of faith to watchful deities, encourage cooperation, contribute to trust, and enable collective action among groups of strangers. It is also consistent with the historical evidence from the written record pointing to the role that these belief-ritual religious complexes played in the establishment of long-distance trade. This hypothesis accounts for the cultural spread of prosocial religions at the dawn of the agricultural revolution by assuming that, at the very least, Big Gods were one critical causal factor that contributed to the rise of large groups unleashed by agriculture. It would also explain the glaring absence of evidence for domesticated grains and animals in Göbekli Tepe.

The Gods of Small Groups

One of the last remaining societies of hunter-gatherers, the Hadza, live in northern Tanzania in an area of East Africa, on and around the shores of Lake Eyasi. There are in total about 1,000 Hadza speakers, although they are spread out in a territory of about 4,000 square kilometers (or 1,544 square miles), and each camp at any given time numbers 30 on average. Like other hunter-gatherers, they hunt with bows and arrows, and forage for wild tubers, berries, nuts, honey, and fruits. Camps are mobile, and agriculture and animal husbandry are unknown. The Hadza are egalitarian and there is no political organization, not within any given camp, nor beyond it. Contact with the outside world and industrialized people is minimal.

The Hadza, and other hunting and foraging groups like them, are of great interest to evolutionary anthropologists such as Frank Marlowe, who has lived among the Hadza, and written an extensive ethnography of their unique way of life and cultural characteristics.[6] For 99.99 percent of their existence, human beings lived in relatively small hunter-gatherer bands. The Hadza, therefore, are a rare, if elusive, glimpse into our past. Evolutionary anthropologists warn us that we should be careful about extrapolating from modern-day hunter-gatherer populations to the ancestral conditions before the Holocene period that marked the start of the agricultural revolution. For one thing, despite some important shared characteristics, there is no such thing as a cookie-cutter hunter-gatherer group; there is considerable variability in the cultural traits of modern-day hunter-gatherers, their social complexity, and group size. Also, it is possible that unlike pre-Holocene foragers, modern-day foragers occupy marginal habitats that were left unclaimed by agricultural societies, who nevertheless influenced them in myriad ways. Another worry is a *survivor bias* that could distort our observations: modern-day hunter-gatherer groups that have survived to this day may be highly unusual relative to most such groups that have existed, for reasons that are lost in the mists of history. Despite these difficulties, anyone interested in human origins must consult the rich ethnographic record about these tragically disappearing modern hunter-gatherers, whose way of life is being threatened by the relentless onslaught of modernity.[7] With their disappearance, we will lose a unique and irreplaceable source of crucial information about human origins. As Marlowe remarks, they provide the only direct (though necessarily imperfect) clues of human existence in the absence of agriculture and the massive cultural, economic, and political transformations that settled, domesticated life unleashed.

This is why groups like the Hadza are crucial for our understanding of the origins of religion, and in particular, the origins of the Big Gods of modern world religions—the powerful, all-knowing, and interventionist deities who care deeply about human morality. And this is where the story gets interesting. What is remarkable about the Hadza, and many other hunter-gatherer groups, is the *absence* of such Big Gods. Here is how Marlowe describes the religious beliefs of the Hadza, after discussing the observations of earlier anthropologists who were unsure whether or not the Hadza had any religious beliefs at all:

> I think one can say that the Hadza do have a religion, certainly a cosmology anyway, but it bears little resemblance to what most of us in complex societies (with Christianity, Islam, Hinduism, etc.) think of as religion. There are no churches, preachers, leaders, or religious guardians, no idols or images of gods, no regular organized meetings, no religious morality, no belief in an afterlife— theirs is nothing like the major religions.[8]

There is little dispute anymore that all hunter-gatherer groups have their spirits and gods who transcend physical, biological, and psychological limitations, at least to some extent. But these deities are not that powerful, have limited knowledge, and are largely indifferent toward human affairs. Hadza foragers have a creator God, called *Haine*, who nevertheless cares little about human morality. Similar observations have come from ethnog-

raphies of other foraging groups. Among the San in the Kalahari, for example, "Man's wrong-doing against man is not left to Gao!na's [the local
god] punishment nor is it considered to be his concern. Man corrects or
avenges such wrong-doings himself in his social context."[9] Pascal Boyer also
reports many cases where the gods of small-scale societies may be tricked by
humans or be manipulated by other rival gods. If they have powers and care,
they typically care about themselves (they want sacrifices), not about the
common good. These are hardly the all-knowing, all-powerful, judgmental,
moralizing Big Gods of the modern world religions.

Even chiefdoms—groups that are larger and more hierarchical than
hunter-gatherers, but much smaller and socially less stratified than
states—do not necessarily have full-scale Big Gods, though their supernatural powers are more than what is found among hunter-gatherers. These
then, are "intermediate" deities that have not fully transformed into Big
Gods. My anthropologist colleague Joseph Henrich, who does his fieldwork
on the remote Yasawa island in Fiji, reports that the local deity, sometimes
referred to as Kalou-vu, is believed to have omniscience, but a limited one.
He perceives things within village boundaries, but not beyond. If someone commits theft within the village, Kalou-vu might know about it. But
Kalou-vu would not be able to track down the same moral transgression if
it was committed on the main island. This led Rita McNamara to wonder
whether Kalou-vu deters acts of cheating. In her fieldwork among Yasawa
villagers, she found that Kalou-vu, similar to the Christian God, discour-
aged cheating among some in an anonymous game held in the village. But
this was only to the extent that the villagers thought Kalou-vu and God
were supernatural punishers.[10]

In this chapter, I argue that this connection between morality and
religion, taken for granted in modern world religions, has in fact emerged
culturally over human history, probably rather recently.[11] If true, this
should be a startling fact that begs for an explanation. As I emphasized
in chapter 1, we now live in a world where the vast majority of human beings are the cultural descendants of Big Gods. If modern hunter-gatherer
groups clue us to the ancestral conditions, even in a limited and oblique
fashion, then we can conclude that these beliefs started as rare forms of
cultural beliefs. If so, then how did we get here from there? What role
did this cultural change play in the growth and stabilization of large-scale
cooperation?

The answer, I suggest, is found in the seventh principle of supernatural monitoring:

Big Gods for Big Groups.

The anthropological record tells us that in moving from the smallest scale human societies to largest and most complex human societies, the following patterns emerge:

- Big Gods go from relatively rare to increasingly common.
- Morality and religion move from largely disconnected to increasingly intertwined.
- Rituals and other credible displays of faith become increasingly organized, uniform, and regular.
- Supernatural punishment becomes increasingly focused on violations of group norms (prohibitions on cheating, selfishness, but also on adultery, food taboos), and the potency of supernatural punishment increases (for example, salvation, eternal damnation, eons of karma, hell).

I present both cross-cultural and historical evidence that speaks to these claims. In discussing history, I also explore whether ancient Chinese religions fit the general historical pattern of increasingly potent supernatural monitoring with the scaling up of societies over time. This chapter lays the final foundation for chapter 10, where I discuss how cultural evolution pushed some societies from prosocial religions to secular ways of organizing large-scale cooperation.

We're among Friends and Family (and Sometimes a Few Strangers)

Why are interventionist and moralizing Big Gods rare in the supernatural worlds of the Hadza, the San, and most other foraging and hunting groups? The answer can be found in the evolutionary logic of cooperation that is constrained by group size. In these relatively transparent societies where face-to-face interaction is the norm, it is hard to escape the social spotlight. The bonds of family and friendship, combined with a set of cultural practices, go a along way in fostering cooperation and cementing the social matrix.

Of course, kin altruism and reciprocity are by no means the only way to maintain social bonds in these groups—a sophisticated repertoire of cultural norms for cooperation and coordination that sometimes involves strangers.[12] Hunting and foraging societies must tackle a wide range of collective action problems including big-game hunting, leveling risk through extended networks, coordinated defense against predators and rival groups, warfare, and extended child care. Moreover, preagricultural groups differ in the degree of social complexity, reflecting varying levels of population size and density, technology, and sedentary lifestyle. The technological record in the Upper Paleolithic (40,000–10,000 years ago) shows that social complexity waxed and waned over time—it was not a straightforward, linear progression from simpler to more complex.[13]

Keeping in mind these important complexities, it is nevertheless true that individuals in these groups do not face the recurrent problem of extensive and regular dependence on anonymous strangers in the way that modern, anonymous societies do. The idea is that smaller-scale societies are able to build local solidarity without appealing to moralizing, powerful supernatural agents. But matters are different for larger groups. In *Treatise on Human Nature*, David Hume recognized that this type of large-scale cooperation doesn't come easily:

> Two neighbours may agree to drain a meadow, which they possess in common; because it is easy for them to know each other's mind; and each must perceive, that the immediate consequence of his failing in his part, is, the abandoning the whole project. But it is very difficult, and indeed impossible, that a thousand persons should agree in any such action; it being difficult for them to concert so complicated a design, and still more difficult for them to execute it; while each seeks a pretext to free himself of the trouble and expence, and would lay the whole burden on others.[14]

Mutual cooperation has tremendous fitness benefits to individuals, but does not come for free. A considerable amount of brainpower is required to get along with one another, and the larger the number of social interactions one must track, the more cortical tissue one needs to navigate the ensuing complexity of the social world. Based on these considerations, the anthropologist Robin Dunbar conducted cross-species comparisons of brain size, and found that, among primates, the best predictor of neocortex volume relative to body size is group size.[15] A wide range of intensely cooperative human behaviors begins to break down as groups get too large—unless additional cultural solutions are injected into the group dynamics. We see this in the smallest hunter-gatherer settlements, the earliest Neolithic farming villages, the basic unit of professional armies since Roman times, and in the breaking point of thriving religious movements. Limits to group size are demonstrated also in ethnographic work among the Arapesh, in remote parts of New Guinea, where villages routinely split once they exceed about 300 people (or 150 adults). The anthropologist Donald Tuzin reports on the historical emergence of an anomalous village of 1,500 people, and explains how additional cultural norms sustaining social organization, marriage, rituals, and morally involved supernatural agents converged to galvanize cooperation in a locale where this scale was previously unknown.[16]

Kin selection and reciprocity cannot produce stable levels of cooperation even in groups as small as 300. Even in these village settlements, there is sufficient social complexity to require a whole package of cultural solutions to life's problems. But it is beyond dispute that these comparatively small groups pale in comparison to the possibly thousands of hunter-gatherers, who, starting 12,000 years ago, congregated in settled farming villages at the dawn of agriculture in the so-called Natufian culture in the Eastern Mediterranean.[17] Let alone the millions who coexist in today's vast metropolises, where large numbers of people cooperate with complete strangers, such as in warfare, trade, volunteerism, or voting.

Big Groups, Big Gods

The ethnographic observations discussed earlier are important, but to reach firmer conclusions, we need more systematic cross-cultural studies. Here is what quantitative analyses tell us. If we confine our sample to hunting and foraging groups, we find that Big Gods are indeed a rarity. Taking a conservative approach, the anthropologist Christopher Boehm analyzed 43 ethnographies covering 18 foraging societies. Specifically, Boehm narrowed his sample to groups that had spatial mobility, economic independence, egalitarianism, and large-game hunting. In this strictly defined subsample, he found that the gods and spirits occasionally intervene, but typically care little about human affairs that we would consider falling under the label *moral.* Despite substantial coverage of each society's religion, few reveal supernatural sanctions for lying, stealing, disrespect to elders, adultery, fighting, or cheating. For example, only four of the eighteen societies have gods that prohibit cheating, and only seven prohibit murder, even though all societies disapprove of and socially sanction these behaviors.[18] We must be careful in extrapolating from hunting and gathering societies of today to ancestral humans, but if these groups tell us anything, it is that ancestral religions did not have a clear moral dimension.

If we broaden our scope to include a wider range of preindustrial world cultures (not just mobile hunter-gatherers), we find that the prevalence of Big Gods increases, but it is still in the minority. Sociologist Rodney Stark found that only 24 percent of the 427 cultures that anthropologists have documented in a large worldwide database acknowledge a god who is active in human affairs and is specifically supportive of human morality.[19]

If Big Gods are a solution to the problem of large-scale cooperation in big groups, then the prevalence of these gods should be rare in small groups and increase with group size. Franz Roes and Michel Raymond tested this idea based on the Standard Cross-Cultural Sample, a representative sample of the world's ethnographic cultures. This database includes all kind of societies, ranging from the smallest foraging groups to modern nation-states. They measured two variables—society size and what is usually referred to as *High Gods.* Measuring size of societies that are not modern states is notoriously difficult, but there is another measure that is a good proxy of size. Societies in the world vary in what anthropologists call *jurisdictional hierarchy*—some societies are *communities*, small bands with no known social hierarchy. The Hadza and many hunter-gatherer groups fit this category. Others are small or large *chiefdoms*, which have larger populations and have a chief. Fiji, for example, has historically been a collection of chiefdoms with big men at the helm. Next are *states*, and finally, *large states*, which have the largest populations with extensive social complexity, and encompass the vast majority of the world's population. Next, Roes and Raymond looked at whether or not each culture had a *High God*, or a deity who is omniscient, powerful, and morally involved in human affairs.[20]

Gods who do double duty as supernatural punishers are found in cultures that have high levels of jurisdictional hierarchy—that is to say, societies with large group size and social complexity. Thus, omniscient, all-powerful, morally concerned deities who directly observe, reward, and punish social behavior are rare in smaller groups, and become increasingly common as societies scale up. This association is obviously *correlational*, meaning that we cannot conclusively determine what causes what. However, when Roes and Raymond controlled for some obvious alternative possibilities, the association remained unchanged. For example, large societies have Big Gods not simply because large groups happen to be more likely to have been exposed to Christian and Muslim missionary activity. Moreover, large groups have Big Gods not just because Big Gods legitimize social and economic inequality. They might have this effect, but when societies are matched on the degree of social and economic stratification, it is still the case that larger societies have bigger and more morally involved gods.

This association makes sense if we realize that as groups gain in size, anonymity invades interactions, which in turn threatens the stability of the group. Beyond kin selection, reciprocity, and other cultural sanctions suitable for small-scale living, additional mechanisms are needed to make anonymous strangers cooperate with one another. One powerful mechanism in cultural evolution is the idea of supernatural monitoring—that gods who know everything and care about human morality are watching and willing to punish. It therefore makes sense that Big Gods who double as supernatural monitors are more prevalent in groups who need them the most—large, socially complex, anonymous, but cooperative groups.

But group size and social complexity aren't the only cooperation and coordination challenges societies as groups face. Another big one is water resource scarcity. When the water supply does not keep up with booming populations, overexploitation, freeriding, and poor social coordination can be catastrophic to a society's ability to survive. When it comes to water, the foolish or selfish actions of a few can jeopardize the survival of the entire community. As an old Russian proverb goes, "A fool may throw into a well a stone which a hundred wise men cannot pull out."

It is just these conditions of water scarcity, soil erosion, and vulnerability to long periods of drought that appear to have contributed to the collapse of the ancient Khmer Empire that revolved around Angkor.[21] The magnificent remains of the main temple, Angkor Wat, can still be appreciated today; so are pieces of the sophisticated hydraulic engineering system dating back to the ninth century. But the society that once thrived in one of the world's largest preindustrial cities exists no more. Therefore, the need to enforce prosocial norms is also acute when water is in short supply—exactly the kinds of conditions where supernatural monitoring would be a useful social mechanism to keep people in line. It is perhaps no coincidence that one of the most culturally successful of all Big Gods, the God of Abraham, was originally a god of the desert.

Sure enough, a study relying on a representative sample of the world's ethnographic cultures found that gods tend to be moralizing in societies with chronic water shortages, compared with societies with abundant water supply.[22] The results did not change if societies exposed to missionary activity were included or excluded. The pattern also held when water scarcity was the result of low levels of rainfall, and when it was the result of inadequate amounts of surface water, such as the presence of streams, rivers, and lakes. These findings nicely parallel those discussed earlier, which indicate that Big Gods are more common as group size and social complexity increases and societies risk fissure. Snarey found one interesting exception to this general pattern, which itself was instructive:

> The one apparent exception among the nine premissioned societies with a morally concerned High God was the Yukaghir who lived along the upper Kolyma River in Eurasia. They were rated as having low precipitation but high surface water and thus an adequate water budget but, nevertheless, their pantheon included a morally concerned and beneficent Supreme Deity. Their Supreme Deity, called "Pon," controlled all visible phenomena of nature: When the evening came, they said "Pon-yulec" (Supreme Deity makes dark); if it began to rain, they said "Pon-tiboi" (Supreme Deity makes rain. . . . The river along which they lived, being located in northern Siberia, was frozen over for eight months of every year. "The Yukaghir territory," in fact, "has the severest climate of all Siberia. . . . Nowhere on the earth's surface does the climate affect so severely vegetable and animal life, including that of man." . . . Although the Yukaghir's water-budget rating used in this study is technically accurate, they obviously lived on the "edge" as much as High God desert peoples.[23]

It is important here to come back to three features of Big Gods that are often associated with supernatural monitoring. The first feature is, from the vantage point of cultural evolution, a critical design feature, but the second and third probably aren't. First, as I discussed in chapter 2, these gods, theologically speaking, are said to know and see everything, but in practice believers have the "theologically incorrect" intuition that these deities have access primarily to "socially strategic" information, and in particular social information about possible moral transgressions such as cheating, lying, and betraying the group. From a psychological point of view, this kind of religious thinking makes eminent sense. A critical design feature of supernatural watchers is that they are interventionist agents who in particular care about moral issues that the group considers socially important.[24]

Big Gods are sometimes equated with monotheism, and are often creator gods, but they need not have either of these two features to be effective supernatural police. I think this is just a cultural bias that has crept into thinking about religion from an Abrahamic cultural perspective. A Big God need not be the only god (hence the emphasis on the plural), and need not be a creator god. Big Gods started as a rare cultural variant of supernatural agents, but the idea of a singular god is even rarer. It so happens that one of the most culturally successful Big Gods is the Abrahamic God (which over time became both a creator and only God), but in principle any Big God can take on the duties of supernatural monitoring. The Kwaio people in the Solomon Islands, for example, believe in ancestor spirits called *adalo*.[25] The *adalo* are interventionist spirits who are constantly monitoring and meddling. They can bring good luck to those who are good and bring misfortune to those who violate group norms. They also appear to be hungry for sacrifices of pig. They take on roles of norm-enforcers, even though clearly there are many of them—in fact, too many, if you ask the Kwaio! They are also not seen as the creators of the universe.[26] Conversely, many hunter-gatherer gods, such as Haine of the Hadza, are in principle creators of the universe, although they are neither powerful, omnisicient, or morally involved. Monotheism and creator status are not at all necessary for supernatural monitoring, and may be historical accidents, rather than critical features of Big Gods.

Rituals seem to follow a pattern similar to that of Big Gods. Anthropologist Harvey Whitehouse has made a distinction between two recurring types of rituals across cultures and history. One mode is *doctrinal*—these are rituals that are repeated frequently, typically do not cause high levels of physiological arousal, and are associated with the cultural transmission of a dogma and are tightly managed by priests and religious authorities. A standard Catholic mass, with its weekly regularity, uniformity, and repetitious movement and song, is a good example of a doctrinal ritual. In contrast, *imagistic* rituals are performed only occasionally, but they are emotionally arousing, and as a result can reflect idiosyncratic, gripping, memorable spiritual experiences. Often a shaman is present who guides the practice, but there is little doctrinal orthodoxy or concern with uniformity. The meaning of the experience is up to the individual, left open to interpretation. Many so-called rites of terror in traditional societies fit this pattern.[27]

Whitehouse, in collaboration with Quentin Atkinson, found that these distinct ritual types are patterned in predictable ways across cultures. Although both types of rituals can co-occur in a group, chances are that if one type is more prevalent, the other is less common. Doctrinal rituals are the stuff of organized religion. They are associated with greater reliance on agriculture, which in turn demands greater levels of ingroup cooperation. These agricultural societies are the ones that were historically shaped by prosocial religious groups. In contrast, rare but emotionally arousing imagistic rituals tended to occur in smaller-scale groups that are less likely to depend on agriculture, and much less likely to be associated with moralistic Big Gods.[28] It's not that the imagistic mode is absent from organized religion. It does occur and can galvanize and renew faith and commitment. However, the imagistic mode is less predictable, and as a result, when it occurs in prosocial religions, it is actively managed by religious authorities and tolerated only to the extent that it doesn't challenge the central dogma or the group's interests.

All of this evidence brings us to a striking conclusion: over time and as groups gain in size, morality and religion move from disconnected to increasingly intertwined. As groups expand, Big Gods emerge, who demand sincere commitment, micromanage humans round the clock, punish transgressions, and reward good behavior. Elaborate, repetitious rituals that coordinate and validate the group's supernatural outlook also become more common.[29] In an earlier assessment of the ethnographic record, anthropologist William Swanson concluded, "The people of modern Western nations are so steeped in these beliefs which bind religion and morality, that they find it hard to conceive of societies which separate the two. Yet most anthropologists see such a separation as prevailing in primitive societies."[30] Small-scale societies of course do have elaborate moral norms that regulate social life. But in those societies, supernatural agents are not typically involved in the enforcement of these norms.

The Rise of Supernatural Monitors: A (Very) Brief Tour of the Historical Record

The anthropological insights gleaned from the ethnographic record converge with the historical record. When it comes to the preliterate archaeological data, we are forced to rely on indirect indicators—namely, material evidence. And this evidence suggests that over time, increasingly elaborate rituals emerge as societies become larger and more complex. There are different possible interpretations for this association, of course. Perhaps elaborate rituals are a reflection of more societal complexity. However, it is also reasonable that these ritual forms inspired faith in gods and created social solidarity, as groups got larger, more anonymous, and therefore more vulnerable to splintering. The archaeological record indicates that the expansion of regularly performed rituals and the construction of religiously significant monumental architecture emerged within the same period with increasing societal size, political complexity, and reliance on agriculture. A case in point is evidence from excavations of Çatalhöyük, a 9,500-year-old Neolithic site in southern Anatolia, not far from Göbekli Tepe, where we see, over time, more evidence of elaborate rituals coinciding with greater reliance on domestication of plants and animals.[31]

The excavation of Göbekli Tepe, discussed earlier, suggests that it may have been one of the world's first temples, where hunter-gatherers engaged in organized religious rituals—possibly predating the rise of settled agriculture in the area. Research on the coevolution of rituals with social changes indicates that rituals became much more formal, elaborate, and costly as societies developed from foraging bands into chiefdoms and states. In ancient Mexico, for example, foraging bands relied on informal, unscheduled rituals just as modern foragers do. With the establishment of chiefdoms consisting of multiple villages, rituals became more regular and a priesthood class emerged, as was the case of state formation in Mexico (2500 BCE). These priests relied on religious calendars and operated in temples built at extravagant costs. This is also true for the earliest societies of Mesopotamia and India, as well as predynastic Egypt and early China (4500–3500 BCE).

Later, in Bronze Age Egypt (ca. 3100 BCE) and China (ca. 1500 BCE), we begin to see changes in tomb architecture and burial practices, indicating the emergence of a highly centralized society bound together by costly public ceremonies. I emphasize that we should be careful about interpretations of these historical data, which cannot conclusively determine causal direction. However, combining these observations with comparative ethnography, and knowing what we know about the effects of religious beliefs on social behavior, it is not unreasonable to argue that these powerful and moralizing gods likely coevolved with costly regularized rituals, creating a mutually reenforcing package capable of enhancing internal cooperation and harmony, while providing opportunities to outcompete smaller and less well-organized outgroups.

Once the written historical record begins, it becomes much easier to establish clear links between large-scale cooperation, elaborate and regular rituals, Big Gods, and morality. This cultural evolution is apparent in the case of the Abrahamic faiths. In *Evolution of God*, Robert Wright documents textual evidence that reveals the gradual evolution of the Abrahamic god from a rather quirky, temperamental, tribal war god among many, to the unitary, supreme, eternally watchful, and moralizing deity of Judaism, Christianity and Islam—the latter two being the world's largest prosocial religious communities.[32] Although important details remain open to debate, the broad patterns of the story of how one Near Eastern tribal god evolved to be the Big God of more than 3 billion people, is reasonably well documented. There has been more confusion and dispute surrounding the role of religion in another massive cultural experiment in history, the unification of China. Did supernatural monitoring play a role in the remarkable scaling up of Chinese society over time?

Did Ancient Chinese Religions Have Supernatural Monitors?

China represents one of the largest-scale civilizations known to us, and early China—and East Asian cultures more generally—have sometimes been portrayed as lacking moralizing gods, or even religion at all. For this reason, early Chinese religion is worth a detour, even if it must be brief. Did early China have supernatural monitoring? This is currently a matter of historical debate. But my colleague and historian of ancient Chinese religions

Edward Slingerland makes a compelling case that supernatural monitoring played a critical role in early Chinese civilization.[33]

Slingerland points out that surveillance by gods appears as a prominent theme in early China. Although there is some debate about the precise nature of the pantheon worshiped by the earliest Chinese culture for which there are written records—that is, the Shang (1600–1046 BCE)—it appears to have included both literal ancestors of the Shang royal line, as well as a variety of nature gods and cultural heroes that are treated as ancestors of a sort, all under the dominion of a supreme deity, the "Lord on High" (*shangdi*). Even from the sparse records from this earliest recorded dynasty, it is apparent that the Lord on High commanded many events in the world, leading the Shang kings to placate this god with proper ritual offerings.

When the Western Zhou Dynasty (1046–771 BCE) replaced the Shang, Lord on High became conflated with the Zhou High God *tian* ("Heaven"), as the two terms were used interchangeably in Zhou sources. Descriptions of Lord on High/Heaven reflect many characteristics of a Big God, controlling the natural world, having powers of omniscience, and caring about moral behavior. Moreover, the ability of the royal family to rule became dependent on possessing the "Mandate" of Heaven, which meant displaying righteous behavior and proper observance of ritual duties. Later, when the Chinese polity began to fragment into a variety of independent, and often competing, states, supernatural surveillance continued to play a role in interstate diplomacy and internal political and legal relations.[34]

Finally, over time, the written record reveals an increasingly clear connection in early China between morality and religion. Heaven dictates norms for moral behavior, and a failure to adhere to norms—either in outward behavior or one's inner life—was to invite instant supernatural punishment. This "heavenly" moral code legitimized the dynasty and provided a shared sense of sacred history and destiny across the growing Zhou polity, facilitating the Zhou's unprecedented ability to expand militarily and politically.

Although there is room for debate about the extent and importance of supernatural monitoring in ancient China, it appears that there is less doubt about the fact that it played some role in the formation of Chinese civilization. The idea in this book that groups with belief in powerful supernatural monitors scaled up and eclipsed other groups does not say that supernatural monitoring is the *only* mechanism that can push groups to expand. Perhaps the Chinese managed to create secular alternatives to religion earlier and more successfully than Western civilization. That would be interesting and important, but not incompatible with the idea of Big Gods pushing groups to expand. Either way, the general pattern of the argument would remain if it turns out that supernatural monitoring was not as central to the formation of Chinese civilization as for others.

Is Supernatural Policing a Naturally Selected Adaptation?

I have outlined a cultural evolutionary framework that gives a central role to supernatural monitoring and punishment in the emergence of large-scale cooperation. Readers might have noticed similarities between this idea and another proposal by Jesse Bering, Dominic Johnson, and their colleagues, an adaptationist account that is often called the *supernatural punishment hypothesis*.[35] This view, which has generated a great deal of interest and research, argues that a belief in gods as supernatural police is a naturally selected adaptation. Dominic Johnson summarizes the key argument in this way:

> Humans may gain a fitness advantage from a bias in which they tend to assume that their every move (and thought) is being watched, judged, and potentially punished by supernatural agents. Although such a belief would be costly because it constrains freedom of action and self-interested behaviors, it may nevertheless be favored by natural selection if it helps to avoid an error that is even worse: committing selfish actions or violations of social norms when there is a high probability of real-world detection and punishment by victims or other group members. Simply put, supernatural beliefs may have been an effective mindguard against excessively selfish behaviour—behavior that became especially risky and costly as our social world became increasingly transparent due to the evolution of language and theory of mind.[36]

Johnson and Bering point out that the fear of supernatural watchers emerged in response to the ability that humans developed to communicate information about reputations. In an intensely social, gossiping species such as ours, individual survival has heavily depended on cooperative group-living. With the advent of capacities for theory of mind, coupled with language, which allows for communication to absent parties, people were able to detect and transmit social transgressions to other group members. Committing selfish actions would have therefore risked detection by the social group, which could have led to punishment, resulting in loss of Darwinian fitness. The wholesale suppression of selfish behavior would therefore become ultimately adaptive at the individual level.

There are important similarities between this hypothesis and the framework in this book that is grounded in cultural evolution. Both see supernatural punishment as a key driver of human prosociality, both are grounded in evolutionary logic, and both draw from some of the same evidence I have been reviewing in this book. However, the two also differ in several key details. First, whereas in the cultural evolutionary framework Big Gods were culturally selected for the advantages they afforded social groups, the supernatural punishment hypothesis argues for an innate fear of divine retribution that is a *genetic adaptation*; these beliefs function to restrain individuals from defection or cheating that would incur fitness costs. In the cultural evolutionary scenario, gods become more powerful and morally involved as anonymity invades relationships; in the supernatural punishment hypothesis, there is no such prediction. Instead, the idea is that supernatural punishment is a human universal.

So how do these two approaches fare given the observations we have reviewed in this book? A key challenge to this hypothesis is that small-scale societies, and especially foragers, don't tend to have moralizing or omniscient gods. This runs exactly counter to the predictions of this gene-only hypothesis. The peculiar distribution of Big Gods and supernatural punishment around the world is not consistent either with the idea that these beliefs are universal. Might it be that supernatural punishment was naturally selected, and then culturally elaborated in larger groups where freeriding is more acute? This sounds plausible, but what's problematic to this latter account is that the deities of many small-scale societies tend to be neither fully omniscient nor morally concerned. Going deeper into the evidence, interventionist gods, when they appear in the supernatural pantheon of a culture, are not just concerned about cooperation and honesty—they vary considerably on what behaviors they care about: they show concern about cheating and selfishness, while also intervening in case of violations of food taboos, laziness, and incest, and some even care about the behavior of animals in public![37] This is puzzling if supernatural punishment was designed as a genetic adaptation to solve the problem of cooperation. Why then, do moralizing gods also care about other behaviors that the groups care about, that are not about cooperation per se?

Moreover, Boehm's analysis of small foraging groups shows considerable cultural variability in supernatural sanctioning even for transgressions that can be hidden from view, where genetically evolved fear of supernatural punishment ought to be most likely. Many such behaviors (murder, fighting, laziness) are subject to social disapproval, but *not* subject to supernatural sanctioning. Only four of the eighteen societies considered have gods that prohibit cheating, and only in seven of them, they prohibit murder. Moreover, it appears that these moralizing gods, when they intervene, do so to enforce local cultural norms (which vary across groups), not only to enforce prosocial norms specifically regarding selfishness and cooperation in situations where transgressions can be hidden from view.

Thus, in foraging societies, where supernatural punishment should be clearly visible if it was a genetic adaptation, many of the gods seem to be amoral beings. In contrast, in evolutionarily recent, large, anonymous social groups, not ancestral hunter-gatherers, there is widespread supernatural monitoring by Big Gods. This pattern we have discussed earlier—increasing moral involvement of gods as groups gain in size is precisely what one would expect from the cultural evolutionary scenario, but not if supernatural punishment was genetically evolved in the Pleistocene.

Cultural evolution can create groups where, under the right conditions, *any* behavior spreads and becomes common, not only *cooperative* behaviors. This is why we often see subcultures or entire cultures stuck in a pattern or "equilibrium" that seems maladaptive and hurts the group and the individuals.[38] A case in point is the mass paranoia and distrust that was seen in police states like the former Soviet Union and its satellite states. Another example is the recent spread of witchcraft and sorcery-based killings in certain parts of Liberia, creating an environment of such pervasive mutual suspicion that even the most basic forms of social cooperation could not flourish.[39] These cases show that not all cultural or religious beliefs and practices lead to prosocial behavior. Many do not, and history is littered with the corpses of moribund religious movements that were cultural failures. While the features of prosocial religions outlined here are often taken to be typical of "religion" in general, there is reason to suspect that they actually represent relatively novel but successful products of a cultural evolutionary process that has forged a linkage between prosociality, morality, rituals, and deep commitments to Big Gods.

Within-group genetic transmission processes are essential part of the story, but by themselves, they cannot provide a complete solution to the dilemma of large-scale cooperation. If we consider the forces of cultural evolution, however, including competition between groups, culturally transmitted beliefs and practices—like the ones found in prosocial religions—can broaden the scale of cooperation. This process is described in the next chapter.

Perhaps more future work will clarify how the adaptationist account of supernatural punishment solves these challenges. For example, if selection pressures were really strong, supernatural punishment could have rapidly evolved in response to life in modern prosocial groups (not in small hunting and foraging groups) in a few thousand years. However, this would imply that supernatural punishment arose as a genetic adaptation more recently, and independently in different groups. Nevertheless, the account provided by the supernatural punishment hypothesis is right that religion's cooperative effects are driven not just by supernatural monitoring, but by monitoring backed up by the threat of divine punishment. Setting aside the issue of whether supernatural monitoring and punishment evolved genetically or culturally, or both, there is much agreement over the psychology behind it.

Taken together, the cross-cultural and historical evidence points to a converging pattern. As groups expand in size and in social complexity, religion acquires a moral dimension. Gods become more powerful, interventionist, and demanding of hard-to-fake commitment. Rituals become more frequent, routinized, and in the service of transmitting dogma. Once belief-ritual complexes begin to take shape, other commitment devices (discussed earlier in chapter 6), are added to the mix by the processes of cultural evolution: synchronous movement (song and dance), practices encouraging self-control (including habitual suppression of self-interest and other socially undesirable behaviors), and a sense of fictive kinship (treating co-religionists as if they were brothers and sisters). Packaged together with supernatural monitoring and extravagant displays of faith, these "cultural gadgets" further ratchet up levels of cooperation and social cohesion in prosocial religious groups, and turn anonymous strangers into moral communities. This process, giving rise to larger and more cohesive groups over time, unfolds in the context of intensifying competition and conflict between groups. This is the topic of chapter 8.

Chapter 8

The Gods of Cooperation and Competition

Dynasties of wide power and large royal authority have
their origin in religion based on ... truthful propaganda. ...
Superiority results from group feeling ... individual desires come
together in agreement, and hearts become united. ... Mutual
cooperation and support flourish. As a result, the extent of the
state widens, and the dynasty grows.

—Ibn Khaldûn[1]

For all its virtues in binding strangers together, religious cooperation is born
out of competition and conflict between groups. It is therefore expected
that religious cooperation in turn fuels the very conflicts, real or imagined,
that are perceived to threaten it. (This is the topic of the next chapter.) This
dynamic helps us understand and resolve the seeming paradox that it is the
handmaiden both of cooperation within the group and of conflict between
groups. Big God religions are both the fire department and the arsonist.

Put another way, when competition between groups is intense, and
when other factors such as war technology and population size are similar, groups that happen to have members who acquire traits favoring self-
sacrifice and subordinate self-interest for group interests—that is, groups
with stronger *social solidarity*—will tend to win out. Of course, when a
whole group wins out, the individuals in that group win out as well, and
the self-sacrificial strategies that led to their groups' success spread. In *The
Descent of Man*, Darwin recognized the unusual importance of social solidarity in shaping human evolution:

> It must not be forgotten that although a high standard of morality
> gives but a slight or no advantage to each individual man and his
> children over the other men of the same tribe, yet that an advance-
> ment in the standard of morality and an increase in the number
> of well-endowed men will certainly give an immense advantage to
> one tribe over another. There can be no doubt that a tribe includ-

ing many members who, from possessing in a high degree the spirit of patriotism, fidelity, obedience, courage, and sympathy, were always ready to give aid to each other and to sacrifice themselves for the common good, would be victorious over other tribes; and this would be natural selection.[2]

In *Darwin's Cathedral*, evolutionary biologist David Sloan Wilson proposes that religion fits Darwin's bill precisely. He echoes Ibn Khaldûn (quoted earlier):

> Groups are acknowledged to evolve into adaptive units, but only if special conditions are met . . . in human groups it is often religion that provides the special conditions. Religion returns to center stage, not as a theological explanation of purpose or order, but as itself a product of evolution that enables groups to function as adaptive units—at least to a degree.[3]

There is evidence that supports the idea that conflict and warfare bolster group social solidarity. In an ambitious cross-cultural investigation spanning 33 nation-states, Michele Gelfand and her colleagues measured something related to social solidarity. They looked at the degree to which nations are "tight"—that is, do they have strict social norms that apply to many situations? How important is conformity to these norms? How much deviation from norms is tolerated and do people get punished for violating these norms? They found several interesting things. First, there was considerable cultural variability, with some cultures such as Turkey, India, and South Korea being very tight, and others, such as Iceland, Ukraine, and New Zealand being "loose." Next, Gelfand and her colleagues set out to understand what factors explain this cultural variability: what explains the strictness of norm-enforcement in some places but not others? They identified a number of important antecedent conditions. Among those factors were historical levels of territorial conflict—that is, they found that, all else being equal, conflict a hundred years ago increased the odds of strict norm-enforcement today. Tighter nations were also more religious—and that makes sense too if world religions are a group-mobilizing force.[4] Of course, there is more to social solidarity than strict norm enforcement, and effective collective action is possible without wholesale suppression of dissent. And as is the case with such broad investigations, it is not always easy to know cause and effect. But Gelfand's findings point to the fact that, when cultural groups feel threatened, they tend to suppress internal discord in order to mobilize the group for collective action against the perceived threat. Often social mobilization takes a life of its own and persists, even after the threat is long gone.

Moreover, as any observer of team sports fans can see, the "cooperate to compete" instinct is particularly strong among that segment of the population that likes war: young men. Psychologist Mark Van Vugt calls this the "male warrior hypothesis." He observes that men are more likely to support wars and to volunteer to fight in them.[5]

In game experiments, Van Vugt and his colleagues first gave men and women money, which they could keep for themselves or contribute to their group's common fund. If enough group members contributed to the group's fund, individual members would get a larger return in the long run by giving to the group. But if few members contributed, individuals would lose by giving to the group. When groups of men were competing against other groups, men were more generous toward their own group. In other words, men are willing to suppress immediate selfishness if the group is under threat. Women, however, were not affected by such intergroup competition. They were generous regardless of whether or not there was conflict.

Richard Sosis and his colleagues looked at this issue from a different angle. They wanted to know whether the prevalence of warfare is linked to another form of group solidarity: participation in costly rites that involve terror, trauma, and painful scarification. In their analyses of nonindustrial societies, they found that the greater the participation in warfare, the more likely there are costly rites for males.[6] They carefully ruled out other possible explanations—for example, they found that costly rites were not predicted by the frequency of violent internal conflict *within* groups, only conflict *between* groups mattered. Neither did intensity of mating competition among men explain the frequency of these costly rites; therefore, these costly behaviors are unlikely to be signals for mating quality.

Sosis sees these painful rites as costly behaviors that signal group commitment. He points out that ritual scarification and violence create male solidarity, which keeps freeriding during warfare under control. But there could also be a cultural evolutionary process at work here that involves intergroup competition. Notice that the key predictor that mattered was the prevalence of warfare *between* groups. It stands to reason that cultural groups that live with a high threat of warfare invent or adopt costly rites to mobilize greater cooperation and solidarity among males. In turn, greater levels of devotion to the group helps men fight better against rival groups. It is also possible that these practices—if they lead to superior fighting success—are imitated more frequently by other groups who find themselves in similar circumstances, leading to the further spread of these costly rites.

Modern evolutionary models of human cooperation support Darwin's intuition: when the forces of intergroup competition are nonexistent or weak, self-interested behavior typically thrives. But as intergroup competition intensifies, strategies that suppress self-interest for the common good win out.[7] Thus, the particular mixture of self-interested and self-sacrificial tendencies we find in a population partly depends on that population's exposure to intergroup conflict. As Scott Atran explains, seemingly irrational tendencies make for stronger groups that can outdo their more rational, self-interested rivals:

> It is not difficult to see why groups formed for purely rational reasons can be more vulnerable to collapse: Background conditions change, and it might make sense to abandon one group in favor of another. . . . For this reason, even ostensibly secular countries and transnational movements usually contain important quasi-religious rituals and beliefs. Think of sacred songs and ceremonies, or postulations that "providence" or "nature" bestows equality and inalienable rights. . . . These sacred values act as moral imperatives that inspire nonrational sacrifices in cooperative endeavors such as war.[8]

Seen in this light, it is not surprising that prosocial religions have been a major force shaping human history. When intergroup rivalries are strong, prosocial religious groups, with their Big Gods and loyalty practices that promote social solidarity, could have a competitive edge over rival groups.[9] And when prosocial religions outcompete or absorb other rival groups, their beliefs and practices proliferate, explaining why most people today are descendants of such groups.

Building Moral Communities of Strangers

In light of the intergroup competition that has marked so much of human history, commitment mechanisms delivered by religious prosociality begin to make sense. They collectively facilitate the sacrificing of self-interest for the common good, a hallmark of prosocial religious groups that binds individuals—often complete strangers—into cohesive moral communities.[10] As Jonathan Haidt shows, much of morality is rooted in social intuitions in the service of gluing individuals together to form "sacred" communities. These moral binds make collective but anonymous social life possible and successful in competition with rival groups. This idea contradicts a long line of thinking in psychology and philosophy, which asserts that moral judgments are the product of abstract decision-making among isolated, rational individuals.[11] For Haidt, it makes more sense then to talk about *moral systems* that serve prosocial functions:

> Moral systems are interlocking sets of values, virtues, norms, practices, identities, institutions, technologies, and evolved psychological mechanisms that work together to supress or regulate self-interest and make cooperative societies possible.[12]

Notice how remarkably similar moral systems are to prosocial religions. If moral systems are in the service of group cohesion, it would be very surprising then if prosocial religions did not have moralizing effects. As Haidt recognizes, not all moral systems are religious, and not all religions are moral systems, but some religious systems—those that have prosocial consequences—have been moral systems throughout time.

Quentin Atkinson and Pierrick Bourrat looked at various aspects of participation in prosocial religions to see if they play a role in encouraging a stricter enforcement of moral norms. In a large global sample of 87 countries, they measured beliefs about two related sources of supernatural monitoring and punishment—God and the afterlife, as well as frequency of religious attendance. They then looked at the justifiability of a range of moral transgressions, such as cheating on taxes, or fare-skipping on public transport. They found that the stronger an individual expressed religious belief and reported high levels of religious participation, the more likely he or she condemned moral transgressions. Importantly, belief in a personal God was more strongly related to these outcomes than belief in an abstract impersonal God, a finding that would be expected if supernatural monitoring is a key element of religious morality.[13] These findings complement results by Shariff and Rhemtulla discussed earlier, who found, all else being equal, lower crime rates in nations with stronger belief in hell than heaven.[14] Big Gods with punishing duties have been enforcers of good behavior within anonymous groups.

Morality without God

This does not mean, of course, that religion is necessary for morality. No doubt core human moral instincts evolved long before religions spread in human groups. Early building blocks of morality—instincts and emotions associated with kinship psychology, reciprocity, and dominance hierarchies, to name a few—predate religion and therefore do not depend on it. Everyone, fervent believers and atheists alike, have them. Kiley Hamlin, Karen Wynn, and Paul Bloom have found that moral-like judgments can be found even in preverbal babies: by six months of age, they show a preference for an individual who helps and an aversion to an individual who obstructs someone else's goal. Hamlin and her colleagues further show the early precursor to another moral tendency that keeps the social order: punishing antisocial behavior. Eight-month-old babies not only prefer prosocial individuals, but they also prefer individuals who act harshly toward an antisocial individual.[15]

Even our primate cousins have vestiges of moral instincts. A long line of research by primatologist Frans de Waal and his colleagues shows capacities for emotional contagion, consolation, and grief in chimpanzees. De Waal cautions us to distinguish between altruism as a behavior, which could be selfishly motivated, and altruism as an experienced motivational state. Most relevant to discussions of the origins of morality is an altruistic motivation that is driven by empathy. De Waal calls this "directed altruism":

> Directed altruism, i.e., altruism in response to another's pain, need, or distress . . . is phylogenetically ancient, probably as old as mammals and birds.[16]

Yet, as de Waal explains, these moral instincts are rooted in the equally ancient evolutionary imperatives to favor the bonds of blood and alliance. They can't explain the key puzzle I am exploring in this book—how intense cooperation among anonymous strangers emerged, why only in human beings, and why only recently in humanity's evolutionary trajectory. The large-scale extension of moral concern to anonymous strangers who demonstrate commitment to the same faith was originally a religious achievement. This milestone has been supplanted by secular ideas of universal morality only recently and only in some societies.[17] We do not need religion to be moral beings. But moral communities of strangers may not have evolved as readily without religions with Big Gods.

Intergroup Competition and Warfare

But this raises the more fundamental question: how much competition and conflict do we see in human history? The trajectory, intensity, and underlying causes of conflict and warfare continue to be debated. Moreover, we still do not know to what extent warfare contributed to the process of scaling up of groups at the dawn of agriculture in the Middle East. Recent archeological evidence at Tel Brak, a prehistoric mass grave in Syria, suggests that it has. There is no shortage of evidence in the historical and ethnographic record showing that violent and nonviolent conflict has been endemic to human existence.[18] In fact, one driver of large group size in cultural evolution is the intensity of between-group competition for resources and habitats. For example, in the 186 societies of the Standard Cross-Cultural Sample (discussed earlier), prevalence of conflict among societies, resource-rich environments, group size, and Big Gods all go together. In places with rich natural resources, there is more intergroup conflict, larger groups, and watchful gods. What causes what is not always easy to know, but one possibility is that conflict over resources led to competition and political expansion of victorious groups, which in turn festered more conflict at the peripheries of these expanding empires. One argument is that these were precisely the antecedent conditions that gave rise to politically centralized states. As Charles Tilly puts it, war made states, and states made war.[19]

Peter Turchin, who has pioneered the scientific study of historical dynamics, emphasizes that the scaling up of social groups happened predominantly in frontiers of states and empires. He calculated that over 90 percent of preindustrial age mega-empires—defined as unified states covering greater than 1 million square kilometers (or 386,100 square miles)—arose in frontier regions, such as the Eurasian steppes. This is exactly where groups came into constant conflict. His calculations reveal that warfare lethality skyrockets as we move from internal regions within expanding and shrinking empires, to borderlands where groups clash. Therefore, conflict, he argues, has been a critical force pushing some groups to expand, others to disappear. But, he explains:

> Human societies did not increase in scale simply by including more and more people. The scaling-up process was accomplished

in a special way: increasing hierarchical complexity by adding levels of administrative control. At each step of the process, lower-
level units had to cooperate with each other, so that together they
could better compete against rival coalitions.[20]

Turchin's observations begin to look like Wilson's group as an adaptive
unit. We are led to the conclusion that groups that develop or acquire cultural traits that are conducive to social solidarity while maintaining large
size outcompete groups lacking these traits. In effect, this is the old adage
that the best way to compete with rivals is to cooperate with allies. Medieval Arab philosopher and historian Ibn Khaldûn, who was a keen observer
of the rise and fall of Islamic dynasties in fourteenth-century North Africa,
saw social solidarity, which he called *asabiya*, as the key to history. He also
recognized religion's potential to create *asabiya*.[21]

This brings us to the eighth and last principle of Big Gods:

Religious groups cooperate in order to compete.

This ancient imperative can help us understand the dramatic rise of prosocial religious groups that assembled through historical time and spread
around the world via population expansions, conversions, and conquest,
taking their beliefs and practices with them. They outcompeted rival groups
that were smaller and had lower rates of social solidarity. Turchin's analysis
predicts that, historically, prosocial religions played a key role in the scaling
up of groups, particularly in borderland areas where conflict was most intense, an idea that remains untested.

How Prosocial Religions Won in the Game
of Intergroup Cultural Competition

Human history, therefore, has been marked with endemic intergroup rivalries,
including constant warfare that led to the preferential cultural survival of some
groups but not others. This observation brings us to the idea that prosocial religions, with their group-beneficial norms that suppress selfishness and increase
social cohesion, outcompeted their rivals. There are good reasons to think that
this process has been driven by cultural—rather than genetic—evolution.

First, compared to genetic evolution, even rapid genetic evolution responding to recent cultural forces,[22] the selective forces in cultural evolution are stronger and operate on faster timescales. Second, between-group variability in cultural traits is by orders of magnitude larger than in genetic traits.[23] Third, even when there is a great deal of genetic flow between groups, such as when there is intermarriage or taking of war brides, cultural differences remain as long as the new migrants adopt the cultural traits of their new groups (which they often do). Internal heterogeneity within groups does not undermine the process either, as long as significant cultural variability is preserved between groups. These are precisely the conditions that give rise to what is called *cultural group selection*,.[24] Scott Atran and Joseph Henrich summarize the idea this way:

> Religious beliefs and practices, like group beneficial norms, can spread by competition among social groups in several ways, including warfare, economic production, and demographic expansion. Such cultural representations can also spread through more benign interactions, as when members of one group preferentially acquire behaviors, beliefs, and values from more successful groups.

Over historical time, demographic and cultural patterns have favored prosocial religious groups. This is why most of human beings today live in, or are the cultural descendants of, these highly successful prosocial religions. The cooperative effects of religious participation in these large anonymous groups are one piece of the explanation. But this fact in and of itself does not give us the complete picture. This expansion brought more and more adherents into the fold, and as a result led to the phenomenal spread of the particular mix of belief-ritual complexes throughout the world. What demographic factors led to this population growth? How did these patterns of demographic superiority and cultural survival play out in intergroup rivalries?

While our knowledge is limited, there are enough strands of evidence from a variety of sources to allow for an outline of an answer. Here I focus on criteria for which compelling, though limited, evidence exists: (1) group stability and longevity; (2) conversions, conquest, and assimilation; and (3) reproductive success and population growth.

Cultural Group Stability

First, let's look at cultural stability of prosocial religious groups. After all, when all is said and done, what matters, in cultural terms, is how well a group weathers storms that might lead to its collapse. World history is littered with the corpses of vast, but short-lived, empires, such as the Assyrian and Mongol conquests that unified large parts of the Middle East and Eurasia, respectively. If we were able to compare, in some precise way, how long groups last over time, what would we find? At least one investigation, discussed earlier, directly tested the prediction that religious groups that incorporate extravagant displays of faith would enjoy an advantage in longevity over groups that do not. Returning to this study of the group longevity of religious and secular communes in nineteenth-century America, Richard Sosis looked at an ideal case study because these communes operated under difficult conditions, facing various internal and external threats to group stability. Communes that were unable to solve "collective action problems"—overcoming internal disputes, preventing members from defecting to rival groups, surviving droughts, and so on, could not prosper. Indeed, some communes were dissolved soon after they were founded, whereas others flourished. For every year considered in a 110-year span, religious communes were found to outlast secular ones by an average factor of four.[25] Not surprisingly, religious communes imposed more than twice as many costly requirements such as food taboos and fasts, than secular ones. Importantly, the number of costly requirements predicted religious commune longevity after accounting for population size, income, and year the commune was founded. Last, the survival advantage of religious communes was statistically explained by the greater costs imposed on their members.

The evidence just discussed leads to two key conclusions: (1) differential rates of group survival favor prosocial religious groups; and (2) the combination of belief in supernatural watchers, extravagant displays, and other commitment devices explains the cultural survival advantage of these groups—precisely what would be expected if prosocial religions were "packaged" by cultural evolutionary processes. It is difficult to see how natural selection at the individual level alone would account for these findings. The outcome, although it can be influenced by fitness benefits to the individual, is a reflection of a group trait that is not reducible to individuals—that is, *cultural stability* over time. Neither could genetic group selection easily explain these effects, given the very short time frames (just over a 110 year span) and the fact that variation in nineteenth-century American commune membership is unlikely to be of genetic origin.

Group survival is a key factor, but not the only measure of cultural success. After all, a group may figure out the means to survive for a long time, but if the group's demographic prospects are dim, then it will have a smaller cultural market share than larger, but equally stable groups. All else being equal, smaller groups are at a disadvantage when competing with larger groups. This brings us to two key demographic factors that give pro-social religious groups an edge: conversions (whether free or coercive) and fertility rates.

Attracting Religious Converts

There is little doubt that the prosocial religions that lay claim to "world religion" status today were, and continue to be, exceedingly good at de-mographic and military expansion at the expense of rival groups by relying on a combination of strategies, involving attracting converts through cultural imitation, coercion, and conquest. In her study of the spread of Islam into Africa, Ensminger argues that Islamic beliefs, supported by powerful displays of faith such as abstaining from alcohol, avoiding pre- and extra-marital sex, not consuming pork, and ritual fasting—permitted greater trust, shared rules of exchange, and the use of credit institutions among converted Muslims.[26] The spread of Islam in turn facilitated more trade and greater economic success. The Orma—a Kenyan pastoralist group, and other African tribes began adopting Muslim religious beliefs along with the associated institutions and rituals. Islam was also imposed on conquered groups, causing the spread of these religious beliefs and practices in Africa.

These processes are certainly not limited to world religions compet-ing with small-scale societies, as it occurred in Africa, or post-Columbian North America. They can be seen in the historical evolution of American religiosity as well. This might come as a surprise to many, but Americans have not been as religious as they are today. Roger Finke and Rodney Stark emphasize the role of religious competition in the dramatic expansion of religiosity in America since 1776.[27] Those familiar with American religious movements today know that competition among religious institutions for membership has been a long-time feature of American life. The devoutness of Americans today, compared to, say, the religiously indifferent Northern Europeans, could be at least partly the result of the open competition of religious institutions found in America. The vibrant evangelical sects, such as the Pentecostal Church, owe much of their success to America's vigorously defended religious freedom. These sects are now spreading and making inroads, via institutional competition for membership, in places like Africa, Southeast Asia, and even Catholic Latin America. One interesting and unintended consequence of this energetic evangelism is that, as Philip Jenkins explains, Christianity's center of gravity is shifting away from Europe and North America toward Africa and Asia. Jenkins estimates that by 2050, a mere 1 in 5 Christians in the world will be of European descent.[28]

Religious Fertility

To survive and prosper, religious groups attract followers, induce adherents to reproduce at rates greater than replacement levels, or, as the demographic expansion of the Mormon Church shows, ideally, do both. The importance of demographic processes in the cultural survival of groups cannot be overstated. The Mormon Church grew, in a time span of just 170 years, from a small group of a few hundred to 15 million followers worldwide. Likewise, Christianity itself grew by leaps and bounds in the Roman Empire, and a once obscure offshoot of Judaism became the state religion of the empire in less than 300 years.[29] A similar story can be told about the rise and spread of Islam.[30] It is these dramatic demographic expansions that make a religion a *world* religion.

The cultural success of prosocial religious groups is therefore aided in no small part by their *reproductive* success, and the more fundamentalist strains of a religious tradition are particularly good at the business of having children (although having children is one thing, and *investing* in children is a different matter). Sociologist Eric Kauffman remarks with irony that, in the culture wars between the religious and secular, arguments fly back and forth, yet neither side seems to have noticed the most important trend that may really settle the dispute. He notes:

> Religious fundamentalists are on course to take over the world through demography. We have embarked on a particular phase of history in which the frailty of secular liberalism will become even more apparent. In contrast to the situation today, the upsurge of fundamentalism will be felt more keenly in the secular West than in developing regions. This is because we are witnessing the historic conjunction of religious fundamentalism and demographic revolution.[31]

Kauffman may sound alarmist, but the numbers he and other researchers report are hard to dispute. In one carefully done study, demographer of religion Michael Blume examined the meticulously recorded Swiss census of 2000, based on almost 7 million respondents. He found that, even after matching respondents on education and income, Christians, Hindus, Muslims, and Jews outbreed the religiously nonaffiliated. The gap in fertility varied, ranging from 50 percent to more than double. But it's not just that religious people have more children than the nonreligious. Religiously nonaffiliated Swiss women are having children at *below replacement* levels, whereas most religiously affiliated Swiss women are at above replacement.

These patterns can also be found globally. A study comparing the fertility rates of European Jews found that the atheists had the lowest birthrate, averaging around 1.5 children per woman (again, below replacement), whereas the religious Jews averaged nearly three, with the Ultra-Orthodox in Israel averaging six to eight children per woman. This trend is strong and robust across cultures. For example, data from 82 countries reveals a linear relationship between frequency of religious worship and number of children, with those who worship more than once a week averaging 2.5 children compared to 1.7 (below replacement!) for those who never worship.[32] Since religious beliefs and practices are importantly, though not exclusively, transmitted vertically from parents to children, these numbers suggest a key force that is pushing religious populations to expand and secular populations to shrink. (However, things get interesting, because there is a countervailing secularizing force: societies become less religious as they get wealthier and more "existentially secure." I discuss this issue in chapter 10).

In their international comparisons of fertility rates, Pipa Norris and Ronald Inglehart find modern-day societies that are more religious have more children than secular societies, even when countries are matched on national income and education levels. Moreover, when fertility rates are plotted over time within the same country, we find the same story: as religiosity declines in a society over the years (reflecting the secularization trend that has occurred in much of Western and Eastern Europe in the second half of the twentieth century), so do fertility rates. Despite strong government incentives in welfare-state countries such as France and Germany to combat low fertility rates, it is hard to find counterexamples. Michael Blume explains:

> Although we looked hard at all available data and case studies back to early Greece and India, we still have not been able to identify a single case of any non-religious population retaining more than two births per woman for just a century. Wherever religious communities dissolved, demographic decline followed suit.[33]

The reason reproductive success is a powerful influence on group survival is that fertility rates decline geometrically—that is, the decline speeds up over time unless something gives. In an article titled "End of History and the Last Woman," a team of researchers at *The Economist* did some calculations to forecast population declines happening in a great number of secular countries. In Hong Kong, for example, 1,000 women are expected to produce just 547 daughters; these, in turn, are expected to be succeeded by 299 daughters, and so on. Unless something changed, it would take just 25 generations for Hong Kong's 3.75 million inhabitants to be reduced to just one person.[34]

It is no accident that religious conservative attitudes on women's rights, contraception, abortion, and sexual orientation are conducive to maintaining high fertility levels. The reproductive advantage of prosocial religions is therefore another key factor that explains the latter's cultural survival and expansion. Culturally transmitted prosocial religious beliefs and practices appear not only to have effects on cooperation and trust, but they also have direct Darwinian fitness consequences that contribute to the demographic growth and stability of large cooperative groups. Of course, not all religions encourage reproductive success (consider the Shakers, who banned sexual intercourse). However, I hope it is clear by now that in the logic of cultural evolution, there is no reason to expect that all religious groups reproduce at high levels. The logic is simply that those religious groups with beliefs and practices that promote population growth (be it by conversions, or higher fertility rates, or both), all else being equal, would outcompete their rivals—including religious rivals like the Shakers and the self-castrating *Skoptsy*—and take a larger share of the religious market, and ultimately the world's population.

While the evidence that religious involvement affects fertility rates is strong, no one knows for sure yet what the reasons are for the religious advantage. To complicate things further, part of the explanation may lie not only in religion per se, but in its close cousins, conservatism and fundamentalism. The more conservative and more fundamentalist a community is, the higher the fertility rates, even when we confine the analysis within religious groups. Whatever the exact causes, I think religion's reproductive advantage, like its effects on cooperation, is best explained as a cultural evolutionary process. This is not to deny that beliefs and attitudes that have effects on reproductive success may have a genetically inherited component. But these values are also, in a very important sense, culturally transmitted. We know this because within the same population, having more or less the same gene pool, there has been dramatic decline of fertility that has followed the decline in religious involvement, sometimes in a matter of just a few decades.

Nevertheless, it is possible that religious fertility is shaped by a process called *gene-culture coevolution*.[35] Just as the lactose-tolerance allele spread in less than 10,000 years in groups that adopted milk-producing cows, goats, and camels, it is conceivable that prosocial religious beliefs and practices adopted by some groups but not others might have exerted selection pressures on the human gene pool of these groups. This provocative idea is just starting to receive attention.[36]

This chapter discussed how prosocial religions became world religions by outcompeting their cultural rivals. This has mostly been a competition among different religious groups, a process that continues to this day. However, the last three centuries have seen the rise of a new cultural idea and a potential alternative to religiously organized cooperation—secular societies. In chapter 9, I discuss religious conflict. In chapter 10, I ask, what are the psychological roots of secularism? What is atheism? And how is cooperation possible without supernatural watchers?

Chapter 9

From Religious Cooperation
to Religious Conflict

Pity the nation that is full of beliefs and empty of religion.
—Khalil Gibran[1]

I am no stranger to religious conflict. The Lebanese civil war erupted in 1975. In the following decade and half, I grew up in Gibran's home country, where one group was pitted against another, in a bloody conflict that left hundreds of thousands dead, and an even larger number became internal refugees. Not unlike Bosnia, a once vibrant, cosmopolitan society turned against itself, and imploded.[2] Coming of age in a war-torn country sparked my curiosity about society. When I would ask the adults around me to explain what was happening, I would hear proclamations about the depravity of the "other side," or I would get puzzled looks. I became a social psychologist largely because I realized that what we cannot explain in ourselves might be our downfall. Conflict, nuclear catastrophe, and ecological devastation are solvable only if we make progress in explaining how human minds create, and in turn reflect, the complex social worlds in which we live today.

What is the relationship between religion and intolerance, conflict, and violence? How could religion promote cooperation and trust and at the same time contribute to hostility and violence? And is there hope for co-opting religion to serve peaceful ends? Given that religious conflict shapes world events and makes the news headlines every day, you would be forgiven to think that we know a great deal about religion's role in human conflict. Remarkably, rhetoric and opinion aside, we know very little in terms of hard scientific facts. What comes in this chapter tries to untangle this highly politicized and hotly debated question. There is much confusion and sloppy thinking. There are many gaps in knowledge and difficult questions that are waiting for proper scientific investigation. A complete answer has to wait, but once we clarify some misconceptions and sharpen the questions, it is possible to sketch some answers.

The first place to start is to ask a simple but difficult question: if we could do a full accounting of world history, how much of a role does religion play in violent conflicts? Critics of religion think that it is a major cause, and there is of course no shortage of examples, historical and contemporary: the Crusades, the early Islamic conquests, the sixteenth-century Catholic-Protestant religious wars, violent Jihadi campaigns of today, Hindu-Muslim violence, Lebanon of the 1970s and 1980s, Bosnia in the early 1990s, Northern Ireland. With these examples in mind, Richard Dawkins argues:

> Religious faith deserves a chapter to itself in the annals of war technology, on an even footing with the longbow, the warhorse, the tank, and the hydrogen bomb.[3]

Critics of secularization have two answers to this charge. One, they offer counterexamples of violent conflicts motivated by secular ideologies that lack a religious dimension: the two World Wars in the twentieth century (including the carnage caused by Fascism and the Nazis), Stalin's and Mao's purges, and the genocidal Pol Pot regime, to name a few. Earlier, starting in 1915, the Committee for Union and Progress, known as the Young Turk Regime, Westernizers who wanted to reform and secularize the ailing (religiously organized) Ottoman Empire, carried out the first genocide of the twentieth century by annihilating most of the Armenian population as well as depopulating the rest of the Ottoman Christians from their ancestral lands. Many of the individual Kurds, Turks, and Arabs who saved some Armenians were pious Muslims.[4]

Moreover, defenders of religion point out that some of the sins attributed to religion are in fact caused by something else that gets entangled with religion. William James, one of the great founders of modern psychology who took a great interest in religion, put it this way:

> The baseness so commonly charged to religion's account are thus, almost all of them, not chargeable to religion proper, but rather to religion's wicked practical partner, the spirit of corporate dominion. And the bigotries are most of them in their turn charge-

able to religion's wicked intellectual partner, the spirit of dogmatic dominion.[5]

It becomes clear quickly that staking a position on this issue, and then picking examples to support the position, would lead us nowhere. To get real answers, we need a systematic approach. If we take all the violent conflicts we know of in a given historical period, and assess the degree to which religious divisions were a factor, what would we find? Such studies are rare, but in the *Encyclopedia of Wars*, Charles Phillips and Alan Axelrod attempted one such comprehensive analysis. They surveyed nearly 1,800 violent conflicts throughout history. They measured, based on historical records, whether or not religion was a factor, and if so, to what degree. They found that less than 10 percent involved religion at all. In a related "God and War" audit commissioned by the BBC, researchers again scrutinized 3,500 years of violent conflicts recorded in history, and rated the degree to which religion was a factor. Wars got high marks if religious leaders expressed support for the war effort, if religion was a mobilizing factor, if religious targets were attacked, and if religious conversion was a key goal of the war. Thus, on a six-point scale of 0 (no religious role) to 5 (central role of religion), the Peloponnesian War (460–445 BCE) was a zero; the Iran-Iraq War (1980–1988) was a 1; the United States and allied second invasion of Iraq was a 3; the Al-Qaeda terror war was a 4; and the Crusades (1097–1291) and the Arab-Muslim conquests (632–732) earned a full 5 points.[6] In the end, religion was a factor in 40 percent of all rated violent conflicts, but rarely as the key motivator of the conflict. Religion is an important player, but rarely the primary cause of wars and violent conflicts. The numbers provided by Phillips and Axelrod and the BBC audit place the question in context, and focus our attention to think of a more nuanced and answerable question: when and how does religion contribute to violent conflict?

Sharpening the Question: Three Clarifications about Religion and Conflict

As we delve deeper into the issue, three things become clear: First, this debate is often couched as a contest among religions for tolerance status. In the popular imagination, there are the tolerant religions (Buddhism gets a lot of votes, and of course, the pacifist Quakers!) and there are intolerant religions (the fundamentalist strains of the Abrahamic faiths). Comedian Al Franken has his own ranking of world religions from best to worst. He suggests to keep the list in a wallet, in case one has to choose a religion in a hurry. At the top is Reform Judaism; at the bottom are fundamentalist branches of Christianity, Judaism, and Islam, and "Buddhism, Hinduism, Confucianism, etc." are somewhere in the middle.[7]

But jokes aside, the fact that some religious groups are more tolerant or less prone to violence than others does not really answer the question—it pushes the question further back: what is it about the particular religious beliefs and practices of a group that contribute to conflict? Today, many people, with more seriousness than Franken, think that radical Islam is the "problem religion" of the twenty-first century, but ten centuries earlier, it was Christianity (mainly Catholicism), and Islamic Spain was a cosmopolitan center of many faiths, a far more tolerant society than medieval Christendom. If some religions are inherently more violent than others, how do we explain these changes within a religious tradition?

This leads us to the second point of clarification. I have argued that "religion" is best seen as a complex amalgam of traits and inclinations, grounded in recurrent, ordinary intuitions and packaged together by cultural evolution over historical time. It makes little sense to ask, then, "does religion cause intolerance and violent conflict?" A much more precise scientific question would be, what part of "religion" is implicated in conflict and intolerance, and why?

Finally, a third related issue that needs clarification is that religious elements must be disentangled from their "wicked partners," as James put it, which are often bound with "religion." Exclusivity, dogmatism, and fundamentalism are not the same thing as religion. This may sound obvious, but they are often seen as interchangeable with religion by its critics. Semantics aside, if we want a more precise understanding of religious roles in human conflict, we must disentangle these tendencies that often go along with the religious bundle. This is not an exoneration of religion—these tendencies are well-known contributors to intolerance and violent conflict, and indeed our job is to understand why they thrive in religions.[8] But they are not unique to religion: many secular ideologies have them too. Eroding the impact of religion would therefore not eliminate conflict, for the simple reason that the myriad sources of human conflict can be found in nonreligion as well.

Religion and Its "Wicked Partners"

"Religious Intolerance Still Plagues World" declared a recent news headline. The piece cited a US State Department yearly report that found a decline in religious tolerance in many parts of the world.[9] Why so much religious intolerance, and does religion itself have something to do with it?

Ian Hansen and I conducted a study that illustrates why it is so important to untangle religion when it comes to understanding its role in religious intolerance. While this study looked at a broad range of questions, I'll focus here on one outcome—religious scapegoating, or the tendency to blame other religions for the problems of the world. We wanted to know: do people who are more religiously devoted scapegoat other religious groups more? Or less? The answer, it turned out, depends on teasing apart "religious devotion" from its "wicked partners."

Hansen and I examined an international sample of over 10,000 people in ten nations: the United States, the UK, Israel, South Korea, India, Indonesia, Lebanon, Russia, Mexico, and Nigeria. As an indicator of religious devotion, we looked at frequency of prayer. We also considered what James called religion's wicked intellectual partner, the "spirit of dogmatic dominion." We got a measure of religious exclusivity: "My God (beliefs) is the only true God (beliefs)." We called this *exclusivity* because it asserts the truth of one's own beliefs to the exclusion of all other beliefs. (These tendencies are related, as James suspected, but not perfectly so. There are many people who pray but don't think that their beliefs are the only true beliefs, and there are those who don't practice a religion but have exclusivist beliefs.)

Hansen and I found that, after matching people on age, gender, occupational status, and other factors, exclusivity increased the odds of scapegoating. No surprise there—more dogmatic people are more scapegoating of other religions. But what was more interesting, holding constant exclusivity, was that prayer frequency *reduced* the odds of scapegoating. This means that people who pray a lot, but do not think that they have a monopoly on the truth, are in fact *less* scapegoating than those who are less devoted and are equally nondogmatic. We found this in the overall sample, and we found the same patterns within each religious group we considered, even among Buddhists.[10] This result would not have surprised psychologist Gordon Allport, who more than half a century ago remarked that religion makes and unmakes prejudice.[11] Decades after Allport, research on religion and prejudice has produced inconclusive results.[12] He was right, because "religion" bundles together psychological tendencies that potentially produce conflicting outcomes. Sociologist of religion Phil Zuckerman agrees with Allport:

> Religion inevitably contains, reflects, and reveals all that is within the realm of humanity: the good and the bad. It is like any other facet of human civilization: some of it is noble and inspirational, much of it is nonsensical and even dangerous. But to condemn it all as poisonous is to be in serious denial.[13]

We are now in a position to attempt a preliminary answer to this question, bearing in mind that our knowledge is limited. Religious tendencies contribute to intolerance and violence in at least three ways. The first one involves the workings of supernatural monitoring as a group-building social device. This leads to a sliding scale of distrust toward those who fall outside of one's own supernatural jurisdiction. Second is the social bonding power of religious participation and ritual that could exacerbate conflict between groups. Third, religion fosters sacred values, making them immune to trade-off, which in turn blocks compromise in conflict situations. Interestingly, within all three pathways to conflict, there is fluidity. There is, seemingly paradoxically, the potential for religion to reduce conflict as much as to create it. Religion appears to be both a maker and an unmaker of conflict.

The Outer Limits of Supernatural Monitoring

The first path is a "soft" one to intolerance and exclusion, rather than to violent conflict. This path lies in the very fact that Big God religions build trust and cooperation *and* contribute to intergroup conflict, for the same underlying reason that these prosocial religions foster social cohesion that helps them compete with rival groups. Social cohesion inevitably involves setting up boundaries between those who can be trusted and those who cannot. After all, and despite some theological teachings about universal love and indiscriminate compassion, a religious community would not be a cooperative community if there were no social boundaries. Supernatural monitoring, then, excludes those who are seen as not following the same norms and believing in the same or similar supernatural watchers. In earlier chapters, we saw that believers' trust of other religious groups declines to the extent that these outsiders are seen to lack proper supernatural monitoring beliefs or dissimilar prosocial norms. In the extreme case, atheists, who do not believe in a god at all, let alone believing in supernatural surveillance, are excluded as people who are beyond the pale.

Azim Shariff and I tested this idea in the well-known Dictator Game. This time, we invited Christian Canadians to choose to transfer money to another player in an anonymous setting. In one condition, they were led to think the other player was Muslim. In a second condition, they thought the other player was a fellow Christian. And finally, in a third, control condition, no information was given about the other player. If Christian folk were good theologians, they would follow Christian doctrine and be "Good Samaritans," being generous equally with everyone. But they were not. Christian participants primed with thoughts of God were most generous toward the Christian receiver, less generous toward a stranger with unknown religious affiliation, and least generous toward the Muslim receiver (playing with a Muslim receiver was the equivalent of not being primed with religious words).[14] While this result is not exactly an indication of intense hostility toward religious outgroups, it does show that making supernatural monitoring salient does lead to a discriminant form of generosity that is sensitive to group boundaries.

Religious Participation, Social Solidarity, and Conflict

Turning to the second path, those very social ties that religious practices and rituals help cement, strengthen communities but at the same time could also widen the divide between who is "in" and who is "out." There is a common belief that social ties are inherently good, and indeed there is a great deal of evidence showing that people with strong community ties are healthier, happier, and more prosocial.[15] However, few talk about the ugly face of strong social ties. The same processes that build community also open the door for exclusion to those who are seen as not belonging, and often, violent opposition to those who are seen as threatening. This could be called the *social solidarity hypothesis* of intergroup violence.

In a series of experiments, psychologists Adam Waytz and Nicholas Epley illustrate how this seeming paradox enables a particularly toxic form of an intergroup attitude: dehumanization of socially distant others. In one version of their studies, some participants were randomly assigned to experience social connection: "write about someone close to you that you interact with often" such as a "close friend, a significant other, or a family member." Others were assigned to a control condition: "write about someone who you see in your daily life, but whom you do not interact with" such as "a person you often pass on the street, someone who you see around work or school, or a total stranger." Then, depending on the specifics of the particular study, all participants were asked about various socially distant outgroups, such as drug addicts, disabled people, or detainees accused of terrorism. Who dehumanizes more: people who feel socially disengaged or socially connected? Their results were counterintuitive but decisive: feelings of stronger social connection to close others led to *more* dehumanization and harsher moral judgment of socially distant others.[16]

This result is especially true when there already is an atmosphere of distrust and conflict that is seen to threaten one's religious community. My own research with Jeremy Ginges and Ian Hansen looked at this process in the case of religion as it plays out in the Israeli-Palestinian conflict. We focused in particular on one of the most devastating forms of modern conflict: suicide attacks.

The political and psychological impact of suicide attacks are hard to underestimate, and as politicians appreciate, their significance is disproportionate to the actual number of victims. Moreover, suicide attacks have been on the rise. For example, between 1983 and 2000, there were a total of 142 suicide attacks worldwide. This number skyrocketed to 312 just within the 3 years between 2000 and 2003, with the numbers growing worldwide.[17] Suicide attacks come in waves, with one act of self-sacrifice inspiring others, creating cultural cycles of violent martyrdom. What better way to inspire and mobilize one's community than to lay down one's life for a cause? As an extreme form of *parochial altruism*—a combination of self-sacrifice and violent attack against perceived enemies—they mobilize society in times of conflict, and nourish it in ways that no other method of violent struggle could accomplish.

No one disputes that a majority of suicide attacks has been carried out by groups who claim to be motivated by a fusion of religious and political goals.[18] Given this, there has been a growing popular debate about religion's role in intergroup violence, with many singling out Islam or religious devotion more broadly as the culprit.[19] This is because, the argument goes, certain religious beliefs denigrate people of other faiths, promise martyrs the reward of an afterlife, or contain narrative traditions that glorify acts of combative martyrdom. In contrast to the *social solidarity hypothesis* discussed earlier, this general class of explanation can be called the *religious belief hypothesis* of intergroup violence—that something about religious belief itself causes intergroup hostility.[20] No doubt religions contain all of these things. But are these beliefs the actual cause? Maybe, but much of this debate has been polemical. Scientific study of this link has been sorely lacking. Does something in religion contribute to suicide attacks, and if so, what and how?

We set out to examine these two alternative explanations. Studying the motivations of actual suicide attackers is not easy, but we were able to do something close to that—we studied support for suicide missions in the subpopulations that produce many suicide attackers. We focused on whether two core elements in the religious bundle—prayer frequency and religious attendance—contribute to popular support for suicide attacks and similar cases of extreme parochial altruism. Prayer and attendance go together—people who pray frequently also attend frequently. But it's an imperfect statistical relationship—there are plenty of cases of prayer without attendance, or vice versa. This gives us an opportunity to do a fine-grained analysis, looking at the relative effects of each religious element.

We focused on two separate samples of Palestinians in the West Bank, where many suicide attackers had been recruited in the past. We found that those who attended mosque often, compared to those who attended rarely or never, were twice to three-and-a-half times more likely to support suicide attacks against the perceived enemy (Israelis). This clearly supports the social solidarity hypothesis. However, contrary to the idea that something about religious belief causes support for violent martyrdom, we found that frequency of prayer was statistically unrelated to such support once attendance was taken into account.

Are these patterns unique to Islam, or more generally applicable to religious attendance and religious belief? In a parallel priming study, we tried to answer this question. Suicide attacks by Israeli Jews are uncommon (only populations that do not have a conventional army use these methods). But to keep our measures comparable, we looked at support for a single act that in many respects resembles a suicide mission. On February 25, 1994, an Israeli settler named Baruch Goldstein died while killing 29 and injuring 60 Muslims at prayer in the Cave of the Patriarchs, a site in the West Bank that is holy to Muslims and Jews. Goldstein's act was widely condemned by the broader Israeli public, but many of his supporters in the settler community refer to him as a martyr.[21]

We asked a representative sample of Israeli West Bank settlers whether or not they thought Goldstein's act was heroic. Instead of measuring prayer and attendance frequencies, we introduced a cognitive priming procedure to get closer at causality: for half of our sample, we asked them to think about prayer to God; for the other half, we asked them to think about synagogue attendance. Then everyone was asked about Goldstein's act. We found that reminders of synagogue attendance increased the odds of approving Goldstein's violent act. Reminders of prayer, if anything, decreased these odds. Once again, we find that some aspects of religion are implicated in violent conflict, others aren't, or may even work to soften conflict. Going further, we found that these patterns are not at all unique to Palestinians and Jews. In an international survey of six major religions in six nations, regular attendance at religious services encouraged a combination of willing martyrdom and outgroup hostility. But regular prayer did not.[22] Religious participation cements social ties and builds group solidarity. But when groups are in conflict, this solidarity translates into the willingness to sacrifice to defend the group against perceived enemies. This is why, as Jonathan Haidt puts it, "religion is therefore often an accessory to atrocity, rather than the driving force of the atrocity."[23]

No doubt, then, religious practices and rituals can add fuel to conflict. But it is important to emphasize that religious participation can also be coopted to work for greater inclusiveness. In a pioneering study, a team of economists led by David Clingingsmith wanted to know what effects, if any, participation in the *hajj*—the annual Muslim pilgrimage to Mecca—has on social attitudes toward various groups. Are people transformed by this powerful experience? This annual pilgrimage brings together millions of practicing Muslims from all over the world and all walks of life into the holy city of Mecca to devote themselves to prayer, fasting, and other ascetic practices. Now, ideally, we would want to randomly assign Muslims to either attend the hajj or do something else unrelated to religion, then measure changes in attitudes. Needless to say, such a true experiment is close to impossible to do, but Clingingsmith and his colleagues found a clever alternative that comes very close. Because there are many more pilgrims than there is space to accommodate them, each year there is a quota system that limits the number of pilgrims who can enter Mecca during the hajj. In some countries, such as Pakistan, there is a random lottery that determines who can go to the hajj. Clingingsmith and his colleagues compared the social attitudes of Sunni Pakistani pilgrims who participated in the hajj by winning a random lottery to those who entered the lottery contest but did not win. This procedure is as close as one can get to random assignment, and effectively eliminates "self-selection," a common problem in this type of research lacking random assignment. Self-selection occurs when any differences found between a "treatment group" and a "control group" may be due to not the treatment itself, but to differences in the type of people who decide to enter the treatment or not. By taking advantage of the lottery, factors that have to do with personality and demographics that could influence attitudes are held constant.

Clingingsmith's findings were complex and wide ranging, but they told a consistent story: hajj participation led to more tolerance toward Muslims and nonMuslims alike. It increased endorsement of equality, harmony, and peace among different ethnic and religious groups. Participation also encouraged more favorable attitudes toward women and their right to education and jobs.

How did hajj participation change these attitudes, and why? It is too early to know, but additional findings give us possible clues: hajj participation reduced local Pakistani practices and beliefs, such as the use of amulets and dowry, and increased "global" Islamic practices that transcend ethnic boundaries. Moreover, the effect on tolerance was strongest among pilgrims who reported interacting with non-Pakistanis during the hajj.[24]

Religious participation among Palestinians and West Bank Jewish settlers increased support for violence against the perceived enemy, whereas in Clingingsmith's results, participation led to more tolerant attitudes. How do we square these two sets of results? I think there are two critical details that, once taken into account, resolve this gap. One is to appreciate that suicide attacks, as appalling and destructive as they are, are a form of altruism—in fact, the ultimate kind that requires sacrificing one's own life for the group. It is only in political contexts where there is asymmetric conflict and there are strong feelings that one's group is under threat that altruism turns violent. In less conflict-prone contexts, when there is no target to attack or adversary to scapegoat, religious attendance would be more about sacrificing and less about attacking.

Second, there is the nature of the religious participation itself. In the case of the former, religious participation was local—it reflected how often Palestinians attended mosque or Jewish settlers remembered attending synagogue in their local neighborhoods. In the hajj, in contrast, participation is global by its very nature. It's an opportunity for Muslims to meet and interact with other Muslims of all stripes from all over the world. I think this is a critically important distinction that could resolve some of the paradoxical effects that religious ritual has on intergroup conflict. Religious ritual is typically enacted in a local context and cements ties with one's immediate neighbors. But religious experiences that push people to interact with a wider range of diverse people broaden the moral circle. In this way, shared rituals can contribute to more tolerance and possibly could also be a tool for conflict reduction.[25]

Religion and the Sacred: Negotiating the Non-Negotiable

Finally, a third path from religion to conflict is something that religions are particularly good at: the creation of sacred values. Although we still don't know exactly how, studies show that involvement in religious ritual, as well as religious reminders of ritual, increase the likelihood of seeing otherwise secular values as sacred.[26] Sacred values in turn are known to make conflicts less tractable. What are sacred values, and why do they matter?

To understand sacred values, and why they matter, we must return to the Western, Educated, Industrialized, Rich, and Democratic (WEIRD) folks who dominate much of the thinking and research about human behavior in the West. Much of WEIRD public policy is grounded in the idea that material or instrumental values are the key drivers of human actions. Instrumental values are motivated by self-interest and involve cost-benefit calculations. For example, if I want to sell my house, and I have two offers, all else being equal, I would accept the higher offer. This is the *rational actor* paradigm. It's the foundation of modern economics that has shaped most policy decisions at the highest levels of power in the West. It guides decisions about the economy, international political relations, decisions to go to war or not, and combatting terrorism. It explains some things about human beings, particularly WEIRD human beings, but goes only so far. What it misses, however, is the cause of a lot of serious trouble in intercultural conflicts, which we do not currently know how to manage.

A great deal of human behavior in the non-WEIRD world is driven by another psychological mindset that is unresponsive to self-interest. In contrast to instrumental values, sacred values involve strong moral convictions that are better seen in the framework of a *devoted actor* model. Sacred values are immune to trade-offs and seem insensitive to outcome. For example, if I consider my house "sacred" because it has a special place in my family history, or if the house was a national or religious monument, I would not sell it no matter what price I was offered. In fact I would take offense to such an offer and get very angry! Interviews show that would-be suicide bombers and their supporters don't care much about how many people are killed— what matters more to them is the meaning of the act and the message it sends to one's community and to one's enemy. A wide range of apparently irrational aspects of human behavior, such as falling in love, emotional attachments people have to objects and places, and why it is so easy for terror groups to recruit young men for suicide missions, defy rational actor models and make much more sense in a devoted actor framework. And many of today's intractable conflicts would make little sense unless we look at them through the lens of sacred values held by devoted actors. Scott Atran and Jeremy Ginges explain:

> Ample historical and cross-cultural evidence shows that when conflict is framed by competing religious and sacred values, intergroup violence may persist for decades, even centuries. Disputes over otherwise mundane phenomena (people, places, objects, events) then become existential struggles, as when land becomes "holy land." Secular issues become sacralized and nonnegotiable.[27]

In a series of groundbreaking studies, Ginges and Atan, along with Douglas Medin and Khalil Shikaki, demonstrated how sacred values can both exacerbate and soften violent opposition to peaceful resolution to conflicts. They questioned hundreds of senior Palestinian and Israeli leaders, Israeli settlers, and Palestinian refugees on hypothetical trade-offs for peace that have been actually discussed in peace negotiations. For example, would Palestinian refugees be willing to abandon their right of return to their formal lands in exchange for massive economic aid? Would Israeli settlers be willing to exchange land for a halt in suicide bombings? The researchers reported a *backfire effect*: when material incentives were offered in return for compromise over sacred values, opposition to compromise actually hardened. However, when the adversary made symbolic gestures such as offering an apology, opposition to compromise softened. People, often those in dominant groups who are asked to do the apologizing, often ask, what is the point of offering a public apology? What difference would it make when what's done is done? The answer is, it makes a significant difference in the realm of the sacred. It turns out that recognition of the other's suffering, or appreciating their core values, even if we on this side do not share them, transforms the dynamic of conflict. Recognizing that sacred values have their own logic can open new doors toward peace.

Because the model organism in psychology, economics, and cognitive science is WEIRD, there is a mountain of scientific research on instrumental values. But we know embarrassingly little about sacred values—how they emerge, operate, and influence actions. However, ignoring sacred values, or treating them as if they are a more expensive or extravagant version of material values, as is often done by policymakers and negotiators in the West, not only does not help resolve conflict, it exacerbates it.

In all three paths from religion to conflict, we notice quite a bit of fluidity. Supernatural monitoring concerns can be dealt with if believers appreciate that other religious groups are also under supernatural surveillance by similar gods. And there is a prayer even for atheists—once believers see that atheists are more common than they think, and that, yes, religion keeps people in line, but it's only one of many paths to good behavior. Clingingsmith's study suggests that when believers are encouraged to reimagine their communities, their moral compass widens to include previously excluded or denigrated groups. And as Scott Atran and Robert Axelrod explain, sacred values are held with absolute conviction and are seen to be inviolable; yet due to ambiguities of interpretation, there is latitude as to how they are applied. This means that sacred values can be reframed, just as the boundaries of one's moral community can be reframed. Does Islam allow or encourage suicide attacks because they are a form of *Jihad* (holy war against the enemies of Islam)? Or does Islam prohibit suicide attacks because the Koran forbids taking one's own life and/or killing innocent noncombatants? When people reimagine their sacred values, their positions soften and opportunities for overcoming conflict emerge.

Psychologists Tom Pyszczynski, Abdolhossein Abdollahi, and Zachary Rothschild showed how even fundamentalist religions can be redirected from conflict to peace. When people are reminded of death, they defensively cling to their cultural beliefs and become more intolerant toward cultural others, including religious others. Yet, even when existential threat is in the air, there is the possibility of transforming jingoism into pacifism. In one study among Iranian Muslims, reminders of death increased support for suicide attacks against Americans. However, when also reminded of Islamic compassionate values ("Do goodness to others because Allah loves those who do good,"), reminders of death *decreased* support for anti-American suicide attacks. In a parallel study with American Fundamentalist Christians, reminders of death again increased support for American military intervention in the Middle East. However, reading compassionate messages from the teachings of Jesus ("love thy neighbor as thyself"), combined with reminders of death, led to *decreased* support for military solutions, down to levels comparable to opinions expressed by liberal Americans.[28]

All of this tells us that parts of the religious bundle can create and intensify conflict, but somewhere in the same bundle there lie seeds that can be coopted to soften and overcome conflict. The relative weight of conflict-producing and conflict-redeeming parts can differ from group to group, and shift over time within the same religious community. Regardless, the complex texture of the religious bundle means that reframing can be a surprisingly powerful tool. It can lead to overlooked opportunities for transmuting religiously motivated hostility into amity.

Chapter 10

Cooperation without God

In the summer of 2007, I visited Denmark's attractive second city, Aarhus, and was surprised to see that anyone can borrow a bicycle, free of charge, at several distribution points throughout the city. You pick up your bicycle, ride it to your destination, and then drop it off at the next distribution point. When I asked my hosts about theft, I got puzzled looks: why would anyone steal a bicycle if anyone can borrow one? Denmark tops the lists of societies high on cooperation, social cohesion, and public trust. Denmark is also synonymous with "welfare state," and in less than a century, has become one of the least religious societies on earth. (A majority of Danes do not believe in God, and few go to church, and if they do, it's only for special occasions.) Denmark presents us with a puzzle: How did Danish society lose its religion so dramatically and so quickly? And how do the Danes keep the wheels of cooperation going without God?

Historically, beliefs and practices that revolved around Big Gods were the driving force behind large cooperative social groups. But in the most secularized corners of the West, and other parts of the world such as in East Asia, an elaborate but fragile set of norms and institutions have emerged that enforce cooperation and encourage trust among strangers.[1] If you suspect that someone is stealing from you, you call the police. If you have a financial dispute with a stranger, you go to an independent court. Trusting the institutions means you can also trust the strangers who obey these institutions. More trust means lower transaction costs and more mutual benefits, which creates a virtuous cycle of trust and cooperation. Sounds familiar? How did secular societies like Denmark come to play the game of cooperation without religion?

To answer this question we need to appreciate how strange these institutions are. As I explained in chapter 3, these evolutionarily novel institutions and societies have shaped a WEIRD psychology that makes people outliers both historically and culturally. In the rest of the non-WEIRD world, euphemistically labeled as *developing*, people don't trust the police, the courts, or for that matter, strangers. In this mostly religious world, what keeps the world going is the ties of blood, honor, and ethnic solidarity. Any cooperation beyond these immediate ties, when it happens, is of a religious nature. Supernatural monitoring by Big Gods is still the only game in town.

The recent spread of secular institutions since the industrial revolution—courts, policing authorities, and effective contract-enforcing mechanisms in modern societies—has raised the specter of large-scale cooperation without God. In these secular societies, Big Gods were replaced by Big Governments. *Quo Modo Deum*, or the Way of God represented as a Big Eye in the Sky, did not disappear—it merely changed shape. The Great Seal of the United States, found on the one-dollar bill, shows a watchful eye on top of a pyramid.

But these social institutions and traditions that replace religion do not come for free—they are costly, fragile, and need constant fine-tuning and upkeep. It is no surprise that in totalitarian communist states, Big Brother in the Sky was quickly replaced by Big Brother in the Party. The Party's eyes and ears were everywhere. These institutions and tactics, which belong to the toolkit of police states, partially suppressed and replaced the functions of religion, but they were far less effective in undermining religion than the social democracies of Northern Europe. In Communist states, unlike Northern Europe, no one believed in the impartiality of the Big Brother. Everyone was under surveillance, but people trusted no one, especially not their next-door neighbor.

There are complex issues at play here—for example, following the fall of the Soviet Union, religion resurged in Russia, but declined further in the former East Germany and the Czech Republic. No doubt, one key factor was that Russians felt a dramatic decline in living standards with the fall of the Soviet Union, whereas Czechs and East Germans saw a gain in living standards. Moreover, in Russia, communism was replaced by yet another totalitarian, corrupt system. In Central European states that merged with the European Union, it was replaced with democracy. As we have seen before, cultural evolution, under the proper conditions, can stabilize any "cultural equilibrium," including dysfunctional systems that benefit a few people or no one. The Communist experiment also is a wake-up call to anyone naïve enough to believe that religion can be abolished by decree. Whatever comes to replace the cultural vacuum left behind by religion must be able to take on the social functions and speak to the deep psychological needs that prosocial religions fulfill.

Climbing the Ladder of Religion, Then Kicking It Away

It turns out that some of the most cooperative, trusting, and well-to-do societies on earth, such as those in Western Europe and Scandinavia, are also the least religious in the world and the most reliant on the government.[2] In these societies there is a very high level of trust, and people who live in societies with strong rule of law show much stronger cooperative tendencies than those who live in places with weak rule of law. In priming experiments, Azim Shariff and I have found that subtle exposure to words such as *police* and *judge* increased generosity between strangers as much as God-related words did. The same secular notions ruptured the mental connection between religion and morality.[3] One of the strengths of a cultural evolutionary explanation of religion—the backbone of the argument in this book—is that it accommodates this significant and far-reaching fact: not only religions take different forms in different cultures and historical periods, but levels of religious commitment wax and wane in a predictable fashion, depending on the social conditions that exist in particular cultures at particular times.

With the benefit of time, when future historians look back at the course of human societies, they may see the prosocial religions as yet another crucial social transition—an intermediate cultural bridge between the small-scale human societies that dominated much of our evolutionary history and the complex secular societies emerging in parts of the modern world. These new institutions and traditions began to erode the foundations of religions with Big Gods. No doubt this is a complex question, and there are many unknowns. Yet there are indications that some societies with strong institutions and material well-being may have passed a threshold, no longer needing religion to sustain large-scale cooperation. In short: secular societies climbed the ladder of religion, and then kicked it away.

Secularism based on science and reason is often portrayed as anathema to religion, particularly among some new atheist thinkers who are critical of religion.[4] But if you have followed the reasoning in this book, you can see that secular societies are really an outgrowth of prosocial religions. Not only because they essentially serve similar functions with comparable methods in sustaining large-scale cooperation. The monotheisms laid the groundwork for the modern secular world in other respects as well. Historian Marcel Gauchet notes two striking continuities between the three monotheisms and the secularisms they ushered. First, it was the monotheistic religions that reduced the role of the sacred and the supernatural from the material world, confining them to a supreme God who created it. Thus, the world, which in polytheism had always been infused with the supernatural, became a material world of cause and effect. In time, this allowed for some to imagine a distant God who created the world but did not actively manage it. It became possible to probe these cause-effect relations by scientific methods. Second, the monotheisms introduced another innovation— other gods were denigrated as false gods. Thus, the monotheisms may have inadvertently planted the seeds of atheism: if people can deny the existence of other gods, it's only a matter of time before they start denying the existence of any gods.[5]

Scott Atran goes further in explaining how most secular ideologies of the nineteenth and twentieth centuries were extensions of monotheisms—in particular, Christianity:

> Universal monotheisms created two new concepts in human thought: individual free choice and collective humanity. People not born into these religions could, in principle, choose to belong (or remain outside) without regard to ethnicity, tribe or territory. The mission of these religions was to extend moral salvation to all peoples, whether they liked it or not. Secularized by the European Enlightenment, the great quasi-religious isms of modern history—colonialism, socialism, anarchism, fascism, communism, democratic liberalism and accompanying forms of messianic atheism—have all tried to harness industry and science to continue on a global scale the Stone Age human imperative "cooperate to compete" (against the other isms, that is). These great secular isms, often relying on the science of the day to justify their moral values, have produced both massive killing to save the mass of humanity as well as great progress in human rights.[6]

Secular sources of authority are a continuation of prosocial religions by other means. This raises the idea that they serve interchangeable functions. If true, this would help us understand how societies come to secularize: one way they do so is by outsourcing religion's functions to new forms of government. Does religion thrive when government is weak? Does belief in God wither when societies invest in policing duties and in efficient governments?

Replacing God with Government and Vice Versa

There is growing evidence showing that both in society and also in peoples' minds, gods and governments occupy a similar niche. Big Gods reign supreme in places where government is corrupt and there is little faith in it. And when trust in government intensifies, religion loses its grip on society. There are at least three explanations for this. First, gods and governments both have surveillance capabilities that facilitate large-scale cooperation and trust. Second, they can both provide comfort in the face of adversity and suffering. Third, they both offer external sources of control and stability when a personal sense of control is under threat.

One piece of evidence for this comes from the work of sociologists. Pipa Norris and Ronald Inglehart find that strong and stable secular institutions erode religion. Religion has declined most steeply in welfare states such as Denmark, Sweden, and France. In these countries, living standards are some of the highest in the world, and government services provide a social safety net from cradle to grave.[7]

But the fluidity of God and government is not just in the social arena. It also plays out inside peoples' heads. Studies by psychologists Aaron Kay, David Moscovitch, and Kristin Laurin show how. Their work explores the basic need to feel "in control." A good way to learn what this need does in human psychology and culture is to see what happens when this sense of control is under threat. Kay and colleagues have found ingenious ways to undermine feelings of control in the laboratory. For example, in one priming study, participants were exposed to control-undermining words such as *chance* and *random*. In the neutral condition, the words were matched for negativity but were unrelated to personal control (*poorly*, *slimy*). In other studies, participants in the threat condition are encouraged to recall an event in their lives that was unpredictable and aroused feelings of losing control. In the comparison condition, participants recall an event that is no more positive or negative, but predictable. Next, participants are asked about their faith in God or in government. When people feel that their grip on life is shaken, they turn to external forms of control: it could be God, or it could be the government. If I'm not in control, the logic goes, at least someone powerful out there is. Things are fine as long as things are under control in one way or another.

Interestingly, faith in government and faith in God appear to compensate for each other. In one study, Aaron Kay and his colleagues had Canadian participants read a news story about government instability in Ottawa. "Nobody can predict when an election will be held," the story went, and "it is not clear what that would mean for the ordinary Canadian." The comparison group read a similarly worded story touting political stability in Canada, and how elections, even if called, would not disturb things. Then participants were asked about their belief in God. Perceptions of political instability increased belief in God. And conversely, in a separate study, perceptions of a strong, stable Canadian government reduced belief in God, particularly among people who saw God as a source of control over the world. Kay and colleagues also found that electoral instability just before national elections undermined faith in the government, which then led to subsequent increases in faith in God.[8]

These findings show, contrary to popular belief, how intertwined divine and secular authority can be. We cannot understand religious belief in isolation from secular cultural beliefs. This insight also points to one of the paths toward secularization: when societies develop strong government institutions that boost peoples' faith in them.

The Problem of Disbelief

Disbelief is a puzzle—historically, when people lost faith, they gravitated to new religions. Yet in the recent past something novel has been happening. Millions of people, and even entire societies, have lost their faith in the very idea of religion. As the forces of secularization have pushed against religion, more and more people in some parts of the world have come to see themselves as atheists, agnostics, or nonbelievers. Some have grown up with little exposure to religion. Others abandoned religion in early adulthood.

Others never really understood or "got" religion. Who are these atheists? How do some people come to lose their religious beliefs, or not have them in the first place?[9]

Unlike historians and sociologists, who have spilled a lot of ink on the origins of secularization, psychologists have said little about it. The current take, offered by several cognitive scientists of religion, is that, while self-reflectively there are atheists, intuitively, everyone is a theist. Paul Bloom, for example, puts it this way:

> People everywhere naturally have some tacit supernatural beliefs; these arise in children regardless of the culture. For instance, even the most sophisticated of cognitive neuroscientists might believe, at an intuitive level, that their mental life is something above and beyond their physical nature.[10]

What Bloom is referring to here is an intuitive belief in mind-body dualism—the idea that there is something immaterial in a person that is separate from the physical body and may survive physical death. It's the feeling of "I" that is distinct from the body and the brain. As we saw in chapter 2, dualism is one of the intuitive building blocks of religious thinking. To believe in a soul, or in various gods and spirits, one has to intuitively get this kind of dualism. Moreover, if such intuitions are the product of fast and automatic sense-making, then our brains have to do some hard work to reject them through reflection and deliberation. Pascal Boyer explains:

> Some form of religious thinking seems to be the path of least resistance for our cognitive systems. By contrast, disbelief is generally the result of deliberate, effortful work against our natural cognitive dispositions—hardly the easiest ideology to propagate.[11]

The logic of this claim goes like this: if the workings of the human mind have factory-installed biases that predispose people toward religion, then disbelief, when it arises, has to work hard against these powerful biases. If our mind-perceiving brains effortlessly infer the existence of invisible agents with mental states, recognize faces in clouds, or see purpose and design, it would be no surprise if atheism—which holds that there are no supernatural agents and events—lacks intuitive support.

Taking this idea in a different direction, philosopher Robert McCauley compares religion's intuitiveness to science's counterintuitiveness. In *Why*

Religion Is Natural and Science Is Not, McCauley points out that whereas religion flows out of easy-to-think intuitions, science involves hard intellectual work that has to push against these same intuitions and replace them with newer concepts. It is not surprising, therefore, that science, like atheism, is a hard sell.[12]

This hypothesis strikes me as partly true, but incomplete. First, atheism is more widespread and enduring than expected if it was merely driven by effortful rejection of intuitive theism. Moreover, while some nonbelievers, some of the time, may be working hard to overcome theistic intuitions, disbelief does not appear to always require hard or explicit cognitive effort. Many nonbelievers simply do not spend time thinking about religious ideas all that much. Third, this view is too narrow to describe all the different kinds of disbelief that we see in the world—in other words, reflective rejection of theism might be just one flavor of atheism. Once we combine insights about cognitive intuitions such as mind-body dualism and mind reading, with an understanding of cultural learning and cultural evolution, we see that there is, actually, not one atheism but multiple flavors of atheism arising from multiple independent pathways.

To appreciate why this is so, let's consider the pathways that give rise to religious belief. For someone to believe in a given deity, he or she must (1) form intuitive mental representations of supernatural agents: (2) be motivated to commit to supernatural agents as real and relevant sources of meaning, comfort, and control; (3) have had prior cultural exposure to the particular deities suggesting that of all the mentally representable supernatural agents, these specific deities should be believed in as real and important; and (4) maintain this commitment without further cognitive processing that could undermine intuitive beliefs. This framework leads to the conclusion that belief and disbelief share the same pathways, and that alterations to any of these four basic pathways could encourage disbelief.

Based on this reasoning, Will Gervais and I have proposed four paths to disbelief: (1) *mind-blind atheism*, which is caused by deficits in understanding God's mind; (2) *analytic atheism*; which arises when habitual analytic thinking encourages religious skepticism; (3) *apatheism*, which is a feeling of indifference to religion found in places where people enjoy safe and secure environments; and (4) closely related to apatheism, *InCREDulous atheism*, which is found in cultural contexts where there is a relative absence of public displays of religious acts—that is, credible displays that one should believe in gods.

Here then, is a story of atheisms in four acts.[13]

Mind-Blind Atheism

Earlier, we saw that religious believers intuitively think of their deities as personified beings with mental states who anticipate and respond to human needs and deeds, and monitor their actions. Entering into a relationship with God therefore requires that people understand God's mind. We saw that when people pray to God, the same mind-reading or mentalizing skills that help people understand other people are recruited to make sense of God:

> The LORD was *grieved* that he had made man on the earth, and his heart was filled with *pain*.

This episode from Genesis (6:6) would not make intuitive sense unless we unconsciously accept that God has mental and emotional states and acts according to them. Similarly, prayer to God would be impossible without the intuitive understanding that the believer has about God's intentions and beliefs. It follows then, that when mentalizing skills are impaired, religious belief is less intuitive. It has long been known that mentalizing or *theory of mind* is compromised at higher levels of the autism spectrum.[14] Autism, and the closely related Asperger syndrome, is a complex, multifaceted developmental condition. Among its symptoms are deficits in nonverbal communication such as lack of eye contact, lack of interest or insensitivity toward other people, repetitive or stereotyped movements, and in many cases, an advanced talent in and curiosity for mechanical systems and numbers. It is best viewed as a spectrum, ranging from mild to severe. At the severe end, the condition can be quite debilitating. At milder levels, however, some individuals with autistic symptoms possess high general intelligence and can be high functioning.

Of all these symptoms, perhaps the most critical aspect of the autism spectrum that causes social difficulties is selective deficits in reasoning about the mental states of others. The higher someone is on the autism spectrum, the more difficulty he or she has in inferring the mental states of others from their actions, telling the difference between what someone says versus means, and understanding emotions. This leads to the surprising idea, hypothesized by virtually all leading cognitive scientists of religion, of an association between autism and religious disbelief.[15] Having difficulties representing mental states, autistic individuals are less likely to conceptualize God or other deities as personlike agents with mental states.[16] Without personalizing God, it is hard for them to get the significance of these beings in their own lives. It becomes harder, although not impossible, to be a believer.

There is quite a bit of anecdotal evidence that autistic individuals seem to be indifferent to religion, and if they do reflect on their religious beliefs, there is a striking absence of a relationship with a personal God who directly enters into relationships with people. After reviewing such autobiographical accounts of autistic individuals reflecting on their religious beliefs (and lack thereof), Jesse Bering concludes:

> What is noticeably absent in the autistic accounts is a sense of deep interpersonal relations between the worshipper and the deity, a sense of emotional dependency on an intentional agent who has control over the experiences and the existence of the individual. God is not presented as an agent who communicates intentions.[17]

For example, Bering cites Temple Grandin, a well-known autistic and animal rights activist:

> In nature, particles are entangled with millions of other particles, all interacting with each other. One could speculate that entanglement of these particles could cause a kind of consciousness for the universe. This is my current concept of God.[18]

Grandin's notion of God is best described as an abstract, impersonal, universal consciousness, hardly a testament of religious fervor.

Will Gervais, Kali Trzesniewski, and I set out to find out if indeed this link exists, and if it does, whether it is explained by deficits in mentalizing. We reasoned that, if God is transformed from a personlike agent to an abstract impersonal force, then it will lose its intuitive appeal. Faith in such a God will erode. Our results matched closely these predictions. People scoring high on the autism spectrum expressed lower levels of belief in a personal God, an association that was due to the lower levels of mentalizing among participants scoring high on the autism spectrum. Other factors, such as personality, age, education, income, IQ, or interest in science were taken into account but did not change the results.[19]

We also tested another closely related idea. Other than people high on the autistic spectrum, what's another group of people whose mentalizing skills aren't as elaborated? These people are called men. Of course, there is a great deal of variability in mentalizing skills among men, but in various tests of mentalizing, men on average score lower than women. Not surprisingly, men also are overrepresented on the high end of the autism spectrum.[20] If mentalizing deficits erode the intuitive support for belief in God, then we should expect more disbelief in men compared to women. Actually, we know this already. Sociologists have known for more than 50 years that on average, men are less religious than women. There are many more atheists among men than among women (atheist conventions are not a good place for bachelors to meet women).[21] There could be several reasons for this gender gap in religiosity, but what we wanted to know was whether differences in mentalizing are a contributing cause. They were. In fact, statistically, we found that the lower levels of belief among men were explained by lower levels of mentalizing, even after taking into account various demographic factors such as age, education, and income.

Of course, we must be cautious with these findings given that all we have are correlations. It is difficult to establish causal direction with certainty, but the overall picture that emerged pointed to one conclusion: mind-blind people are not enamored by the idea of a personal God. Of course, these findings do not show that mind-blindness is the main cause of religious disbelief. They tell us that it is one contributing factor. There are others. I now turn to another psychological factor that could lead to disbelief even when mentalizing tendencies are well-developed.

Analytic Atheism

This second origin story is much closer to the idea found in Boyer's quote earlier—that of implicit theism, arising effortlessly but vetoed by reflection and deliberation. To delve deeper into this scenario, let's first unpack what is meant by *implicit theism*. In chapter 2, I discussed a constellation of intuitions that push our brains toward religious thinking. There is the habitual tendency to mentalize (discussed earlier); mentalizing in turn encourages mind-body dualism, or the feeling that something immaterial exists that is distinct from the physical body; psychological immortality, or the feeling that this "something," being immaterial and distinct, survives the body's death; and teleological thinking, or the feeling that things exist for a purpose, and purpose implies a creator. This cognitive package is typically what's meant by implicit theism.[22] All the ingredients in implicit theism are run by an intuitive system (known as System 1) that is rapid, automatic, and largely unconscious. These are the networks in the brain that produce rapid hunches. Their motto is, "shoot first, ask questions later." What I just described is the scientifically modern version of an insight that seventeenth-century French philosopher and mathematician, devout Christian, and keen observer of the human condition Blaise Pascal had. He said:

> It is the heart which perceives God and not the reason. That is what faith is: God perceived by the heart, not by the reason.[23]

Not surprisingly, Pascal was not fond of the attempts by many medieval Christian theologians, known as *Christian Apologetics*, to prove the existence of God by means of reason and evidence. He thought these attempts were misguided and missed the point. He was on to something: apologetics is doomed to failure as a philosophical enterprise because it fails to capture how our minds accept the plausibility of religious belief.

These attempts at argumentation belong to the realm of doubt, questioning, skepticism. They arise from those parts of our brains that are slower, more deliberative, and reflective (known as System 2). This is the supervisory system that often agrees with the gut reactions from System 1. But it can also sow doubt. Therefore, it occasionally second-guesses, and overrules, these initial reactions.

You might think that System 2 always produces correct answers, and System 1 is always wrong. But this is not true. There are many examples of erroneous intuitions being corrected by reflection. But there are also examples of cases where gut reactions seem to produce better outcomes than deliberation.[24] While the relative merits of intuitive and rational thinking can be debated, what is hard to argue with is that folk theism, rooted in our intuitions, has all the hallmarks of System 1 thinking. Atheism, at least atheism that is characterized by deliberate rejection of belief, is the offspring of System 2.[25]

This line of thinking leads to a number of interesting predictions: First, that people who are habitual intuitive thinkers should be more religious and, conversely, that habitual analytic thinkers should be the skeptical ones who doubt religion. Second, encouraging people to think intuitively should make them more religious, and thinking analytically should lead to a temporary spike in religious doubt. Third, any long-term habits or experiences that cultivate analytic thinking also should encourage religious doubt.

Will Gervais and I set out to test these predictions. Little did we know at the time that two other teams of psychologists were trying to answer the same questions. It turned out that all three teams independently found similar results that converged: Religious belief is the brainchild of intuitive thinking, and one pathway to religious doubt goes through analytic thinking. Amitai Shenhav, David Rand, and Joshua Greene were first to publish their results. In a series of studies, they measured the tendency to think intuitively, the tendency to think deliberatively, and the tendency to endorse belief in God.

In one study, they looked at whether people were inclined to overrule an intuitively appealing, but incorrect, answer in a series of math problems known as the Cognitive Reflection Task. For example: "A bat and a ball cost $1.10 in total. The bat costs $1.00 more than the ball. How much does the ball cost?" The intuitive answer is 10 cents—but it's wrong. A little more reflection reveals that the correct answer is 5 cents.[26]

Participants who were more likely to overrule the intuitive answer were also less likely to believe in God. Shenhav and his colleagues were careful to consider other factors and ruled them out as potential counterexplanations. They showed that the lower levels of belief among the analytic thinkers were not because they had higher education levels, more general intelligence, different personality profiles, or higher income, or were older or younger, more liberal politically, or male. Analytic thinking even explained decreases in religious belief since childhood, suggesting that analytic thinkers tend to lose their religious fervor even if they were raised in a religious environment. Finally, in a subsequent study, participants were encouraged to think about a time when they had to make an important decision, and acted on intuition. In the analytic condition, they thought about a time when they had to make an important decision, and acted reflectively. Intuitive thinking, relative to reflective thinking, temporarily increased belief in God. Research by a team led by Gordon Pennycook found that religious skepticism and skepticism about paranormal phenomena were more prevalent among analytic thinkers, holding constant other potentially confounding factors. Going further, they showed that analytic thinkers, if they do endorse religious belief, show more unconventional and less fervent inclinations, such as the belief in a distant, nonintervening God (Deism), and the belief that the universe and God are identical (Pantheism).[27]

Will Gervais and I were unaware of these findings when we set out to test whether analytical thinking was actually causing a decline in belief. We used a variety of well-tested techniques to induce analytical thinking, then measured subsequent levels of belief in God. Importantly, none of our techniques had any content that is related to debates about religion's rationality or truth. These were not rational arguments against religion. What we did was to prod people to think in an analytical style before reporting their religious convictions.

In one study, for example, we had randomly assigned participants look at various images of Auguste Rodin's sculpture *The Thinker* (figure 10.1). Other participants were shown images of an ancient Greek statue of a discus thrower, *Discobolus*. We picked these two sculptures because they are in many ways similar, except that *The Thinker* is emblematic of a thinking pose. This was a novel technique, so we did a separate test and found that, as expected, merely viewing *The Thinker*, compared to viewing *Discobolus*, caused participants to override intuitive answers in favor of logic in a subsequent syllogistic reasoning task. In this study, those who viewed *The Thinker* expressed less belief in God—they scored an average of about 41 on a 100-point scale, compared with an average of 61 for the group that viewed *Discobolus*.

In another experiment, we relied on a more subtle method to encourage analytic thinking. We induced participants to experience what psychologists call *perceptual disfluency*. This happens when information is difficult to process or understand. When information doesn't flow smoothly through the cognitive system, people are more reflective and skeptical. They are also more eager to question and learn. Not surprisingly, many studies show that disfluency—for example, presenting information in a difficult-to-read font—improves performance in tasks that involve analytic thinking, including syllogistic reasoning as well as the Cognitive Reflection Task discussed earlier.[28] We randomly assigned participants to read our questionnaire in a typical, easy-to-process font (sample) or a difficult-to-process font (sample). The experience of disfluency also produced a dip in belief in God, angels and the Devil. Interest-

(a)   (b)

Figure 10.1. *Panel a*: Rodin's *The Thinker* (photo courtesy of Marie-Lan Nguyen). *Panel b*: *Discobolus of Myron* (photo courtesy of Cyberjunkie). Viewing *The Thinker* compared to *Discobolus* produced a dip in religious belief. A variety of evidence shows that analytic thinking is one source of religious skepticism.

ingly, we also found that analytic thinking reduced belief at every level of prior religious conviction.[29]

These findings are easy to misunderstand, so let's start by clarifying what they don't mean. We observed a dip in religious belief; we certainly did not turn fervent believers into atheists by a single visit to our lab. Moreover, these results don't mean that we can dispose of religion altogether by simply encouraging analytical thinking. Why? Because many flames sustain the fire of religious faith. The fire keeps burning even if one of the flames (intuitive appeal) is subdued. Some of these other flames lie deep in perennial human anxieties, such as anxieties about death and randomness. Others are equally powerful cultural forces that push people toward faith. (I turn to these next.)

Nevertheless, these findings shine light on one path that leads to disbelief. In our lab studies, we had merely one opportunity to encourage analytic thought, and that was enough to produce a dip in religious belief. But Shenhav, Pennycook, and their collaborators showed that habitual analytic thinkers are also habitual disbelievers. We can go further and ask, what happens when people are encouraged to think analytically on a regular basis? What about entire subcultures where analytic thinking is the gold standard, inculcated every day? These subcultures are called universities. And indeed, this link between analytic thought and disbelief might explain the overrepresentation of disbelievers among the more educated classes. Some of this is surely self-selection (atheists are drawn to higher education, particularly to science), but exposure to university education also in turn undermines religious belief. Analytic thinking might also explain why, once demographic factors are taken into account, there is a small but reliable connection between measures of general intelligence and lower levels of religious belief. Intelligence fosters critical thinking, which in turn contributes to religious skepticism. However, we would not expect this connection to be overwhelming, because, as I said earlier, other factors feed the flames of religious faith even among analytic thinkers.[30]

Apatheism and InCREDulous Atheism

I now turn to two additional paths to atheism, *apatheism* and *InCREDulous atheism*. Earlier, we saw that religion declines as societies develop strong institutions that take on the social functions of prosocial religions. Equally important, as social and economic conditions improve, societies become, in the words of Pipa Norris and Ronald Inglehart, *existentially secure*. Life expectancy and income levels increase, and with better nutrition and health care, infant mortality becomes a thing of the past. Moreover, with unemployment and retirement support, universal medical care, as well as poverty reduction strategies, people are rescued by social safety nets in times of trouble or uncertainty.

These are exactly the changes that some countries, particularly in Northern and Western Europe, underwent over the last 100 years. There is strong evidence that this constellation of social forces that level life's playing field precipitate religion's decline. Norris and Inglehart report two key pieces of evidence that support this claim: nations with stronger existential security are less religious by a large margin; and over time, as existential security improves in a given society, religiosity declines in step. Closely related to existential security, cross-cultural comparisons show that societies with more economic equality—that is, with a more egalitarian distribution of wealth—are also less religious, even after a host of other economic and demographic factors, such as gross domestic product, are accounted for.[31] These patterns are seen even within the United States. Psychologists Kurt Gray and Dan Wegner surveyed life conditions state by state, such as rates of infant mortality, cancer deaths, the prevalence of infectious diseases, and the incidence of violent crime. They found that where there is less human misery, there is also less religiosity.[32] Combined with strong secular institutions that keep the cooperative engines going, existential security is the nemesis of religion.[33]

This is perhaps why Al Franken, in his book, *Oh the Things I Know!* devotes an entire chapter to religion titled *Oh Pick a Religion, Any Religion!* He gives this advice to newly minted university graduates:

> Religion is like a fire extinguisher. You never know when you're going to need it. So it's best to have one handy.

He goes on with his advice:

> I don't care what kind of nonsense you believe, I can tell you that religion will be a crutch which you can lean upon in times of adversity.[34]

Big thinkers of modernity, from Freud to Feuerbach, would have agreed with Franken: religious belief thrives partly because it soothes our deepest existential fears. Reason, logic, or science have little to give us when we face intense anxieties about death, chaos, loneliness, or meaninglessness. It's not that religion originates from the need to soothe existential worries. Of course, gods and spirits have to first pass a cognitive hurdle—they have to be intuitively appealing notions to begin with. But once they resonate with common intuitions, they can take on additional features and relieve these anxieties. Those versions of gods that guarantee immortality, order, social connection, and meaning become more attractive in the cultural landscape.

The notion that death and suffering intensify religiosity is surprising to some—shouldn't these conditions make people lose faith and turn into apostates? This is the well-known problem of *theodicy* that has troubled some theologians and philosophers: how can we reconcile the existence of human suffering with a God who is omnipotent, omniscient, and benevolent? But of course, such a rational response to suffering is a luxury few can afford. In the face of existential angst, believers typically seek refuge in religion. Experimental studies from psychology show that when existential worries intensify, religious inclinations increase. And conversely, when these worries are appeased, religious conviction wanes. In one series of experiments I did with Ian Hansen, we first reminded American and Canadian participants of their imminent mortality by asking participants to write about their own death in vivid detail, or in another study, read a graphic story about a child victim of a car accident who later dies in the hospital. Participants in the control conditions wrote about aversive topics unrelated to death (for example, dental pain), or read the same story with the child surviving the car crash. Then, under the guise of a different task that asked people about their opinions regarding a newspaper article about supernatural events, we asked them to tell us how strongly they believed in God. We found that death awareness caused a temporary spike in belief in God. When reminded of death, Christians were more devoted to their Christian God, but they also became a little more enamored by, and a little less suspicious of, even alien gods such as Buddha and Shamanic spirits. There is a truth to the old saying that "when in a storm, voyagers pray to any God."[35]

These effects mirror what typically happens in the world when disaster strikes. In a rare study, Chris Sibley and Joseph Bulbulia compared levels of religious faith before and after a devastating earthquake that hit Christchurch, New Zealand, on February 22, 2011, killing 185 people and causing extensive damage, including to the city's landmark Anglican Cathedral. In the rest of the country, religious devotion declined a little between 2009 and 2011, consistent with an overall secularization trend that has been observed in New Zealand over the last half-century. However, among citizens who reported being directly affected by the earthquake, in that same period, devotion increased. As they put it, "where the church spires had fallen, faith soared."[36]

There is more evidence that external threats to life and well-being encourage religiosity. In a global analysis of 800 geographic regions in the world, people who are exposed to natural disasters (such as earthquakes, volcano eruptions, tropical storms) were found to be more religious, even after other factors, such as income, education, and denomination are taken into account. Moreover, immigrants in Europe whose mothers came from disaster-prone areas are more religious. This latter finding speaks against the alternative idea that the reason for why there is more religiosity in disaster-prone areas is because religious people are more likely to stay put (perhaps because they may see these uncontrollable events as God's will).[37]

Death might be the ultimate existential worry, but it is not the only one. Fears of chaos and loneliness appear to have the same religion-promoting effect. Earlier, I discussed work by Aaron Kay and his colleagues, who showed that, like reminders of death, incidental reminders of randomness also amplify belief in God. Bastiaan Rutjens and colleagues found that the same feelings of randomness make staunchly secular Dutch participants gravitate towards arguments for intelligent design (a more subtle creationist stance cloaked in scientific jargon). And when feelings of loneliness are aroused, people report a stronger belief in a personal God. It appears that this spike in religious conviction following distress has palliative effects. One study found that religiosity spikes during bereavement, and moreover, those who turned to religion more experienced less grief later.[38]

This is why evolutionary psychologist Lee Kirkpatrick sees gods and spirits as attachment figures providing safety and comfort in times of distress. And just as our parents and significant others can be both the cause and the solution to our anxieties, God's love can be comforting, but God's wrath can be anxiety provoking. Fear of sinning is a major religious preoccupation. Religions are populated with scary creatures who torment souls. This raises an interesting puzzle—how to explain the wide-ranging evidence (discussed earlier) that in the face of existential threats, people embrace religion, and not only the feel-good parts? It could be that a disturbing but predictable world is still more comforting than a chaotic, senseless one. Moreover, not all religions are equally good at soothing these anxieties. It is likely that religions that succeed, all else being equal, offer even greater succor in the face of these, as well as other, graver threats. This brings us back full circle to the delicate balancing act between supernatural punishment, which makes people be nice to each other, and supernatural benevolence, which helps people cope with their deepest anxieties. Once again, true to its paradoxical effects, religion is both the arsonist and the fire department.[39]

It follows then, in places where life is stable, long, controllable, and enjoyable, religion is a crutch that people do not want or need. This then is the third path to disbelief. This disbelief is not so much an opposition to religion, but an indifference to it. I don't know who coined the term *apatheism*, but I think it captures this kind of irreligion quite well. Here is how the journalist and writer, and possible inventor of the term, Jonathan Rauch describes apatheism:

> Apatheism—a disinclination to care all that much about one's own religion, and an even stronger disinclination to care about other people's—may or may not be something new in the world, but its modern flowering... is worth getting excited about.[40]

Rauch extols the virtues of apatheism as a principled and tolerant alternative to the culture wars pitting dogmatic religion against religion, or religion against secularism. In his interviews with Danes, Phil Zuckerman rarely found antagonism toward religion, which is common among some atheists in America. Instead, he found a widespread attitude of benign neglect of religion—in essence, in Denmark Zuckerman found a nation of apatheists.[41]

Last, a close cousin of apatheism is *InCREDulous atheism*. This term of course draws on the work of Joseph Henrich, who, you might recall, coined the term CREDs (credibility-enhancing displays), to point out that many of the extravagant practices and rituals found in prosocial religions and other cultural groups serve a persuasive function. When observers witness acts that reveal sincere commitment or belief—that is, when actions speaker louder than words—they are more inclined to see these beliefs as genuine and more willing to adopt them. In turn, this causes them to display the same CREDs to others. In this way, repeated waves of belief-behavior packages may turn into cultural epidemics. This is what we mean when we say religion spreads in a population. But when children grow up in families with parents who claim to be Christian but hardly ever spend a Sunday morning at church, they are less likely themselves to feel or express religious fervor. There arises a reverse cascade of irreligion. Consistent with this, anthropologist Jonathan Lanman studied the reasons behind the decline of religion in Scandinavia, and found that adults who recalled being raised by such parents—even if the parents claimed to believe in God—grew up to be nonbelievers.[42]

Strong, reliable governments might be another potent factor underlying inCREDulous atheism. We know that belief in watchful gods who monitor and intervene in human affairs may culturally spread by encouraging cooperative tendencies that allow anonymous groups of strangers to expand in size. However, reliable secular institutions such as governments, courts, and the police can serve these same functions and therefore supplant religion. We saw earlier that people perceive God and government as interchangeable sources of external control and stability. Belief in God, commitment to supernatural monitoring, and distrust of atheists all decline as societies develop strong secular alternatives to religion. Combined with conditions of existential security and relative absence of sincere religious displays, effective secular institutions undermine religion and its place in society. As religion plays a less prominent role in society, it declines further still, as there is simply less opportunity for religious displays to influence cultural learners.

Bringing the Varieties of Atheisms Together

So to summarize, mind-blind atheism does not *get* religion; analytical atheism *rejects* religion; apatheism and inCREDulous atheism are *indifferent* toward religion. I discussed these four pathways to irreligion separately, because they do have different flavors and have different origins. But it would be a mistake to think that they are unrelated to each other in the world. In fact, chances are, these paths criss-cross all the time. To illustrate, consider why scientists tend to be much less religious than the general population.[43] To begin with, analytic thinkers are drawn to science more than intuitive thinkers. Scientific training in turn further cultivates the habitual use of analytic thinking. Additionally, the scientific enterprise relies on tendencies and abilities, such as systemizing, categorizing, careful attention to detail, and generally the willingness to see the world in material terms, devoid of purpose and intention. This means that the high end of the autism spectrum, where these talents and tendencies are abundantly available, is over-sampled, particularly in the hard sciences.[44] Once scientists come together in the relative security and predictability of their social circles, the end result is a subculture of atheists where religious faith is unintuitive to begin with, seen to be irrational when entertained at all, and in any case, rarely observed among fellow scientists in the form of passionate public displays.

Similarly, the confluence of several of these pathways might explain why Scandinavian societies are some of the least religious in the world. While the intuitions that support theistic beliefs—such as mind-body dualism and teleology—may have stayed intact, changes to the other pathways have led to widespread disbelief. These societies of apatheists and inCREDulous atheists enjoy high levels of existential security, strong and stable governments with social safety nets, and the absence of widespread passionate displays of religiosity in public life. Once again, these factors were likely mutually reinforcing: increases in existential security reduced motivations to attend religious services, in turn causing further declines of religious belief, leading to a retreat of religious displays from the public sphere. These developments were likely reinforced by widespread access to science education in these societies, which further encourages analytic thinking that fosters religious skepticism.

So is atheism a hard sell as many evolutionary scientists of religion have proposed? I think they are right that in human brains, religion has a head start over atheism and science. But once we broaden our scope to accommodate the many paths to disbelief, and appreciate that these paths can be mutually energizing, we can see that, under the right conditions, atheism can flourish and become a viable cultural equilibrium. Consider literacy as an analogy. Illiteracy is more intuitive and easier to arise than literacy, and humanity has been illiterate for 99.99 percent of its evolutionary history. But while literacy is initially hard to get off the ground, once all the conditions for literacy are there, it can be a culturally stable pattern, and indeed, we now have, for the first time in human history, entire populations with universal literacy. Similarly, we might be on the verge of a new phenomenon—cooperative societies without God.

I am not underestimating the point that Robert McCauley and others have made, that our minds give an easy ride to religion and a hard one to science and atheism. Unlike religion, which is historically ubiquitous, science arose only three times—in ancient Greece, in medieval Islam, and in the modern West. And these three sproutings of science were culturally dependent—Greece inspired Islamic science, which in turn rescued it from oblivion, replanting roots again in its modern Western version, which then took off. In the first line of *Anna Karenina*, Tolstoy famously said, "Happy families are all alike; every unhappy family is unhappy in its own way."[45] Literacy, atheism, and science obey the same *Anna Karenina Principle*: they are hard to arrive at. They are alike in their fragility and complexity; they need many things at once to be viable, and the absence of one critical factor can doom the whole enterprise. But once all the necessary conditions are firmly established, they can flourish.

The Future of Religion

Nevertheless, it is far from clear to me that secular societies will win the race for cultural longevity. On one hand, we have the powerful forces of secularization gaining ground in some places—more economic prosperity, greater existential security, strong secular institutions, and mass exposure to higher learning, science, and analytic thinking. This means that people in these societies are on the verge of moving beyond prosocial religions. But prosocial religions have one crucial advantage over secular ones—the demographic windfall of more children. And that religious advantage is the secularists' Achilles' heel—in fact, the most secularized societies are having the fewest children. This means that what prosocial religious groups lose against the forces of secularization, they gain in reproduction. Today, most of the world remains religious, with the overwhelming majority belonging to a handful of big prosocial religions worshipping Big Gods. We are beginning to understand how we got here. We don't know enough to forecast religion's future, but we can be more certain that the tension between various competing religious movements, and between religion and secular ways of life, will continue to shape the world in the coming century.

Notes

Chapter 1   Religious Evolution

1. The Mormon Church: Ostling and Ostling, 1999.

2. Growth of the Mormon Church: Stark, 2005; for estimates of Christian demographic expansion in the Roman Empire, see Stark, 1996.

3. Growth of Fundamentalist Christianity in particular: Jenkins, 2002.

4. Religious beliefs among Americans: Newport and Strausberg, 2001.

5. There is a long tradition in the humanities of debating definitions of religion. Interested readers can consult, for example, Horton, 1960, and Clarke and Byrne, 1993. For a psychological approach, see Saroglou, 2011. Sidestepping definitional debates, Taves (2009) takes a "building-block" approach to religion. The approach that I develop in this book follows a similar logic, but goes even further; it is precise about operationalizing specific constituent elements of *religion* but departs from broader definitional issues and is not concerned with semantic debates and conceptual boundaries. First, religion is a family resemblance construct, not a natural kind category; therefore no necessary or sufficient features are needed or expected. Second, the argument rooted in cultural evolution specifies the particular combination of elements that coalesce as a result of increasing social scale over time and across groups. In other words, the package of traits that gets labeled *religion* shares recurrent features, but also this package evolves, taking different shapes in different groups and at different historical times.

6. The growth, number, and distribution of all religions in the world: (Barrett et al., 2001); for an in-depth exploration of the origins and growth of world religions, see Bellah, 2011; for an entertaining discussion of the cultural dynamism of the religious landscape, see Lester, 2002. Lester observes: "New religions are born

all the time. Old ones transform themselves dramatically. Schism, evolution, death, and rebirth are the norm."

7. Utopian religious movements in America: Pitzer, 1997; Oved, 1997.

8. Quantitative analysis of American utopian communes: Sosis, 2000; Sosis and Bressler, 2003; see also Kitts, 2009.

9. In the study of the varying cultural survival rates of religious ideas, traditions and groups, we must be careful not to conflate cultural superiority and moral superiority—a version of the well-known naturalistic fallacy that erroneously derives *ought* from *is*. A cultural tradition or group that disappears is no more or less moral than a cultural group or tradition that survives. History shows that some of the most culturally resilient human practices, such as slavery or warfare, are also known as the most morally objectionable ones, and conversely, some of the most morally elevating ones, such as protecting civilians during wars, or accountable government institutions, have dubious records of cultural success.

10. Oneida Perfectionists: (Klaw, 1993; see also Bering, 2010).

11. Sometimes called *imagined communities*: Anderson, 1983.

12. The rise of large-scale cooperation: Seabright, 2004; Henrich and Henrich, 2007. The extent of cooperation in preagricultural hunting and foraging groups in the early Holocene likely varied from group to group and across time—there is evidence that at least some of these groups engaged in cooperative practices that went beyond the immediate band, such as trading, collective hunting, and warfare. This suggests dependence on some forms of cultural institutions to foster cooperation among strangers, at least some of the time (see for example, Kelly, 1995; Klein, 2009; see also Powell et al., 2009). However, the debate about the scale of preagricultural cooperation and social complexity, as important as it is, does not fundamentally change the argument in this book. Big God religions, without being a necessary condition, dramatically expanded the cooperative scale of societies; but other cultural institutions could have similar effects.

13. Kin selection: Hamilton, 1964.

14. Reciprocal altruism: Trivers, 1971); Axelrod, 1984; Fehr and Fischbacher, 2003.

15. This is often called the *assortment problem* that the evolution of cooperation has to solve. For cooperation to get off the ground, cooperators have to find other cooperators and selectively interact with them. There are many solutions to this problem; see for example, Chudek and Henrich, 2011.

16. Costly punishment as a stabilizer of large-scale cooperation: Henrich et al., 2006)

17. Kummerli, 2011.

18. Food sharing in vampire bats: Wilkinson, 1990. Adoption in chimpanzees: Boesch et al., 2010.

19. *Gemeinschaft* and *Gesellschaft*: Tonnies, 1887/2001.

20. Some evolutionary researchers propose to solve this puzzle by arguing that kin and reciprocity psychology are simply overextended to cause cooperation with strangers (Dawkins, 2006; Burnham and Johnson, 2005). Therefore in this view, large-scale cooperation is a "big mistake." No doubt, kinship and reciprocity explain a significant amount of human cooperation, but these processes fall short of a complete explanation. This argument doesn't easily explain why this happens only in humans, despite the fact that other primate groups also interact with kin and reciprocating partners. And it doesn't explain why this process occurred only in the last 12,000 years but not before. Finally, this view is silent about the massive population variability in the scale of cooperation and ultrasociality found in humans, and has difficulty explaining why we find *less* prosociality toward strangers in small face-to-face societies, where kinship and reciprocity, if anything, should be more potent (see for example, Henrich et al., 2006).

21. Some have singled out Buddhism as a world religion without supernatural beings. Granted, these "nontheistic" belief-systems reject personifying the divine. However, these assertions confuse theological dogma with "natural religion" as lived by adherents every day. Angels and devils are legion in Buddhist worship. Buddhist monks ritually ward off malevolent deities by invoking benevolent ones, and common folk deify Buddha contrary to theological teachings (Pyysiäinen, 2003). In India, Nepal, China, Japan, Thailand, and Vietnam, there are magic mountains and forests that are infused with Buddha's powers, and the folklore of every Buddhist tradition recounts supernatural events surrounding the Buddha and the Buddhas (Atran and Norenzayan, 2004).

22. I am using 10,000–12,000 years as a convenient starting point when the first human groups in the Middle East (known as Natufian villages) began to rapidly scale up. This is also where Diamond, 2005, p. 512, starts his survey of divergent cultural evolution. However, this process unfolded at different times in different geographic regions. Moreover, this broad pattern of history masks a great deal of fluctuation in the size and social complexity of human groups even during the Pleistocene. These details are important, but do not change the overall argument that some human societies scaled up and expanded at the expense of rival groups that did not.

23. The gods of hunter-gatherer bands vary in the degree of their involvement in human affairs, but typically are morally indifferent; see for example, Marshall, 1962; Marlowe, 2010. For an entertaining, accessible review of the ethnographic literature on this, see Wright, 2009; Swanson, 1966. See chapter 7 for a detailed exploration of this issue.

24. The spread of world religions at the dawn of the agricultural revolution: Cauvin, 1999.

25. Joseph Bulbulia, 2009, p. 519, independently makes a similar point, when he writes: "the puzzle of large-scale cooperation and the puzzle of religion's fascinating endurance contain each other's solution."

26. Cognitive foundations of religion: Atran and Norenzayan, 2004; Barrett, 2004; Boyer, 2001; Lawson and McCauley, 1990; Pyysiäinen and Hauser, 2010.

27. Dualism as a natural intuition: Bloom, 2004, chapters 7–8.

28. This debate is also couched in modern *adaptationist* versus cognitive by-product theories of religion. For adaptationist accounts, see Bering, 2011; Johnson and Bering, 2006; Johnson, 2009; Johnson, 2011; Sosis and Alcorta, 2003; Bulbulia, 2004. For cognitive by-product theories, see Boyer, 2001; Lawson and McCauley, 1990; Barrett, 2004.

29. See Haidt, 2012, chapter 11, for a synthesis that also sees religion as the merging of belief and social solidarity.

30. Intergroup cultural competition: Khaldûn, 1958; Atran and Henrich, 2010; Turchin, 2007; Durkheim, 1912/1915; Wilson, 2002.

31. E. O. Wilson, 1998; for a comprehensive volume on the promises and challenges of consilience, see Slingerland and Collard, 2012.

Chapter 2   Supernatural Watchers

1. Trial by ordeal: Leeson, 2010a and 2010b.

2. Cognitive foundations of religion: Atran and Norenzayan, 2004; Barrett, 2004; Boyer, 2001; Lawson and McCauley, 1990; Pyysiäinen and Hauser, 2010.

3. Mind perception, mentalizing, or theory of mind; see Waytz et al., 2010; Bloom, 2004, chapter 1; Birch and Bloom, 2004; Frith and Frith, 2003; Mitchell, 2009.

4. Dualism as a natural intuition: Bloom, 2004, chapters 7–8.

5. For a discussion of psychological immortality, see Bering, 2006, 2011; see also Bloom, 2004.

6. See Kelemen, 2004; Kelemen and Rosset, 2009; Kelemen et al., in press. For creationist thinking, see Evans, 2001.

7. Willard and Norenzayan, in press. Interestingly, the tendency to project human traits onto nature—*anthropomorphism*—was not associated with belief, possibly because this tendency is suppressed in Christianity. This finding moderates the idea, developed by Stewart Guthrie and others, that religious thinking is rooted in anthropomorphism; it is right in the sense that believers anthropomorphize spirits and gods. It is not necessarily true, however, that the tendency to "see human" everywhere increases the odds of believing in God, at least not among Christians.

8. See chapter 10 for an account of how these factors, in combination, give rise to various forms of atheism.

9. Attributing human-like mental states to God: Guthrie, 1993; Barrett and Keil, 1996.

10. This claim should not be confused with another that sees religion as a product of the general tendency to anthropomorphize the world. Some argue that seeing human-like beings everywhere is a "better-safe-then-sorry" hyperactive strategy, encouraging the belief that the world is populated with gods and spirits (see Guthrie, 1996; Barrett, 2000). This might describe animistic beliefs of many cultures to some extent. However, empirical work has painted a different picture regarding the origins of anthropomorphism. Rather than showing that this tendency is promiscuous, rapid, and automatic, studies have shown that people project human minds to nonhuman entities sometimes, under some conditions. They do so when an entity behaves unpredictably (think of your computer malfunctioning), when the idea of human is prominent (a robot with human-like features), and when people desire human connection (lonely people who anthropomorphize their pets); for reviews, see Epley et al., 2007; Waytz et al., 2010.

11. Neuroimaging evidence: Schjoedt et al. 2009; Kapogiannis et al., 2009.

12. Autism linked to seeing less mind in God: Gray et al., 2011. Link between deficits in mind perception and disbelief: Norenzayan et al., 2012.

13. Ground of Being: Tilich, 1951.

14. In economic games, some degree of cooperation is found at least among some people, even when reputational incentives or social monitoring are absent. This is sometimes known as *strong reciprocity*, although the term is controversial in evolutionary biology. See Fehr and Henrich, 2003; Gintis et al., 2003; see also Warneken and Tomasello, 2009.

15. Anonymity makes people more selfish: Hoffman et al., 1994.

16. So does the lack of repeated interactions: Fehr and Gaechter, 2000; Fehr and Fischbacker, 2003; Nowak and Sigmund, 1998.

17. Ambient darkness and wearing dark glasses increase dishonesty and selfish tendencies: Zhong et al., 2010.

18. Fusiform networks of the brain: Tong et al., 2000.

19. Inability to suppress attention to gazing eyes: Driver et al., 1999. The question often arises: are people paying attention to faces? Or to eyes, which happen to be at the center of faces? While both eyes and faces are important, recent work seems to show that eyes are psychologically privileged over faces. When participants are shown monsters with eyes on other parts of the body, they instinctively look at their eyes first, then the faces. See "Monsters Are People Too," Levy et al., in press.

20. Sensitivity to eyes in birds: Stevens, 2005; and fish: Neudecker, 1989.

21. Subtle exposure to drawings of human eyes increases prosocial behavior in anonymous economic games: Haley and Fessler, 2005; Rigdon et al., 2009. For a critique of these studies, see Fehr and Schneider, 2010.

22. Rigdon et al., 2009.

23. Evidence that exposure to human eyes decreases cheating in naturalistic settings: Bateson et al., 2006.

24. Supernatural monitoring: Norenzayan and Shariff, 2008; Bering, 2006, 2011.

25. The Abrahamic God: Peters and Esposito, 2006.

26. Buddha Eyes: Coleman, 1993.

27. Horus of Two Eyes and Eye of Ra in ancient Egyptian religion: Wilkinson, 2003.

28. Virachocha god of the Inca Empire: Steele and Allen, 1994.

29. *Adalo* ancestor spirits among the Kwaio people: Keesing, 1982.

30. Anthropomorphizing God and believing in God: Norenzayan et al., 2012; Waytz et al., 2010; Guthrie, 1993.

31. God is anthropomorphized in everyday thinking: Barrett and Keil, 1996; Epley et al., 2007; Guthrie, 1993.

32. For an in-depth discussion of "theological incorrectness": Barrett, 2004; Slone, 2004.

33. "Full access strategic social agents": Boyer, 2001, pp. 156–157.

34. Believers respond faster to God knowing socially strategic information: Purzycki et al., 2012.

35. For the President Carter quote, and studies comparing Jewish and Protestant moral intuitions about sinful thoughts: see Cohen and Rozin, 2001.

36. God is up: Meier et al., 2007; see also Chasteen et al., 2010.

37. See E. O. Wilson, 2012, for an account of humanity's colonization of the Earth that is rooted in human ultrasociality.

38. Cultural learning and cultural evolution: Richerson and Boyd, 2005; Henrich and Henrich, 2007; for related but distinct views on cultural evolution, see Sperber, 1996; Cavalli-Sforza and Feldman, 1981.

39. For a discussion of this issue, see Sperber, 1996; Atran, 2001; Henrich and Boyd, 2002.

40. Demonstrations of content biases in supernatural beliefs: Boyer and Ramble, 2001; Barrett and Nyhof, 2001; Norenzayan et al., 2006.

41. Boyer quote: Boyer, 2001, pp. 78–79.

42. The role of various cultural learning biases in religion: Gervais et al., 2011.

43. Credibility-enhancing displays: Henrich, 2009; for the importance of credible testimony in how children adopt new beliefs from others, see also Harris and Koenig, 2006; Harris, 2012. Wide-ranging evidence for epistemic vigilance: see Sperber et al., 2010.

44. Extravagant religious behaviors as costly signals: Sosis and Alcorta, 2003; Bulbulia, 2004.

Chapter 3   Pressure from Above

1. This chapter title can be found in a news story that discusses some of the research found here. See Chin 2007.

2. These survey findings can be found in Brooks, 2006, and in Putnam and Campbell, 2010. These findings are correlational, and therefore cannot tell us about causal direction. Moreover, they are based on self-reports of religious attendance, belief, and charitability. However, whether consciously or unconsciously, survey respondents may inflate their frequency of church attendance, as well as the number of charitable acts they engage in. What's more troubling, these tendencies are especially exaggerated among more religious people. See for example, Sedikides and Gebauer, 2010. For evidence that religious Americans exaggerate church attendance, see Brenner, 2011. For a critique of these findings, see Norenzayan and Shariff, 2008.

3. Princess Alice Study: Bering, 2006; Piazza et al., 2011.

4. Subliminal cheating study: Randolph-Seng and Nielsen, 2007.

5. Ten commandment study: Mazar et al., 2008.

6. Religious priming increases generosity and cooperation: Shariff and Norenzayan, 2007; Norenzayan and Shariff, 2008; Ahmed and Salas, 2009; Pichon et al., 2007. Religious priming increases costly punishment of selfishness: McKay et al., 2011; Laurin et al., 2012b.

7. Sunday Effect: Edelman, 2009; Malhotra, D., 2008.

8. Behavior is embedded in a Lewinian "social field": Ross and Nisbett, 1991.

9. Fundamental attribution error: Ross and Nisbett, 1991.

10. Marrakech "call to prayer" study: Duhaime, 2011.

11. Mauritius study: Xygalatas, in press.

12. Religious priming effects on attribution of external agency: Dijksterhuis et al., 2008; on public self-awareness and social desirability, see Gervais and Norenzayan, 2012b.

13. Atheism thought to be skin-deep: Boyer, 2008, p. 1039; Bloom, 2007, p. 148. In a recent statistical analysis of all known religious priming studies, we found that religious priming reliably increases prosocial behavior for believers, but the effect was inconsistent and unreliable overall for non-believers (Shariff, Willard, Andersen, & Norenzayan, unpublished data).

14. Mean Gods make good people: Shariff and Norenzayan, 2011; Debono et al., 2012; Shariff and Rhemtulla, 2012.

15. Laurin et al., 2012.

16. Personal communication, July 24, 2012.

17. Shariff and Rhemtulla, 2012. See also McCleary and Barro, 2006, for evidence that, even though religiosity declines with greater economic development, belief in hell in particular is associated with greater economic productivity.

18. For ideomotor explanations of priming: Bargh et al., 2001; Bargh and Chartrand, 1999; Bargh et al., 1996.

19. Good Samaritan study: Darley and Batson, 1973.

20. Studies of religiosity and helping behavior in the lab: Batson et al., 1993.

21. Israeli Kibbutz study: Sosis and Ruffle, 2003; two other studies found similar results. Candomble study: Soler, 2012; Madrassah study: Ahmed, 2010.

22. Fifteen-society cross-cultural study: Henrich et al, 2010.

23. WEIRD: Henrich et al., 2010; see also Norenzayan and Heine, 2005; Arnett, 2008. Population variability in psychology does not mean, of course, that there are no regularities or principles of human behavior. What it means is that these regularities cannot be discovered, unless the full range of human diversity is considered in constructing explanations and theories of human behavior.

Chapter 4   In Big Gods We Trust

1. Maa Tarini Coconut Temple courier service: Jena, 2006.

2. The role of gods in commerce, in Roman Delos: Rauh, 1993, quote p. 129.

3. New Julfa Armenian trade networks, sixteenth to nineteenth centuries: Aslanian, 2011, quote p. 110.

4. Jewish Maghrebi trade networks, eleventh to twelfth centuries, Greif, 1993.

5. Spread of Islam in Africa: Ensminger, 1997, quote pp. 7–8.

6. Weber quote: Gerth and Wrigh Mills, 1946, p. 303.

7. Schlessinger quote: Blumner, 2011.

8. Religious people are trusted more: Edgell et al., 2006; Sosis, 2005.

9. Most Americans think religiosity and morality are connected: Hout and Fisher, 2001; see also Pew Research Center, 2007.

10. Worldwide trust of religion: Inglehart et al., 2004.

11. For evidence of discriminatory laws and policies towards atheists worldwide, see International Humanist and Ethical Union, 2012.

12. Cooperation games in Eugene, Oregon, versus Utah: Orbell et al., 1992.

13. A good discussion of religion and trust can be found in Sosis, 2005.

14. New Yorkers trust Mormon nannies: Frank, 1988.

15. Trustworthy Sikhs: see Sosis, 2005.

16. Locke, J., 1689/1983, quote p. 51.

17. Secular Coalition of America: Harris, P., 2011. Kyrsten Sinema, who won election to the US Congress from Arizona in 2012, was initially thought to be the only remaining openly atheist member of Congress after Stark's departure. However, her campaign has "clarified" that the openly bisexual Sinema does not wish to define her religious beliefs or the lack thereof. See Lombrozo, 2012. See also Ryan, 2012.

18. 2008 Pew Forum Poll: Pew Forum, 2008.

19. 1999 Gallup poll: see Edgell et al., 2006.

20. Franklin, 1757, quote p. 293.

21. Anti-atheist prejudice in America: Edgell et al., 2006, relevant quote on pp. 217–218.

22. Number of atheists in the world: Zuckerman, 2007. Chapter 10 discusses the varieties of atheism in further depth.

23. Ricky Gervais quote: Gervais, 2010.

24. Empathy and compassion: Keltner and Haidt, 2001; Haidt, 2007.

25. Expanding the moral circle: Singer, 2011.

26. Compassionate prosociality in nonbelievers: Saslow et al., 2013. Results also showed that among people reporting low feelings of compassion, believers were more prosocial than nonbelievers. However, this trend, if anything, was reversed among people reporting high levels of compassion. Religiosity and feelings of compassion were statistically unrelated—neither religion, nor atheism, appear to have a monopoly on these feelings. The implication is that supernatural monitoring and compassion can independently encourage nice behavior toward others.

27. Atheists have other prosocial motivations: Beit-Hallahmi, 2010; Saslow et al., 2013.

28. Sunday Effect in charitability: Malhotra, 2009.

29. Religious individuals are no more likely to be altruistic than nonreligious ones: Batson et al., 1993.

30. Good Samaritan study: Darley and Batson, 1973.

31. More charitable behavior during Muslim call to prayers: Duhaime, 2011.

32. Religious involvement predicts prosocial behavior in countries with weak institutions: Ahmed, 2009; Soler, 2011.

33. Cross-cultural study shows adherence to religions with Big Moral Gods increases prosocial behavior in economic games: Henrich et al., 2010.

34. For religious badges, see Sosis, 2006.

35. Denmark and Sweden: Zuckerman, 2008. The only exception to these trends is the high suicide rates in Scandinavian societies.

Chapter 5   Freethinkers as Freeriders

1. Dostoevsky, 1990, quote p. 589.

2. Psychology of anti-atheist prejudice: Gervais et al., 2011; Gervais and Norenzayan, 2012c.

3. "Linda problem" and the representativeness heuristic: Tversky and Kahneman, 1983.

4. Implicit Association Test (IAT): Greenwald et al., 1998.

5. Asymmetry between believers distrusting nonbelievers but not the other way around: Gervais et al., 2011.

6. Ethnographic interviews in Denmark and Sweden show little distrust of religion by atheists: Zuckerman, 2008.

7. Believing in belief: Dennett, 2006.

8. For a review of the literature on the complex relationship between religious involvement and various forms of prejudices, see Hansen and Norenzayan, 2006.

9. The stereotype content model: Fiske, 2010; Cuddy et al., 2007; Fiske et al., 2007.

10. Perceiving outgroup members as threats to morality: Leach et al., 2007.

11. The evolutionary psychology of cultural norms: Henrich and Henrich, 2007; Sripada and Stich, 2005.

12. Overall levels of religiosity have remained stable in the last century: Norris and Inglehart, 2004.

13. People in societies with strong institutions have higher levels of trust, behave more prosocially, and are more likely to punish freeriders: Kauffman et al., 2003; Knack and Keefer, 1997; Herrmann et al., 2008.

14. Reminders of secular authority increase generosity in the lab: Shariff and Norenzayan, 2007.

15. Cross-cultural evidence that believers living in countries with strong secular institutions distrust atheists less: Norenzayan and Gervais, in press.

16. Anti-black prejudice involves a fear reaction: Cottrell and Neuberg, 2005.

17. Racial prejudice in America increases with perceived or actual outgroup size: Allport, 1954; Fosset and Kiecolt, 1989.

18. Increased perceived prevalence of atheists reduces distrust of atheists: Gervais, 2011, quote p. 553.

19. Another possible factor might be the degree to which a religious tradition prioritizes belief rather than practice. Adam Cohen and his colleagues point out that unlike in Protestant denominations, in some traditions such as Judaism, religious participation is as important, and sometimes more important, than religious belief. Some of the Orthodox branches of Christianity are similar to Judaism in this regard. It is possible that in these traditions, concerns about supernatural monitoring are dampened and replaced by other mechanisms. Hence in these traditions, there might be comparatively less prejudice against atheists. See Cohen et al., 2005.

Chapter 6   True Believers

1. Parable of the Weeds: see Matthew 13:24–30.

2. *Tartuffe* by Molière, trans. Martin Sorrel, 2002.

3. For a thoughtful evolutionary analysis of religious hypocrisy, see Schloss, 2008.

4. Cybele religious revival in the early Roman Empire: Burkert, 1982.

5. Skoptsy self-castrating religious movement in nineteenth-century Russia: Engelstein, 1999.

6. Thaipusam festival among Tamil Hindus: Ward, 1984. Participation in, or witnessing the intense Cavadee rituals in Thaipusam increases generosity toward the temple among Tamil Hindus in Mauritius, See Xygalatas et al., in press.

7. Irrationality of falling in love signals commitment: Gonzaga and Haselton, 2008.

8. Credibility-enhancing displays, or CREDs: Henrich, 2009. Sperber and his colleagues (2010) propose that human minds are equipped with a variety of cognitive biases that make us vigilant toward the dangers of being duped or misinformed.

9. Cultural cycles of religious commitment: Finke and Stark, 2005.

10. Costly signaling theory of animal behaviors: Maynard Smith and Harper, 2003.

11. Costly signaling theory of extravagant religious behaviors: Irons, 2001; Sosis and Alcorta, 2003; Bulbulia, 2004, 2008.

12. For critical discussions of costly signaling theories of religion, see Henrich, 2009; Schloss, 2008, 2009; and Bulbulia, 2008. Joseph Bulbulia offers a reformulation of costly signaling approaches, which he calls "commitment-signaling," to address some of these concerns. For example, signaling can be credible if it is hard to fake, even if it is not costly. Examples include involuntary expressions of religious sentiment, such as convulsive weeping, shaking and trembling, and speaking in tongues.

13. See Xygalatas et al., in press.

14. Evidence that strict churches are strong: Iannacone, 1992.

15. Restrictions on behavior and commune longevity: Sosis and Alcorta, 2003; Sosis and Bressler, 2003. For further evidence that religious communes outsurvive secular ones, see Kitts, 2009. Cristine Legare and André Souza (2012) have found that people, especially believers, see rituals that are associated with a supernatural agent to be more effective, which might also explain why rituals are more potent when combined with religion.

16. Costly behaviors in Islam may have promoted its spread in Africa: Ensminger, 1997, pp. 26–27.

17. For an account of religious belief as a cognitive by-product, see Boyer, 1994 and 2001; see also Barrett, 2004; Pyysiäinen and Antonnen, 2002.

18. A great deal of the discussion in this section is drawn from Gervais et al., 2010.

19. Beliefs are initially processed as true: Gilbert, 1991; Gilbert et al., 1993.

20. Emotionally evocative information is remembered better and culturally transmitted more: Heath et al., 2001.

21. The transmission advantage of mad cow disease: Sinaceur and Heath, 2005.

22. For inferential potential, see Boyer, 2001.

23. See Sperber, 1996.

24. See Legare et al., 2012.

25. Minimal counterintuitions in Brothers Grimm folktales: Norenzayan et al., 2006.

26. Minimal counterintuitiveness in religion and culture: Barrett and Nyhof, 2001; Boyer and Ramble, 2001; Atran and Norenzayan, 2004.

27. Relevant mysteries: Sperber, 1996, quote p. 73.

28. For the Mickey Mouse problem, see Atran and Norenzayan, 2004; for the related Zeus problem and the Santa Claus problems, see Gervais and Henrich, 2010; Gervais et al., 2011.

29. Skepticism in children: Birch et al., 2010; Harris and Koenig, 2006; Harris, 2012; Bergstrom et al., 2006.

30. Collective effervescence: Durkheim, 1915/1995.

31. Synchrony in fire-walking ritual: Konvalinka et al., 2011.

32. Rowing together increases pain tolerance: Cohen et al., 2009.

33. Synchrony increases prosocial behavior within groups: Wiltermuth and Heath, 2009. Effects of synchrony on social affiliation: Hove and Risen, 2009; see also Valdesolo et al., 2010. For historical examples, see McNeill, 1995.

34. Not all rituals involve synchrony: Whitehouse, 2004.

35. Religious involvement contributes to self-regulation: McCullough and Willoughby, 2009, quote p. 88.

36. For experimental evidence: Rounding et al., 2012; Laurin et al., 2012a; see also Inzlicht and Tullett, 2010.

37. Religion partly derived from fictive kinship: Nesse, 1999; Robertson Smith, 1891/1972, quote p. 44, note 2; see also Atran and Norenzayan, 2004.

Chapter 7   Big Gods for Big Groups

1. Klaus Schmidt, 2000, quote p. 5.

2. For an accessible account of the fascinating mysteries surrounding Göbekli Tepe, see Mann, 2011. For a detailed scientific account and progress reports, see Schmidt, 2000, 2010.

3. For a discussion of the evidence, see for example, Clark, 2007.

4. An account of how religious thinking contributed to agricultural civilizations: Cauvin, 1999.

5. Analysis of blades in Göbekli Tepe: Carter et al., 2012.

6. The Hadza: Marlowe, 2010, Apicella et al., 2011.

7. For a critical discussion of the promises and pitfalls of relying on modern hunter-gatherers as a plausible model for preagricultural hunter-gatherers: Marlowe, 2005. For evidence of significant social complexity among some hunter-gatherers, see Powell et al., 2009. See also Diamond, 2012, for a discussion of foraging societies and what modern societies can learn from them.

8. Quote on Hadza religion: Marlowe, 2010, p. 61.

9. Marshall, 1962, quote p. 245.

10. See McNamara, 2012.

11. This tendency to assume that religions are universally concerned with morality is another blind spot that is the unintended result of seeing the world through a WEIRD lens (discussed earlier in chapter 3). Psychologists who work in a WEIRD paradigm often equate "religion" with the most familiar religion they see, which happens to be the religion of the Abrahamic God. The ethnographic evidence on the deities of foraging groups, which clues us about the origins of religion, becomes crucially important.

12. See for example, Apicella et al., 2011; Hill et al., 2011; see also Kelly, 1995; Klein, 2009.

13. See Powell et al., 2009.

14. Hume, 1888, quote p. 538.

15. Social group size correlates with brain size across primate species: Dunbar, 2003. This general trend is well-documented. However, the claim that there is a "natural limit" to the size of human social groups is open to question. For a critique, see Smith, 1996.

16. Groups fissure in New Guinea: Tuzin, 2001.

17. Bar-Yosef, 1990.

18. Boehm selected these groups based on what he calls their suitability for modeling "Late-Pleistocene" social conditions. However, this should not be confused to mean that late Pleistocene hunter-gatherer and foraging societies were all small. In fact, they varied in size and social complexity. Nevertheless, the point remains that in the smallest-scale foraging societies, many gods and spirits have limited or little concern for human moral behavior. See Boehm, 2008.

19. The prevalence of Big Gods across cultures: Stark, 2001.

20. Big Gods are more prevalent in big and more socially complex groups: Roes and Raymond, 2003; Sanderson and Roberts, 2008; see also Johnson, 2005. For earlier work, see Underhill, 1975, and Swanson, 1964.

21. Collapse of Angkor, the seat of the Khmer Empire, due to water scarcity: Day et al., 2012.

22. Water scarcity and Big Gods: Snarey, 1996.

23. Snarey, 1996, quote pp. 93–94.

24. Gods as "full access strategic agents": Boyer, 2001; for experimental evidence: Purzycki et al., 2012.

25. Kwaio beliefs about *adalo* ancestor spirits: Keesing, 1982.

26. Interventionist ancestor gods nevertheless are unlike Big Gods in some important respects: they tend to be limited to specific places and often influence some people but not others. Such gods have more limited omniscience and supernatural powers. See, for example, Wright, 2009; Boyer, 2001. Purzycki (2011), for example, reports that in Tyvan (or Tuvan) culture, a Russian republic in Siberia, local "spirit masters," known as *Cher eezi*, are generally indifferent about peoples' interpersonal behavior. However, they are pleased by ritual offerings, and are angered by overexploitation of resources that they control. They exert their (limited) powers in designated locations found in ritual cairns (*ovaa*). They are unable to see or intervene in distant places.

27. Two modes of religious rituals, "doctrinal" and "imagistic": see Whitehouse, 2004.

28. The two ritual modes follow predictable cross cultural patterns: Atkinson and Whitehouse, 2011.

29. Big Gods co-evolved with big groups: Norenzayan and Shariff, 2008; Shariff, 2011; Shariff et al., 2010; Atran and Henrich, 2010.

30. Swanson, 1966, quote p. 153.

31. Monumental architecture co-emerged with increasing societal size, political complexity, and reliance on agriculture: Marcus and Flannery, 2004. For a discussion of Çatalhöyük in particular: Whitehouse and Hodder, 2010. Historical evolution of rituals in Mexico: Marcus and Flannery, 2004; in China: Thote 2009.

32. The cultural evolution of the Abrahamic God over historical time: Wright, 2009).

33. Claims that China lacked moralizing gods or even religion: Granet, 1934; see also Rosemont and Ames, 2009. For critiques of these claims, and historical evidence for supernatural monitoring in ancient Chinese religions, see Slingerland, 2013; Slingerland et al., in press; Clark and Winslett, 2011. For the Shang religion, see Eno (2009); for the Eastern Zhou period, see Poo, 2009. See Paper, 2012, for a critical discussion.

34. In the "Mohist" period (fifth century BCE), we see Mohist philosophers arguing for the existence of supernatural punishment. Many Mohist philosophers believed that much of the chaos of their time could be traced to what they saw as the loss of belief in watchful ghosts who dole out punishment and reward. Modern scholars debate the meaning of these arguments. Did the Mohists themselves believe in supernatural monitoring, or did they think that it was an effective social tool, even if not literally true? Either way, for such ar-

guments to be relevant, they must have been occurring against the background of some cultural belief in supernatural punishment. See Wong and Loy, 2004; Hansen, 2000.

35. The supernatural punishment hypothesis as a genetic adaptationist account: Johnson, 2009; Bering, 2006; Bering, 2011. For discussions, see Schloss and Murray, 2011 (with related commentaries); Shariff et al., 2010.

36. Johnson, 2009, pp. 169–170.

37. See Boehm, 2008; Wright, 2009.

38. See Henrich et al., 2006; Henrich and Henrich, 2007; Panchanathan and Boyd, 2004. D. Cohen (2001) also sees cultural variability as the result of multiple stable equilibriums. Herrmann et al. (2008) demonstrate, in cross-cultural game experiments, the existence in some cultures, such as Turkey, Greece, and Saudi Arabia, of what they call "antisocial punishment," where cooperators, not freeriders, are punished! Antisocial punishment is rare in Western societies, and without cross-cultural comparisons, would have been missed.

39. See *The Economist*, February 5, 2011, "Nasty Business: Killings in Liberia."

Chapter 8   The Gods of Cooperation and Competition

1. Ibn Khaldûn, 1377/2005, quote chapter 3, section 3, p. 125.

2. Darwin, 1871, quote p. 166.

3. D. S. Wilson, 2002, quote p. 6.

4. See Gelfand et al., 2011.

5. Male warrior hypothesis: see Van Vugt et al., 2007; see also Connor, 2006.

6. See Sosis et al., 2007.

7. See for example, Bowles, 2008; Choi and Bowles, 2007.

8. Atran, 2012.

9. For historical examples, see D. S. Wilson, 2002.

10. Morality as an adaptation for group living: Graham and Haidt, 2010; Haidt et al., 2008: Haidt, 2012.

11. Moral judgment as the product of individual reasoning: see Turiel, 1983; Kohlberg et al., 1983. For a critical account of this view, see Haidt et al., 2008; Graham and Haidt, 2010; Haidt, 2012.

12. Haidt, 2012, quote p. 270.

13. Religious involvement is tied to moral judgment: Atkinson and Bourrat, 2011.

14. Shariff and Rhemtulla, 2012.

15. Hamlin et al., 2007, 2011. For a good discussion of religion and morality, see Bloom, 2012.

16. Moral emotions in primates: see for example, de Waal, 2006; for a discussion of the evolutionary origins of empathy, see de Waal, 2008; van Wolkentenet al., 2007; de Waal, 2008, quote p. 279.

17. For a historical account of secularization, see Taylor, 2007.

18. Intergroup violence and parochial altruism: Alexander, 1987; Bowles, 2008; Turchin, 2003. War as the ultimate cooperative act: Tilly, 1975; Otterbein, 1970; Keeley, 1996. For evidence regarding the decline of violence over time, see Pinker, 2011. For a recent discussion of archeological evidence in the Middle East, and particularly Tel Brak, see Lawler, 2012.

19. Intergroup conflict, group size, and resource-rich ecologies co-occur: Roes and Raymond, 2003. The origin of politically centralized states: see Carneiro, 1970; Turchin, 2003; Tilly, 1975.

20. Turchin, 2010, quote p. 25.

21. The idea of *asabiya* or social solidarity as a major force in history: see Ibn Khaldûn, 1318/1958; Turchin, 2007.

22. Voight et al., 2006.

23. See Richerson and Boyd, 2005; Soltis et al., 1995; For a comparison of genetic versus cultural intergroup variation, see Bell et al., 2009.

24. Cultural group selection, within the rubric of "multilevel selection," is supported by mathematical models, and with evidence from ethnography, history, and experiments. There is also large agreement that models that incorporate multilevel selection and those that do not can be mathematically equivalent. See for example, Henrich and Henrich, 2007; Turchin, 2010; Sigmund et al., 2010; D. S. Wilson, 2007; Hayek, 1988; and see also Atran and Henrich, 2010, quote p. 26. For a critique, responses, and discussion, see Pinker, 2012, and associated commentaries.

25. Sosis, 2000; Sosis and Bressler, 2003; Sosis and Alcorta, 2003.

26. Ensminger, 1997.

27. Finke and Stark, 2005.

28. Jenkins, 2002; see pp. 2–3 for projections of the demographic composition of the Christian population in the world.

29. See Stark, 1996.

30. Levy, 1957.

31. Kaufmann, 2010, quote p. ix.

32. Religion and fertility: Blume, 2009; Norris and Inglehart, 2004.

33. Personal e-mail communication, January 4, 2013.

34. *The Economist*, 2011.

35. For a discussion and evidence for culture-gene coevolution, see Laland et al., 2010. It remains to be shown whether religious beliefs and practices have exerted

enough selection pressures on the human genome for particular psychological traits that may be found in some cultural groups but not others.

36. For one such account, see Rowthorn, 2011.

Chapter 9   From Religious Cooperation to Religious Conflict

1. Kahlil Gibran quote: Gibran, 1985, from his poem, *Pity the Nation*.

2. For a detailed account of the complex events of the Lebanese civil war, see Fiske, 1990.

3. Dawkins, 1989, quote pp. 330–331.

4. For an account of the Armenian Genocide and Turkey's persistent state policy of denial, see Akcam, 2007.

5. James, 1982/1902, quote p. 337.

6. Religion and war; Phillips and Axelrod, 2007; BBC report: Austin et al., 2003.

7. Franken, 2002, p. 50.

8. One reason these tendencies thrive in religion is that religious belief can serve as an ideology that buffers people against uncertainty and anxiety; see for example, Inzlicht et al., 2009.

9. Radio Free Europe Radio Liberty, 2012.

10. For further details and more analyses, and for a discussion of religion and prejudice, see Hansen and Norenzayan, 2006.

11. Allport, 1950.

12. The literature on religion and prejudice has found inconclusive results. For reviews, see Batson et al., 1993; Kirkpatrick and Hood, 1990; Hansen and Norenzayan, 2006. Results often depend on the type of prejudice and the particular variables that are controlled for. A recent comprehensive analysis (Hall et al., 2010) that included 55 studies with mostly White Christian participants in the United States found a small but reliable association between self-reported religiosity and racial prejudice.

13. Zuckerman, 2011.

14. Shariff and Norenzayan, 2012.

15. For example, see House et al., 1988; Putnam, 2000.

16. Waytz and Epley, 2012.

17. See Atran, 2003; Pape, 2005.

18. See Atran, 2006.

19. For a wholesale condemnation of religion, see for example, Harris, 2005. See Atran, 2010, for an empirically based critical discussion of the links between religion and violent extremism.

20. For examples of this line of thinking, see Harris, 2005; Dawkins, 2003; Gambetta, 2005.

21. See Sprinzak, 2000.

22. See Ginges et al., 2009, for further details. These findings are a blow to the religious belief hypothesis of intergroup hostility, especially because prayer was a more decisive factor than participation in how important people felt religion was in their lives. Results held controlling for obvious demographic variables such as age, gender, and occupational status. Degree of support for *sharia* (Islamic law), for the Oslo peace process, and for major Palestinian groups that sponsor terror were taken into account, but did not change the findings.

23. Haidt, 2012, quote p. 268.

24. Hajj study: Clingingsmith et al., 2009.

25. For a similar point, see Bulbulia, 2009. Xygalatas and his colleagues (in press) found that participation in a painful Hindu ritual (known as the Kavadi or Cavadee), increased identification with the multiethnic Mauritian national identity, suggesting again, that rituals, when they encourage interactions with a broader community of diverse people, have the potential to unite people across ethnic and religious lines.

26. Religious ritual makes values sacred: Sheikh et al., 2012. Rational versus devoted actors, and how sacred values can be reframed: Atran and Axelrod, 2008; Tetlock, 2003.

27. Atran and Ginges, 2012, quote p. 857; Ginges et al., 2007. Scott Atran points out that poor scientific understanding of sacred values and religion has led to serious errors in Western policy combatting religious extremism. See Atran, 2010, for a discussion of how sacred values can be harnessed to soften opposition to peace.

28. See Pyszczynski et al., 2009.

Chapter 10   Cooperation without God

1. The word *secular* has different meanings and has a rich intellectual history. Here I am using it to mean the decline or absence of religious belief and practice, synonymous with *irreligious*. However, secular societies are not necessarily incompatible with religion, as when there is a separation of religion and state. For an in-depth exploration of secularism, see for example, Taylor, 2007; Gauchet, 1997.

2. Secular societies with high trust and cooperation: see Zuckerman, 2008; Norris and Inglehart, 2004.

3. Rule of law predicts prosocial behavior in games: see Herrmann et al., 2008. Priming secular authority: Shariff and Norenzayan, 2007; Norenzayan and Shariff, 2008; see also Gervais and Norenzayan, 2012.

4. See for example, Dawkins, 2006; S. Harris, 2010.

5. See Gauchet, 2007.

6. Atran, 2011.

7. See Norris and Inglehart, 2004.

8. For evidence that threats to control undermine faith in God, see Kay et al., 2010. For a review, see Kay et al., 2010. For the interchangeability of God and government, see Kay et al., 2008, 2010; see also Purzycki, 2012.

9. For new discussions of evolutionary explanations of atheism, see Johnson, 2012, and related commentaries. See also Geertz and Markússon, 2010, and replies.

10. Bloom, 2007, quote p. 148.

11. Boyer, 2008, quote p. 1039.

12. McCauley, 2011.

13. This section on the origins of religious disbelief draws from Norenzayan and Gervais, 2013. Lanman (2011) also argues that atheism comes in different flavors and arise from multiple sources.

14. There is an extensive literature on mentalizing deficits in autism. See for example, Baron-Cohen et al., 2001; Badcock, 2009; Crespi and Badcock, 2008.

15. For example, Bering, 2001, 2011; McCauley, 2011; Bloom, 2004; Barrett, 2004.

16. For evidence, see Gray et al., 2011.

17. Bering, 2002, quote p. 14.

18. Grandin, 1995, quote p. 200.

19. See Norenzayan et al., 2012. Similar findings have been reported by Caldwell-Harris et al., 2011. We considered other explanations for this link. For example, it could be that high levels of autism give rise to social difficulties, leading to lower levels of religious attendance, which in turn could cause lower levels of religious belief. Contrary to this explanation, the effect of autism on belief in God remained strong even after statistically removing the role of religious attendance; neither could general intelligence or IQ, or personality factors linked to autism and religiosity, explain the link. Mentalizing was the key variable that explained the autism-disbelief link.

20. See Baron-Cohen et al., 2001; Badcock, 2009. These differences begin to emerge early in boys and girls. For a discussion of the evidence, see Bloom, 2004.

21. There is a large sociological literature exploring the gender gap in religiosity. See for example, Roth and Kroll, 2007; Stark, 2002; Walter and Davie, 1998. The size of the gap varies from population to population, but it is typically found in a wide range of studies using different survey questions. While the gender difference is well established, the reasons behind it are hotly debated.

22. There are other, related residual theistic intuitions that can be found among nonbelievers. Jesse Bering (2011) for example, argues that many, if not all, nonbelievers would claim that their own life has a purpose, even if they would explicitly

agree that human beings are the product of purposeless natural processes. Similarly, the intuition that important life events are fated is more prevalent among believers, but can be found among nonbelievers as well (Norenzayan and Lee, 2010).

23. Pascal quote: O'Connell, 1997, p. xi.

24. Psychologists seem to be divided on this question, and the findings are mixed. One view is that gut feelings can produce a superior outcome to deliberation under specific conditions—that is, when the decision maker is an expert, and when the decision domain itself is complex. For a classic study on this question, see Wilson and Schooler, 1991; see also Dijksterhuis et al., 2000. For case examples, see Gladwell, 2005. See Kahneman, 2011, for a lucid and nuanced discussion of System 1 and System 2 thinking, from one of the leading researchers in this area of psychology.

25. There is evidence that believing in any proposition, not just religious ones, is rapid and automatic, but disbelief and skepticism require cognitive effort. See Gilbert, 1991.

26. This is the Cognitive Reflection Task: see Frederick, 2005. It is very important to appreciate that this task is a measure of the degree to which analytic tendencies overrule intuitive tendencies. It is *not* a measure of general intelligence (although the two are related).

27. Shenhav et al., 2011; Pennycook et al., 2012.

28. See for example, Alter et al., 2007; for the effect of perceptual disfluency on judgments of pleasantness and beauty, see Reber et al., 1998.

29. See Gervais and Norenzayan, 2012a.

30. For the link between education and disbelief in Canada, see Hungerman, 2011; for intelligence and disbelief, see: Lewis et al., 2011; Zuckerman et al., 2013. There are, however, lively debates surrounding both findings, which are affected by various other factors.

31. Norris and Inglehart, 2004; see also Inglehart and Baker, 2000. Decline in economic inequality leads to lower levels of religiosity: see Solt et al., 2011. People who live in existential insecurity are more religious, but interestingly, living in societies with economic inequality increases the odds of religiosity for both the poor and the wealthy.

32. See Gray and Wegner, 2010.

33. A glaring exception to this international trend is the United States, of course, which has one of the world's richest societies. There are several explanations for this. The United States had founders with strong religious convictions, and high rates of poverty. Perhaps more importantly, despite its economic wealth, the United States is an outlier among advanced industrialized nations, as it ranks at the top of inequality rankings and has very limited social safety nets (see Solt et al., 2011).

34. Franken, 2002, quotes chapter 9, pp. 47, 52.

35. Reminders of death increase faith: see Norenzayan and Hansen, 2005; see also Vail et al., 2012. Interestingly, Vail and colleagues show that awareness of death moves faith among agnostics, but not atheists. Religion as an attachment system: Kirkpatrick, 2005.

36. See Sibley and Bulbulia, 2012.

37. See Bentzen, 2013.

38. For randomness, see Kay et al., 2010; Rutjens et al., 2010. Tracy et al. (2011) showed that reminders of death, like randomness, increase the attractiveness of arguments for intelligent design. For loneliness, see Epley et al., 2008. For religion as a coping device in bereavement, see Brown et al., 2004.

39. The idea that religion offers solace in the face of adversity and suffering has been criticized as implausible because, the argument goes, we can't satisfy a need for something by simply imagining that we have it. However, I am not claiming the far-fetched idea that religious belief *arises from* wishful thinking. It arises from ordinary cognitive operations and is intuitively compelling to begin with, even before our motivations shape their content. True, we don't have brains that when hungry, imagine a refrigerator full of food. But neither do we have brains that see the world the way it is, undistorted by irrational hopes and wishful thinking. Indeed, hungry people see food-related words faster and more clearly than people who have just eaten (Radel and Clément-Guillotin, 2012). Studies show evidence for such unconscious *wishful seeing* (Dunning and Balcetis, 2013), and people are notoriously bad at separating reasoning from deeply held motivations, hope from expectation (see for example, Kunda, 1990). For discussions of the pervasiveness and evolutionary adaptiveness of various "misbeliefs," see McKay and Dennett, 2009.

40. Rauch, 2005. See also Joseph Bulbulia, in press, for the similar concept of *ennuitheism*, which is characterized by a certain boredom toward religious matters, particularly metaphysical questions about religion.

41. Zuckerman, 2008.

42. For CREDs, see Henrich, 2009; for the importance of religious CREDs in secularization in Scandinavia, see Lanman, 2012.

43. Atheists are overrepresented among scientists, and the more elite scientists are the least religious; see Larson and Witham, 1998.

44. See Baron-Cohen et al., 2001.

45. First line of *Anna Karenina*: see Tolstoy, 1886.

References

Ahmed, A. M. (2009). Are religious people more prosocial? A quasi-experimental study with Madrasah pupils in a rural community in India. *Journal for the Scientific Study of Religion, 48*, 368–374.

Ahmed, A. M., and Salas, O. (2011). Implicit influences of Christian religious representations on dictator and prisoner's dilemma game decisions. *Journal of Socio-Economics, 40*, 242–246.

Akcam, T. (2007). *A Shameful Act: The Armenian Genocide and the Question of Turkish Responsibility.* New York: Holt.

Alexander, R. (1987). *The Biology of Moral Systems.* New York: Aldine De Gruyter.

Allport, G. (1950). *The Individual and His Religion.* New York: Macmillan Press.

———. (1954). *The Nature of Prejudice.* Cambridge, MA: Addison-Wesley.

Alter, L., Oppenheimer, D. M., Epley, N., and Eyre, R. N. (2007). Overcoming intuition: Metacognitive difficulty activates analytic reasoning. *Journal of Experimental Psychology: General, 136*, 569–576.

Anderson, B. (1983). *Imagined Communities: Reflections on the Origin and Spread of Nationalism.* New York: Verso.

Apicella, C. L., Marlowe, F., Fowler, J. H., and Christakis, N. A. (2012). Social networks and cooperation in hunter-gatherers. *Nature, 481*, 497–501.

Arnett, J. (2008). The neglected 95%: Why American psychology needs to become less American. *American Psychologist, 63*, 602–614.

Aslanian, S. D. (2011). *From the Indian Ocean to the Mediterranean: The Global Trade Networks of Armenian Merchants from New Julfa.* Berkeley: University of California Press.

Atkinson, Q. D., and Bourrat, P. (2010). Beliefs about God, the afterlife and moral-
    ity support the role of supernatural policing in human cooperation. *Evolution
    and Human Behavior, 32*, 41–49.

Atkinson, Q. D., and Whitehouse, H. (2011). The cultural morphospace of ritual
    form: Examining modes of religiosity cross-culturally. *Evolution and Human
    Behavior, 32*, 50–62.

Atran, S. (2001). The trouble with memes: Inference versus imitation in cultural
    creation. *Human Nature, 12*, 351–381.

———. (2003). Genesis of suicide terrorism. *Science, 299*, 1534–1535.

———. (2006). The moral logic and growth of suicide terrorism. *The Washington
    Quarterly, 29*, 127–147.

———. (2010). *Talking to the Enemy: Faith, Brotherhood and the (Un)making of
    Terrorists*. New York: Harper Collins.

———. (2011, February). Sam Harris' guide to nearly everything. *The National
    Interest*. Available at http://nationalinterest.org/bookreview/sam-hariss
    -guide-nearly-everything-4893 (accessed 03/12/2013).

———. (2012, August). God and the ivory tower: What we don't understand about
    religion just might kill us. *Foreign Policy Online*. Available at http://www
    .foreignpolicy.com /articles /2012/08/06/god_and_the_ivory_tower?   (ac-
    cessed 03/12/2013).

Atran, S., and Axelrod, R. (2008). Reframing sacred values. *Negotiation Journal,
    24*, 221–246.

Atran, S., and Ginges, J. (2012). Religious and sacred imperatives in human con-
    flict. *Science, 336*, 855–857.

Atran, S., and Henrich, J. (2010). The evolution of religion: How cognitive by-
    products, adaptive learning heuristics, ritual displays, and group competition
    generate deep commitments to prosocial religions. *Biological Theory: Integrat-
    ing Development, Evolution, and Cognition, 5*, 18–30.

Atran, S., and Norenzayan, A. (2004). Religion's evolutionary landscape: Coun-
    terintuition, commitment, compassion, communion. *Behavioral and Brain
    Sciences, 27*, 713–770.

Austin, G., Kranock, T., and Oommen, T. (2003). God and war: An audit and
    exploration. Available at http://news.bbc.co.uk/2/shared/spl/hi/world/04/
    war_audit_pdf/pdf/war_audit.pdf (accessed 03/12/2013).

Axelrod, R. (1984). *The Evolution of Cooperation*. Cambridge, MA: Basic Books.

Badcock, C. (2009). *The Imprinted Brain: How Genes Set the Balance between Au-
    tism and Psychosis*. London: Jessica Kingsley Publishers.

Bargh, J. A., and Chartrand, T. L. (1999). The unbearable automaticity of being.
    American Psychologist, 54, 462–479.

Bargh, J. A., Chen, M., and Burrows, L. (1996). Automaticity of social behavior: Direct effects of trait construct and stereotype activation on action. *Journal of Personality and Social Psychology, 71*, 230–244.

Bargh, J. A., Gollwitzer, P. M., Lee-Chai, A., Barndollar, K., and Troetschel, R. (2001). Automating the will: Nonconscious activation and pursuit of behavioral goals. *Journal of Personality and Social Psychology, 81*, 1014–1027.

Baron-Cohen, S., Wheelwright, S., Skinner, R., and Clubley, E. (2001). The autism spectrum quotient (AQ): Evidence from Asperger syndrome/high functioning autism, males and females, scientists and mathematicians. *Journal of Autism and Developmental Disorders, 31*, 5–17.

Barrett, D. B., Kurian, G. T., and Johnson, T. M. (eds.). (2001). *World Christian Encyclopaedia*, 2nd ed. Oxford, UK: Oxford University Press.

Barrett, J. L. (2004). *Why Would Anyone Believe in God?* Walnut Creek, CA: Alta-Mira Press.

Barrett, J. L., and Keil, F. C. (1996). Conceptualizing a nonnatural entity: anthropomorphism in god concepts. *Cognitive Psychology, 31*, 219–247.

Barrett, J. L., and Nyhof, M. A. (2001). Spreading nonnatural concepts: The role of intuitive conceptual structures in memory and transmission of cultural materials. *Journal of Cognition and Culture, 1*, 69–100.

Bar-Yosef, O. (1998). The Natufian culture in the Levant, threshold to the origins of agriculture. *Evolutionary Anthropology, 6*, 159–177.

Bateson, M., Nettle, D., and Roberts, G. (2006). Cues of being watched enhance cooperation in a real-world setting. *Biology Letters, 2*, 412–414.

Batson, C. D., Schoenrade, P., and Ventis, W. L. (1993). *Religion and the Individual: A Social-psychological Perspective*. New York: Oxford University Press.

Beit-Hallahmi, B. (2010). Morality and immorality among the irreligious. In *Atheism and Secularity*, ed. P. Zuckerman, pp. 113–148. Westport, CT: Greenwood Publishing Group.

Bell, A. V., Richerson, P. J., and McElreath, R. (2009). Culture rather than genes provides greater scope for the evolution of large-scale human prosociality. *Proceedings of the National Academy of Sciences, 106*, 17671–17674.

Bellah, R. (2011). *Religion in Human Evolution: From the Paleolithic to the Axial Age*. Cambridge, MA: Harvard University Press.

Benjamin, D. J., Choi, J. J., and Fisher, G. (2010). *Religious Identity and Economic Behavior*, Working Paper No. 15925. Cambridge, MA: National Bureau of Economic Research.

Bentzen, J. S. (2013, February). Origins of religiousness: The role of natural disasters. University of Copenhagen, Department of Economics, Discussion Paper No. 13-02. Available at http://ssrn.com/abstract=2221859 (accessed 03/12/2013).

Bergstrom, B., Moehlmann, B., and Boyer, P. (2006). Extending the testimony problem: Evaluating the truth, scope and source of cultural information. *Child Development, 77*, 531–538.

Bering, J. (2002). The existential theory of mind. *Review of General Psychology, 6*, 3–24.

———. (2010, December). God's little rabbits: Religious people out-reproduce secular ones by a landslide. *Scientific American*. Available at http://blogs .scientificamerican.com/bering-in-mind/2010/12/22/gods-little-rabbits -religious-people-out-reproduce-secular-ones-by-a-landslide/   (accessed 03/12/2013).

———. (2011). *The Belief Instinct: The Psychology of Souls, Destiny, and the Meaning of Life*. New York: W. W. Norton.

———. (2006). The folk psychology of souls. *Behavioral and Brain Sciences, 29*, 453–498.

Birch, S. A., and Bloom, P. (2004). Understanding children's and adult's limitation in mental state reasoning. *Trends in Cognitive Science, 8*, 255–260.

Birch, S. A., Akmal, N., and Frampton, K. L. (2010). Two-year-olds are vigilant of others' non-verbal cues to credibility. *Developmental Science, 13*, 363–369.

Bloom, P. (2004). *Descartes' Baby*. New York: Basic Books.

———. (2007). Religion is natural. *Developmental Science, 10*, 147–151.

———. (2012). Religion, morality, evolution. *Annual Review of Psychology, 63*, 179–199.

Blume, M. (2009). The reproductive benefits of religious affiliation. In *The Biological Evolution of Religious Mind and Behavior*, ed. E. Voland and W. Schiefenhövel, pp. 117–126. Berlin: Springer-Verlag.

Blumner, R. E. (2011, July). Goodness without God. *St. Petersburg Times*.

Boehm, C. (2008). A biocultural evolutionary exploration of supernatural sanctioning. In *The Evolution of Religion: Studies, Theories, and Critiques*, ed. J. Bulbulia, R. Sosis, C. Genet, R. Genet, E. Harris, and K. Wyman, pp. 143–150. Santa Margarita, CA: Collins Foundation Press.

Boesch, C., Bolé, C., Eckhardt, N., and Boesch, H. (2010). Altruism in forest chimpanzees: The case of adoption. *PLoS ONE, 5*, e8901.

Bowles, S. (2006). Group competition, reproductive leveling, and the evolution of human altruism. *Science, 314*, 1569–1572.

———. (2008). Conflict: Altruism's midwife. *Science, 456*, 326–327.

Boyer, P. (1994). *The Naturalness of Religious Ideas: A Cognitive Theory of Religion*. Berkeley: University of California Press.

———. (2001). *Religion Explained*. New York: Basic Books.

———. (2008). Religion: Bound to believe? *Nature, 455*, 1038–1039.

Boyer, P., and Ramble, C. (2001). Cognitive templates for religious concepts: Cross-cultural evidence for recall of counter-intuitive representations. *Cognitive Science, 25,* 535–564.

Brenner, P. S. (2011). Exceptional behavior or exceptional identity? Overreporting of church attendance in the US. *Public Opinion Quarterly, 75,* 19–41.

Brewer, M. B., and Brown, R. (1998). Intergroup relations. In *The Handbook of Social Psychology,* 4th ed., ed. D. T. Gilbert, S. T. Fiske, and G. Lindzey, pp. 554–594. New York: McGraw-Hill.

Brooks, A. C. (2006). *Who Really Cares: The Surprising Truth about Compassionate Conservatism.* New York: Basic Books.

Brown, S. L., Nesse, R. M., House, J. S., and Utz, R. L. (2004). Religion and emotional compensation: Results from a prospective study of widowhood. *Personality and Social Psychology Bulletin, 30,* 1165–1174.

Bulbulia, J. (2004). Religious costs as adaptations that signal altruistic intention. *Evolution and Cognition, 10,* 19–38.

Bulbulia, J. (2008). Free love: Religious solidarity on the cheap. In *The Evolution of Religion: Studies, Theories and Critiques,* ed. J. Bulbulia, R. Sosis, R. Genet, E. Harris, K. Wynan, and C. Genet, pp. 153–160. Santa Margarita, CA: Collins Foundation Press.

———. (2009). Charismatic signalling. *Journal for the Study of Religion, Nature, Culture, 3,* 518–551.

———. (in press). *Ennuitheism.* In *Science and the World's Religions. Volume II: Religion, Disease, and Health,* ed. W. Wildman and P. McNamara. Westport, CT: Greenwood Publishing Group.

Burkert, W. (1982). *Ancient Mystery Cults.* Cambridge, MA: Harvard University Press.

Burnham, T. C., and Johnson, D. D. (2005). The biological and evolutionary logic of human cooperation. *Analyse and Kritik, 27,* 113–115.

Byrne, R. W., and Whiten, A. (1988). *Machiavellian Intelligence: Social Expertise and the Evolution of Intellect in Monkeys, Apes and Humans.* Oxford, UK: Oxford University Press.

Caldwell-Harris, C., Murphy, C. F., Velazquez, T., and McNamara, P. (2011). Religious belief systems of persons with high functioning autism. *Proceedings of the Thirty-third Annual Meeting of the Cognitive Sciences Society.* Available at http://www.academia.edu/628798/Religious_Belief_Systems_of_Persons_with_High_Functioning_Autism (accessed 03/12/2013).

Carneiro, R. L. (1970). A theory of the origin of the state. *Science, 169,* 733–738.

Carter, T., Le Bourdonnec, F.-X., Poupeau, G., and Schmidt, K. (2012, February). Towards an archaelogy of pilgrimage: Sourcing obsidian from the PPN Temple Complex of Göbekli Tepe. Presented at the 7th International Conference on the Chipped and Ground Stone Industries of the Pre-Pottery Neolithic, Barcelona, Spain.

Cauvin, J. (1999). *The Birth of the Gods and the Origins of Agriculture*, trans. T. Watkins. Cambridge, UK: Cambridge University Press.

Cavalli-Sforza, L. L., and Feldman, M. (1981). *Cultural Transmission and Evolution*. Princeton, NJ: Princeton University Press.

Chasteen, A. L., Burdzy, D. C., and Pratt, J. (2010). Thinking of god moves attention. *Neuropsychologia, 48*, 627–630.

Chin, G. (2007, September). Pressure from above. *Science, 317*, 1473.

Choi, J. K., and Bowles, S. (2007). The coevolution of parochial altruism and war. *Science, 318*, 636–640.

Chudek, M., and Henrich, J. (2011). Culture-gene coevolution, norm-psychology, and the emergence of human prosociality. *Trends in Cognitive Science, 15*, 218–226.

Clark, G. (2007). *A Farewell to Alms: A Brief Economic History of the World*. Princeton, NJ: Princeton University Press.

Clark, K. J., and Winslett, J. T. (2011). The evolutionary psychology of Chinese religion: Pre-Qin high gods as punishers and rewarders. *Journal of the American Academy of Religion, 79*(4), 928–960.

Clarke, P., and Byrne, P. (1993). *Religion Defined and Explained*. London: Macmillan Press.

Clingingsmith, D., Khwaja, D., and Kremer, M. (2009). Estimating the impact of the hajj: Religion and tolerance in Islam's global gathering. *The Quarterly Journal of Economics, 124*, 1133–1170.

Cohen, A. B., Hall, D. E., Koenig, H. G., and Meador, K. G. (2005). Social versus individual motivation: Implications for normative definitions of religious orientation. *Personality and Social Psychology Review, 9*, 48–61.

Cohen, A. B., and Rozin, P. (2001). Religion and the morality of mentality. *Journal of Personality and Social Psychology, 81*, 697–710.

Cohen, D. (2001). Cultural variation: Considerations and implications. *Psychological Bulletin, 127*, 451–471.

Cohen, E., Ejsmond-Frey, R., Knight, N., and Dunbar, R.I.M. (2010). Rowers' high: behavioural synchrony is correlated with elevated pain thresholds. *Biology Letters, 6*, 106–108.

Coleman, G. (ed.). (1993). *A Handbook of Tibetan Culture*. Boston: Shambhala Publications, Inc.

Connor, S. (2006, September). "Male warrior" effect makes men more likely to support war. *The Independent*. Available at http://www.independent.co.uk/news/science/male-warrior-effect-makes-men-more-likely-to-support-war-415239.html (accessed 03/12/2013).

Cottrell, C. A., and Neuberg, S. L. (2005). Different emotional reactions to different groups: A sociofunctional threat-based approach to prejudice. *Journal of Personality and Social Psychology, 88,* 770–789.

Crespi, B. J., and Badcock, C. (2008). Psychosis and autism as diametrical disorders of the social brain. *Behavioral and Brain Sciences, 31,* 284–320.

Cuddy, A.J.C., Fiske, S. T., and Glick, P. (2007). The BIAS map: Behaviors from intergroup affect and stereotypes. *Journal of Personality and Social Psychology, 92,* 631–648.

Darley, J. M., and Batson, C. D. (1973). "From Jerusalem to Jericho": A study of situational and dispositional variables in helping behavior. *Journal of Personality and Social Psychology, 27,* 100–108.

Darwin, C. (1871). *The Descent of Man, and Selection in Relation to Sex.* London: John Murray.

Dawkins, R. (1989). *The Selfish Gene.* Oxford, UK: Oxford University Press.

———. (2003). *A Devil's Chaplain: Reflections on Hope, Lies, Science, and Love.* Boston: Houghton Mifflin.

Day, M. B., Hodell, D. A., Brenner, M., Chapman, H. J., Curtis, J. H., Kenney, W. F., Kolata, A. L., et al. (2012). Paleoenvironmental history of the West Baray, Angkor (Cambodia). *Proceedings of the National Academy of Sciences, 109*(4), 1046–1051.

Debono, A., Shariff, A. F., and Muraven, M. (2012). Forgive us our trespasses: Priming a forgiving (but not a punishing) god increases theft. Unpublished manuscript, Winston-Salem State University.

Dennett, D. C. (2006). *Breaking the Spell.* New York: Viking.

de Waal, F. (2006). *Primates and Philosophers: How Morality Evolved.* Princeton, NJ: Princeton University Press.

———. (2008). Putting the altruism back into altrusim: The evolution of empathy. *Annual Review of Psychology, 59,* 279–300.

Diamond, J. (2005). *Guns, Germs, and Steel: The Fates of Human Societies.* New York: W.W. Norton and Company.

———. (2012). *The World until Yesterday: What Can We Learn from Traditional Societies?* New York: Viking Press.

Dijksterhuis, A., Preston, J., Wegner, D. M., and Aarts, H. (2008). Effects of subliminal priming of self and God on self-attribution of authorship for events. *Journal of Experimental Social Psychology, 44,* 2–9.

Dijksterhuis, B., Van, D. L., and Baaren, V. (2000). Predicting soccer matches after unconscious and conscious thought as a function of expertise. *Psychological Science, 20*(11), 1381–1387.

Dostoevsky, F. (1990). *The Brothers Karamazov,* trans. R. Pevear and L. Volokhonsky. San Francisco: North Point Press.

Driver, J., Davis, G., Ricciardelli, P., Kidd, P., Maxwell, E., and Baron-Cohen, S. (1999). Gaze perception triggers reflexive visuospatial orienting. *Visual Cognition*, *6*, 509–540.

Duhaime, E. (2011). Did religion facilitate the evolution of large-scale cooperative societies? Religious salience and the "Ritual Effect" on prosocial behavior. Unpublished MA thesis, Cambridge University.

Dunbar, R.I.M. (2003). The social brain: Mind, language, and society in evolutionary perspective. *Annual Review of Anthropology*, *32*, 163–181.

Dunning, D. and Balcetis, D. (2013). Wishful seeing: How preferences shape visual perception. *Current Directions in Psychological Science*, *22*, 33–37.

Durkheim, E. (1915). *The Elementary Forms of the Religious Life*. New York: New York Free Press.

The Economist (2011). Nasty business: A spate of ritual killings unnerves Liberia. Available at http://www.economist.com/node/18073315 (accessed 03/12/2013).

Edelman, J. (2009). Red light states: Who buys online adult entertainment? *Journal of Economic Perspectives*, *23*, 209–220.

Edgell, P., Gerteis, J., and Hartmann, D. (2006). Atheists as "other": Moral boundaries and cultural membership in American society. *American Sociological Review*, *71*, 211–234.

Engelstein, L. (1999). *Castration and the Heavenly Kingdom: A Russian Folktale*. Ithaca, NY: Cornell University Press.

Eno, R. (2009). Shang state religion and the pantheon of the oracle texts. In *Early Chinese Religion: Part One: Shang through Han (1250 BC–22 AD)*, ed. J. Lagerwey and M. Kalinowski, pp. 41–102. Leiden: Brill.

Ensminger, J. (1997). Transaction costs and Islam: Explaining conversion in Africa. *Journal of Institutional and Theoretical Economics*, *153*, 4–28.

Epley, N., Akalis, S., Waytz, A., and Cacioppo, J. T. (2008). Creating social connection through inferential reproduction: Loneliness and perceived agency in gadgets, gods, and greyhounds. *Psychological Science*, *19*, 114–120.

Epley, N., Waytz, A., and Cacioppo, J. T. (2007). On seeing human: A three-factor theory of anthropomorphism. *Psychological Review*, *114*, 864–886.

Evans, E. M. (2001). Cognitive and contextual factors in the emergence of diverse belief systems: Creation versus evolution. *Cognitive Psychology*, *42*, 217–266.

Fehr, E., and Fischbacher, U. (2003). The nature of human altruism. *Nature*, *425*, 785–791.

Fehr, E., and Gächter, S. (2000). Fairness and retaliation: The economics of reciprocity. *Journal of Economic Perspectives*, *14*, 159–181.

Fehr, E., and Henrich, J. (2003). Is strong reciprocity a maladaptation? In *Genetic and Culture Evolution of Cooperation*, ed. P. Hammerstein, pp. 55–82. Cambridge, MA: MIT Press.

Fehr, E., and Schneider, F. (2010). Eyes are on us, but nobody cares: Are eye cues relevant for strong reciprocity? *Proceedings of the Royal Society B, 277*, 1315–1323.

Finke, R., and Stark, R. (2005). *The Churching of America, 1776–2005: Winners and Losers in Our Religious Economy*. New Brunswick, NJ: Rutgers University Press.

Fiske, R. (1990). *Pity the Nation: The Abduction of Lebanon*. New York: Nation Books.

Fiske, S. T. (2010). *Social Beings: Core Motives in Social Psychology*. New York: Wiley.

Fiske, S. T., Cuddy, A.J.C., and Glick, P. (2007). Universal dimensions of social cognition: Warmth, then competence. *Trends in Cognitive Sciences, 11*, 77–83.

Fosset, M. A., and Kiecolt, K. J. (1989). The relative size of minority population and white racial attitudes. *Social Science Quarterly, 70*, 820–835.

Frank, R. H. (1988). *Passions within Reason: The Strategic Role of the Emotions*. New York: W. W. Norton.

Franken, A. (2002). *Oh, the Things I Know!* New York: Dutton.

Franklin, B. (1757). The papers of Benjamin Franklin. *The American Philosophical Society*. Available at http://franklinpapers.org/franklin/ (accessed 03/12/2013).

Frederick, S. (2005). Cognitive reflection and decision making. *Journal of Economic Perspectives, 19*, 25–42.

Frith, U., and Frith, C. D. (2003). Development and neurophysiology of mentalizing. *Philosophical Transactions of the Royal Society B: Biological Sciences, 358*(1431), 459–473.

Gambetta, D. (ed.). (2005). *Making Sense of Suicide Missions*. New York: Oxford University Press.

Gauchet, M. (2007). *The Disenchantment of the World: A Political History of Religion*. Princeton, NJ: Princeton University Press.

Geertz, A. W., and Markusson, G. I. (2010). Religion is natural, atheism is not: On why everybody is both right and wrong. *Religion, 40*, 152–165.

Gelfand, M. J., Raver, J. L., Nishii, L., Leslie, L. M., and Lun, J. (2011). Differences between tight and loose cultures: A 33-nation study. *Science, 332*, 1100–1104.

Gerth, H., and Mills, W. (eds.). (1946). *From Max Weber: Essays in Sociology*. New York: Oxford University Press.

Gervais, R. (2010). Does God exist? Ricky Gervais takes your questions. *The Wall Street Journal*. Available at http://blogs.wsj.com/speakeasy/2010/12/22/does-god-exist-ricky-gervais-takes-your-questions/ (accessed 03/12/2013).

Gervais, W. M. (2011). Finding the faithless: Perceived atheist prevalence reduces anti-atheist prejudice. *Personality and Social Psychology Bulletin, 37*, 543–556.

Gervais, W. M., and Henrich, J. (2010). The Zeus problem: Why representational content biases cannot explain faith in gods. *Journal of Cognition and Culture, 10*, 383–389.

Gervais, W. M., and Norenzayan, A. (2012a). Analytic thinking promotes religious disbelief. *Science, 336*, 493–496.

———. (2012b). Like a camera in the sky? Thinking about God increases public self-awareness and socially desirable responding. *Journal of Experimental Social Psychology, 48*, 298–302.

———. (2012c). Reminders of secular authority reduce believers' distrust of atheists. *Psychological Science, 23*, 483–491.

Gervais, W. M., Shariff, A. F., and Norenzayan, A. (2011a). Do you believe in atheists? Distrust is central to anti-atheist prejudice. *Journal of Personality and Social Psychology, 101*, 1189–1206.

Gervais, W. M., Willard, A. K., Norenzayan, A., and Henrich, J. (2011b). The cultural transmission of faith: Why innate intuitions are necessary, but insufficient, to explain religious belief. *Religion, 41*, 389–410.

Gibran, K. (1985). *The Treasured Writings of Kahlil Gibran.* Seacaucus, NJ: Castle.

Gilbert, D. (1991). How mental systems believe. *American Psychologist, 46*, 107–119.

Gilbert, D., Tafarodi, R., and Malone, P. (1993). You can't not believe everything you read. *Journal of Personality and Social Psychology, 65*, 221–233.

Ginges, J., Atran, S., Medin, D., and Shikaki, K. (2007). Sacred bounds on rational resolution of violent political conflict. *Proceedings of the National Academy of Sciences, 104*, 7357–7360.

Ginges, J., Hansen, I., and Norenzayan, A. (2009). Religion and support for suicide attacks. *Psychological Science, 20*(2), 224–230.

Gintis, H., Bowles, S., Boyd, R., and Fehr, E. (2003). Explaining altruistic behavior in humans. *Evolution and Human Behavior, 24*, 153–172.

Gladwell, M. (2005). *Blink: The Power of Thinking without Thinking.* New York: Back Bay Books.

Gonzaga, G., and Haselton, M. G. (2008). The evolution of love and long-term bonds. In *Social Relationships: Cognitive, Affective, and Motivational Processes,* ed. J. P. Forgas and J. Fitness, pp. 39–54. New York: Psychology Press.

Graham, J., and Haidt, J. (2010). Beyond beliefs: Religions bind individuals into moral communities. *Personality and Social Psychology Review, 14*, 140–150.

Grandin, T. (1995). *Thinking in Pictures: And Other Reports from My Life with Autism.* New York: Doubleday.

Granet, M. (1934). *La Pensée Chinoise.* Paris: La Renaissance du livre.

Gray, K., Jenkins, A. C., Heberlein, A. H., and Wegner, D. M. (2011). Distortions of mind perception in psychopathology. *Proceedings of the National Academy of Sciences, 108*, 477–479.

Gray, K., and Wegner, D. M. (2010). Blaming God for our pain: Human suffering and the divine mind. *Personality and Social Psychology Review, 14*, 7–16.

Greenwald, A. G., and Banaji, M. (1995). Implicit social cognition: Attitudes, self-esteem, and stereotypes. *Psychological Review, 102*, 4–27.

Greenwald, A. G., McGhee, D. E., and Schwartz, J. L. (1998). Measuring individual differences in implicit cognition: The implicit association test. *Journal of Personality and Social Psychology, 74*, 1464–1480.

Greif, A. (1993). Contract enforceablity and economic institutions in early trade: The Maghribi traders. *American Economic Review, 83*, 525–548.

Guthrie, S. (1993). *Faces in the Clouds.* Oxford, UK: Oxford University Press.

Haidt, J. (2007). The new synthesis in moral psychology. *Science, 316*, 998–1002.

———. (2012). *The Righteous Mind: Why Good People Are Divided by Politics and Religion.* New York: Pantheon Books.

Haidt, J., and Graham, J. (2009). Planet of the Durkheimians, where community, authority, and sacredness are foundations of morality. In *Social and Psychological Bases of Ideology and System Justification*, ed. J. Jost, A. C. Kay, and H. Thorisdottir, pp. 371–401. New York: Oxford University Press.

Haidt, J., Seder, J. P., and Kesebir, S. (2008). Hive psychology, happiness, and public policy. *Journal of Legal Studies, 37*, 133–156.

Haley, K. J., and Fessler, D.M.T. (2005). Nobody's watching? Subtle cues affects generosity in an anonymous economic game. *Evolution and Human Behavior, 26*, 245–256.

Hall, D. L., Matz, D. C., and Wood, W. (2010). Why don't we practice what we preach? A meta-analytic review of religious racism. *Personality and Social Psychology Review, 14*, 126–139.

Hamilton, W. D. (1964). The genetical evolution of social behavior. *Journal of Theoretical Biology, 7*, 1–52.

Hamlin, J. K., Wynn, K., and Bloom, P. (2007). Social evaluation by preverbal infants. *Nature, 450*, 557–559.

Hamlin, J. K., Wynn, K., Bloom, P., and Mahajan, N. (2011). How infants and toddlers react to antisocial others. *Proceedings of the National Academy of Sciences, 108*, 19931–19936.

Hansen, C. (2000). *A Daoist Theory of Chinese Thought: A Philosophical Interpretation.* Oxford, UK: Oxford University Press.

Hansen, I. G., and Norenzayan, A. (2006). Between yang and yin and heaven and hell: Untangling the complex relationship between religion and intolerance. In *Where God and Science Meet: How Brain and Evolutionary Studies Alter*

Our Understanding of Religion, ed. P. McNamara, vol. 3, pp. 187–211. Wesport, CT: Greenwood Press-Praeger Publishers.

Harris, P. (2011). Rising atheism in America puts religous right on the defensive. *The Guardian*. Available at http://www.guardian.co.uk/world/2011/oct/01/atheism-america-religious-right (accessed 03/12/2013).

Harris, P. L. (2012). *Trusting What We're Told: How Children Learn from Others*. Cambridge, MA: Harvard University Press.

Harris, P. L., and Koenig, M. A. (2006). Trust in testimony: How children learn about science and religion. *Child Development, 77*, 505–524.

Harris, S. (2005). *The End of faith: Religion, Terror and the Future of Reason*. New York: W.W. Norton and Company.

———. (2010). *The Moral Landscape: How Science Can Determine Human Values*. New York: New York Free Press.

Hayek, F. (1988). *The Fatal Conceit*. Volume I in *The Collected Works of F. A. Hayek*, ed. W. Bartley. Chicago: University of Chicago Press.

Heath, C., Bell, C., and Sternberg, E. (2001). Emotional selection in memes: The case of urban legends. *Journal of Personality and Social Psychology, 81*, 1028–1041.

Henrich, J. (2006). Cooperation, punishment, and the evolution of human institutions. *Science, 312*, 60–61.

———. (2009). The evolution of costly displays, cooperation and religion: Credibility enhancing displays and their implications for cultural evolution. *Evolution and Human Behavior, 30*(4), 244–260.

Henrich, J., and Boyd, R. (2002). On modeling cognition and culture: Why replicators are not necessary for cultural evolution. *Journal of Cognition and Culture, 2*, 87–112.

Henrich, J., Ensimger, J., McElreath, R., Barr, A., Barrett, C., Bolyanatz, A., Cardenas, J., et al. (2010a). Markets, religion, community size, and the evolution of fairness and punishment. *Science, 327*, 1480–1484.

Henrich, J., Heine, S. J., and Norenzayan, A. (2010b). The weirdest people in the world? *Behavioral and Brain Sciences, 33*(2–3), 61–83.

Henrich, J., McElreath, R., Barr, A., Ensimger, J., Barrett, C., Bolyanatz, A., Cardenas, J., et al. (2006). Costly punishment across human societies. *Science, 312*, 1767–1770.

Henrich, N. S., and Henrich, J. (2007). *Why Humans Cooperate: A Cultural and Evolutionary Explanation*. Oxford, UK: Oxford University Press.

Herrmann, B., Thoeni, C., and Gaechter, S. (2008). Antisocial punishment across societies. *Science, 319*, 1362–1367.

Hill, K. R., Walker, R. S., Božičević, M., Eder, J., Headland, T., Hewlett, B., Hurtado, A. M., et al. (2011). Co-residence patterns in hunter-gatherer societies show unique human social structure. *Science, 331*(6022), 1286–1289.

Hoffman, E., McCabe, K., Shachat, K., and Smith, V. (1994). Preferences, property rights, and anonymity in bargaining games. *Games and Economic Behavior, 7,* 346–380.

Horton, R. (1960). A definition of religion, and its uses. *Journal of the Royal Anthropological Institute, 90,* 201–226.

House, J. S., Landis, K. R., and Umberson, D. (1988). Social relationships and health. *Science, 241,* 540–545.

Hout, M., and Fischer, C. (2001). Religious diversity in America, 1940–2000: A century of difference. Available at http://ucdata.berkeley.edu/rsfcensus/papers/Fischer-Hout_Ch7_June05.pdf (accessed 03/12/2013).

Hove, M. J., and Rise, J. L. (2009). It's all in the timing: Interpersonal synchrony increases affiliation. *Social Cognition, 27,* 949–961.

Hume, D. (1888). *A Treatise of Human Nature.* Oxford, UK: Clarendon Press.

Hungerman, D. M. (2011). The effect of education on religion: evidence from compulsory schooling laws. *NBER Working Paper 16973.* Available at http://papers.nber.org/papers/w16973 (accessed 03/12/2013).

Iannacone, L. R. (1992). Sacrifice and stigma: Reducing free-riding in cults, communes, and other collectives. *The Journal of Political Economy, 100,* 271–291.

———. (1994). Why strict churches are stong. *American Journal of Sociology, 99,* 1180–1211.

Inglehart, R., and Baker, W. (2000). Modernization, cultural change, and the persistence of traditional values. *American Sociological Review, 65,* 19–51.

Inglehart, R., Basanez, M., Diez-Medrano, J., Halman, L., and Luijkx, R. (eds.). (2004). *Human Beliefs and Values: A Cross-Cultural Sourcebook Based on the 1999–2002 Value Surveys.* Mexico City: Siglo XXI.

International Humanist and Ethical Union (2012). Freedom of thought report 2012. *iheu.org.* Available at http://www.iheu.org/files/IHEU%20Freedom%20of%20Thought%202012.pdf (accessed 03/12/2013).

Inzlicht, M., McGregor, I., Hirsh, J. B., and Nash, K. (2009). Neural markers of religious conviction. *Psychological Science, 20,* 385–392.

Inzlicht, M., and Tullett, A. M. (2010). Reflecting on God: Religious primes can reduce neuropsychological response to errors. *Psychological Science, 21,* 1181–1190.

Irons, W. (2001). Religion as a hard-to-fake sign of commitment. In *Evolution and the Capacity for Commitment,* ed. R. Nesse, pp. 292–309. New York: Russell Sage Foundation.

James, W. (1902/1982). *The Varieties of Religious Experience.* New York: Penguin Books.

Jena, S. (2006, February). The coconut temple courier service. *BBC News*.

Jenkins, P. (2002). *The Next Christendom*. Oxford, UK: Oxford University Press.

Johnson, D.D.P. (2009). The error of God: Error management theory, religion and the evolution of cooperation. In *Games, Groups and the Global Good*, ed. S. A. Levin, pp. 169–180. Berlin: Springer-Verlag.

Johnson, D.D.P., and Bering, J. M. (2006). Hand of God, mind of man: Punishment and cognition in the evolution of cooperation. *Evolutionary Psychology*, *4*, 219–233.

Kahneman, D. (2011). *Thinking, Fast and Slow*. New York: Farrar, Straus, and Giroux.

Kapogiannis, D., Barbey, A. K., Su, M., Zamboni, G., Krueger, F., and Grafman, J. (2009). Cognitive and neural foundations of religious belief. *Proceedings of the National Academy of Sciences*, *106*, 4876–4881.

Kauffman, D. A., Kraay, A., and Mastruzzi, M. (2003). Governance matters III: Governance indicators for 1996–2002. *World Bank Economic Review*, *18*, 253–287.

Kaufmann, E. (2010). *Shall the Religious Inherit the Earth?: Demography and Politics in the Twenty-first Century*. London: Profile Books.

Kay, A. C., Gaucher, D., McGregor, I., and Nash, K. (2010a). Religion conviction as compensatory control. *Personality and Social Psychology Review*, *14*, 37–48.

Kay, A. C., Gaucher, D., Napier, J. L., Callan, M. J., and Laurin, K. (2008). God and the government: Testing a compensatory control mechanism for the support of external systems. *Journal of Personality and Social Psychology*, *95*, 18–35.

Kay, A. C., Moscovitch, D. M., and Laurin, K. (2010b). Randomness, attributions of arousal, and belief in God. *Psychological Science*, *21*, 216–218.

Kay, A. C., Shepherd, S., Blatz, C. W., Chua, S. N., and Galinsky, A. D. (2010c). For God (or) country: The hydraulic relation between government instablity and belief in religious sources of control. *Journal of Personality and Social Psychology Review*, *99*, 725–739.

Keeley, L. H. (1996). *War before Civilization: The Myth of the Peaceful Savage*. Oxford, UK: Oxford University Press.

Keesing, R. (1982). *Kwaio Religion: The Living and the Dead in a Solomon Island Society*. New York: Columbia University Press.

Kelemen, D. (2004). Are children "intuitive theists?": Reasoning about purpose and design in nature. *Psychological Science*, *15*, 295–301.

Kelemen, D., and Rosset, E. (2009). The human function compunction: Teleological explanation in adults. *Cognitive Development*, *111*, 138–143.

Kelemen, D., Rottman, J., and Seston, R. (in press). Professional physical scientists display tenacious teleological tendencies: Purpose-based reasoning as a cognitive default. *Journal of Experimental Psychology: General*.

Kelly, R. L. (1995). *The Foraging Spectrum: Diversity in Hunter-Gatherer Lifeways.* Washington, DC: Smithsonian Institution Press.

Keltner, D., and Haidt, J. (2001). Social functions of emotions. In *Emotions: Current Issues and Future Directions*, ed. T. Mayne and A. Bonanno, pp. 192–213. New York: Guilford.

Khaldûn, I. (1958). *The Muqaddimah: An Introduction to History*, trans. F. Rosenthal. London: Routledge and Kegan Paul.

Kirkpatrick, L. A. (2005). *Attachment, Evolution and the Psychology of Religion.* New York: Guilford.

Kirkpatrick, L. A., and Hood, R. W. (1990). Intrinsic-extrinsic religious orientation: The boon or bane of contemporary psychology of religion? *Journal for the Scientific Study of Religion, 29*, 442–462.

Kitts, J. A. (2009). Paradise lost: Age-dependent mortality of American communes, 1609–1965. *Social Forces, 87*, 1193–1222.

Klaw, S. (1993). *Without Sin: The Life and Death of the Oneida Community.* New York: Penguin Books.

Klein, R. G. (2009). *The Human Career: Human Biological and Cultural Origins*, 3rd ed. Chicago: University of Chicago Press.

Knack, S., and Keefer, P. (1997). Does social capital have an economic payoff? *Quarterly Journal of Economics, 112*, 1251–1288.

Kohlberg, L., Levine, C., and Hewer, A. (1983). *Moral Stages: A Current Formulation and a Response to Critics.* Basel, Switzerland: Karger.

Konvalinka, I., Xygalatas, D., Bulbulia, J., Schjoedt, U., Jegindo, E.-M., and Wallot, S. (2001). Synchronized arousal between performers and related spectators in a fire-walking ritual. *Proceedings of the National Academy of Sciences, 108*, 8514–8519.

Krebs, D. (1975). Empathy and altruism. *Journal of Personality and Social Psychology, 32*, 1134–1146.

Kummerli, R. (2011). A test of evolutionary policing theory with data from human societies. *PLoS ONE, 6*(9), e24350.

Kunda, Z. (1990). The case for motivated reasoning. *Psychological Bulletin, 108*, 480–498.

Kurzban, R., and Leary, M. R. (2001). Evolutionary origins of stigmatization: The functions of social exclusion. *Psychological Bulletin, 127*, 187–208.

Laland, K. N., Odling-Smee, J., and Myles, S. (2010). How culture shaped the human genome: bringing genetics and the human sciences together. *Nature Reviews Genetics, 11*(2), 137–148.

Lanman, J. (2011, March). Thou shalt believe—or not. *New Scientist, 2805*, 38–39.

———. (2012). The importance of religious displays for belief acquisition and secularization. *Journal of Contemporary Religion, 27*, 49–65.

Larson, E. J., and Witham, L. (1998). Leading scientists still reject God. *Nature*, *394*, 313–314.

Laurin, K., Kay, A. C., and Fitzsimons, G. M. (2012a). Divergent effects of activating thoughts of god on self-regulation. *Journal of Personality and Social Psychology*, *102*, 4–21.

Laurin, K., Shariff, A. F., Henrich, J., and Kay, A. C. (2012b). Outsourcing punishment to god: Beliefs in divine control reduce earthly punishment. *Proceedings of the Royal Society B: Biological Sciences*, *279*, 3272–3281.

Lawler, A. (2012). Civilization's double-edged sword. *Science*, *336*, 832–833.

Lawson, E. T., and McCauley, R. N. (1990). *Rethinking Religion: Connecting Cognition and Culture*. Oxford, UK: Oxford University Press.

Leach, C. W., Ellemers, N., and Barreto, M. (2007). Group virtue: The importance of morality (vs. competence and sociability) in the positive evaluation of ingroups. *Journal of Personality and Social Psychology*, *93*, 234–249.

Leeson, P. (2010a, January). Justice, medieval style. *The Boston Globe*.

———. (2010b). Ordeals. Available at http://www.peterleeson.com/Ordeals.pdf (accessed 03/12/2013).

Legare, C. H., Evans, E. M., Rosengren, K. S., and Harris, P. L. (2012). The coexistence of natural and supernatural explanations across cultures and development. *Child Development*, *83*, 779–793.

Legare, C. H., and Souza, A. (2012). Evaluating ritual efficacy: Evidence from the supernatural. *Cognitive Development*, *124*, 1–15.

Lester, T. (2002, February). Oh, Gods! *The Atlantic Monthly*, 37–45.

Levine, R. A., and Campbell, D. T. (1972). *Ethnocentrism*. New York: Wiley.

Levy, J., Foulsham, T., and Kingstone, A. (in press). Monsters are people too. *Biology Letters*.

Lewis, G. J., Ritchie, S. J., and Bates, T. C. (2011). The relationship between intelligence and multiple domains of religious belief: Evidence from a large adult US sample. *Intelligence*, *39*, 468–472.

Locke, J. (1983). *A Letter Concerning Toleration*. Indianapolis: Hackett.

Lombrozo, T. (2012, November). Would you vote for an atheist? Tell the truth. *NPR: National Public Radio*. Available at http://www.npr.org/blogs/13.7/2012/11/13/164963163/would-you-vote-for-an-atheist-tell-the-truth (accessed 03/12/2013).

Mann, C. C. (2011, June). The birth of religion. *National Geographic Magazine*. Available at http://ngm.nationalgeographic.com/2011/06/gobekli-tepe/mann-text (accessed 03/12/2013).

Malhotra, D. (2008). (When) Are religious people nicer? Religious salience and the "Sunday effect" on prosocial behavior. *Judgment and Decision Making*, *5*, 138–143.

Marcus, J., and Flannery, K. V. (2004). The coevolution of ritual and society: New C-14 dates from ancient Mexico. *Proceedings of the National Academy of Sciences, 101*, 18257–18261.

Marlowe, F. W. (2005). Hunter-gatherers and human evolution. *Evolutionary Anthropology, 14*, 54–67.

———. (2010). *The Hadza: Hunter-Gatherers of Tanzania*. Berkeley: University of California Press.

Marshall, L. (1962). !Kung bushman religious beliefs. *Journal of the International African Institute, 32*, 221–252.

Maynard Smith, J., and Harper, D. (2003). *Animal Signals*. Oxford, UK: Oxford University Press.

Mazar, N., Amir, O., and Ariely, D. (2008). The dishonesty of honest people: A theory of self-concept maintenance. *Journal of Marketing Research, 45*, 633–644.

McCauley, R. (2011). *Why Religion Is Natural and Science Is Not*. Oxford, UK: Oxford University Press.

McCleary, R. M., and Barro, R. J. (2006). Religion and political economy in an international panel. *Journal for the Scientific Study of Religion, 45*, 149–175.

McCullough, M. E., and Willoughby, B.L.B. (2009). Religion, self-regulation, and self-control: Associations, explanations, and implications. *Psychological Bulletin, 135*, 69–93.

McKay, R. T., and Dennett, D. C. (2009). The evolution of misbelief. *Behavioral and Brain Sciences, 32*, 493–510.

McKay, R., Efferson, C., Whitehouse, H., and Fehr, E. (2011). Wrath of God: Religious primes and punishment. *Proceedings of the Royal Society B: Biological Sciences, 278*, 1858–1863.

McNamara, R. A. (2012). When does it matter that God is watching? Differential effects of large and small gods on cheating as a function of material insecurity in Yasawa, Fiji. MA dissertation, University of British Columbia.

McNeill, W. H. (1995). *Keeping Together in Time*. Cambridge, MA: Harvard University Press.

Meier, B. P., Hauser, D. J., Robinson, M. D., Friesen, C. K., and Schjeldahl, K. (2007). What's "up" with God?: Vertical space as a representation of the divine. *Journal of Personality and Social Psychology, 93*, 699–710.

Mitchell, J. (2009). Inferences about mental states. *Philosophical Transactions of the Royal Society B: Biological Sciences, 364*, 1309–1316.

Molière. (2002). *Tartuffe*, trans. M. Sorrel. London: Nick Hern Books.

Nesse, R. (1999). Evolution of commitment and the origins of religion. *Science and Spirit, 10*, 32–36.

Neudecker, S. (1989). Eye camouflage and false eyespots: Chaetodontid responses to predators. *Environmental Biology of Fishes, 25*, 143–157.

Newport, F., and Strausberg, M. (2001). Americans' belief in psychic and paranormal phenomena is up over the last decade. Available at http://www.gallup.com/poll/4483/americans-belief-psychic-paranormal-phenomena-over-last-decade.aspx (accessed 03/12/2013).

Norenzayan, A., Atran, S., Faulkner, J., and Schaller, M. (2006). Memory and mystery: The cultural selection of minimally counterintuitive narratives. *Cognitive Science, 30*, 531–553.

Norenzayan, A., and Gervais, W. M. (in press). Secular rule of law erodes believers' political intolerance of atheists. *Religion, Brain, & Behavior*.

———. (2013). The origins of religious disbelief. *Trends in Cognitive Science, 17*, 20–25.

Norenzayan, A., Gervais, W. M., and Trzesniewski, K. (2012). Mentalizing deficits constrain belief in a personal God. *PLoS ONE, 7*, e36880.

Norenzayan, A., and Hansen, I. G. (2006). Belief in supernatural agents in the face of death. *Personality and Social Psychology Bulletin, 32*, 174–187.

Norenzayan, A., and Heine, S. J. (2005) Psychological universals: What are they and how can we know? *Psychological Bulletin, 131*, 763–784.

Norenzayan, A., and Lee, A. (2010). It was meant to happen: Explaining cultural variations in fate attributions. *Journal of Personality and Social Psychology, 98*, 702–720.

Norenzayan, A., and Shariff, A. F. (2008). The origin and evolution of religious prosociality. *Science, 322*, 58–62.

Norris, P., and Inglehart, R. (2004). *Sacred and Secular: Religion and Politics Worldwide*. Cambridge, UK: Cambridge University Press.

Nowak, M. A., and Sigmund, K. (2005). Indirect reciprocity. *Nature, 437*, 1291–1298.

O'Connell, M. R. (1997). *Blaise Pascal: Reasons of the Heart*. Grand Rapids, MI: Wm. B. Eerdmans Publishing.

Orbell, J., Goldman, M., Mulford, M., and Dawes, R. (1992). Religion, context and constraint towards strangers. *Rationality and Society, 4*, 291–307.

Ostling, R. N., and Ostling, J. K. (1999). *Mormon America: The Power and the Promise*. San Francisco: Harper San Francisco.

Otterbein, K. F. (1970). *The Evolution of War: A Cross-Cultural Study*. New Haven, CT: HRAF Press.

Oved, Y. (1997). The lesson of the communes. In *Kibbutz: An Alternative Lifestyle*, ed. D. Leichman and I. Paz, pp. 159–165. Efal, Israel: Yad Tabenkin.

Panchanathan, K., and Boyd, R. (2003). A tale of two defectors: The importance of standing for the evolution of indirect reciprocity. *Journal of Theoretical Biology, 224*, 115–126.

Pape, R. A. (2005). *Dying to Win: The Strategic Logic of Suicide Terrorism*. New York: Random House.

Paper, J. (2012). Response to Kelly James Clark and Justin T. Winslett, "The evolutionary psychology of Chinese religion: Pre-Qin high gods as punishers and rewarders." *Journal of the American Academy of Religion, 80*, 518–521.

Paulhus, D. L. (1984). Two-component models of socially desirable responding. *Journal of Personality and Social Psychology, 46*, 598–609.

Pennycook, G., Cheyne, J. A., Seli, P., Koehler, D. J., and Fugelsang, J. A. (2012). Analytic cognitive style predicts religious and paranormal belief. *Cognitive Development, 123*, 335–346.

Peters, F. E., and Esposito, J. L. (2006). *The Children of Abraham: Judaism, Christianity, Islam*. Princeton, NJ: Princeton University Press.

Pew Forum. (2008). Many Americans say other faiths can lead to eternal life. Available at http://pewforum.org/Many-Americans-Say-Other-Faiths-Can-Lead-to-Eternal-Life.aspx (accessed 03/12/2013).

Pew Research Center. (2007). Voters remain in neutral as presidential campaign moves into high gear. Available at http://www.people-press.org/2007/02/23/voters-remain-in-neutral-as-presidential-campaign-moves-into-high-gear (accessed 03/13/2013).

Phillips, C., and Axelrod, A. (2007). *Encyclopedia of Wars*. New York: Facts on File.

Piazza, J., Bering, J. M., and Ingram, G. (2011). "Princess Alice is watching you": Children's belief in an invisible person inhibits cheating. *Journal of Experimental Child Psychology, 109*, 311–320.

Pichon, I., Boccato, G., and Saroglou, V. (2007). Nonconscious influences of religion on prosociality: A priming study. *European Journal of Social Psychology, 37*, 1032–1045.

Pinker, S. (2011). *The Better Angels of Our Nature: Why Violence Has Declined*. New York: Viking.

———. (2012). The false allure of group selection. *Edge*. Available at http://edge.org/conversation/the-false-allure-of-group-selection (accessed 03/12/2013).

Pitzer, D. (1997). *America's Communal Utopias*. Chapel Hill: University of North Carolina Press.

Poo, M.-C. (2009). *Rethinking Ghosts in World Religions*. Leiden: Brill.

Powell, A., Shennan, S., and Thomas, M. G. (2009). Late Pleistocene demography and the appearance of modern human behavior. *Science, 324*, 1298–1301.

Purzycki, B. G. (2011). Tyvan *cher eezi* and the sociological constraints of supernatural agents' minds. *Religion, Brain and Behavior, 1*, 31–45.

Purzycki, B. G., Finkel, D. N., Shaver, J., Wales, N., Cohen, A. B., and Sosis, R. (2012). What does God know? Supernatural agents' access to socially strategic and non-strategic information. *Cognitive Science, 36*, 846–869.

Putnam, R. (2000). *Bowling Alone: The Collapse and Revival of American Community*. New York: Simon and Schuster.

Putnam, R., and Campbell, R. (2010). *American Grace: How Religion Divides and Unites Us*. New York: Simon and Schuster.

Pyszczynski, T., Abdollahi, A., and Rothschild, Z. (2009). Does peace have a prayer? The effects of mortality salience, compassionate values, and religious fundamentalism on hostility towards out-groups. *Journal of Experimental Social Psychology, 45*, 816–827.

Pyysiäinen, I. (2003). Buddhism, religion, and the concept of "god." *Numen, 50*, 147–171.

Pyysiäinen, I., and Antonnen, V. (eds.). (2002). *Current Approaches in the Cognitive Science of Religion*. New York: Continuum.

Pyysiäinen, I., and Hauser, M. (2010). The origins of religion: Evolved adaptation or by-product? *Trends in Cognitive Sciences, 14*, 104–109.

Radel, R., and Clément-Guillotin, C. (2012). Evidence of motivational influences in early visual perception: Hunger modulates conscious access. *Psychological Science, 23*, 232–234.

Radio Free Europe Radio Liberty (2012, July). U.S.: Religion intolerance still plagues globe. Available at http://www.rferl.org/content/us-says-religious-intolerance-still-plagues-globe/24661614.html (accessed 03/12/2013).

Randolph-Seng, B., and Nielsen, M. E. (2007). Honesty: One effect of primed religious representations. *International Journal for the Psychology of Religion, 17*, 303–315.

Rauch, J. (2003, May). Let it be: Three cheers for apatheism. *The Atlantic Monthly*. Available at http://www.theatlantic.com/magazine/archive/2003/05/let-it-be/2726/ (accessed 03/12/2013).

Rauh, N. K. (1993). *The Sacred Bonds of Commerce: Religion, Economy, and Trade Society at Hellensitic Roman Delos, 166–87 B.C.* Amsterdam: Gieben.

Reber, R., Winkielman, P., and Schwarz, N. (1998). Effects of perceptual fluency on affective judgments. *Psychological Science, 9*, 45–48.

Richerson, P. J., and Boyd, R. (2005). *Not by Genes Alone: How Culture Transformed Human Evolution*. Chicago: University of Chicago Press.

Rigdon, M. L., Ishii, K., Watabe, M., and Kitayama, S. (2009). Minimal social cues in the dictator game. *Journal of Economic Psychology, 30*, 358–367.

Robertson Smith, W. (1972). *The Religion of the Semites: Lectures on the Religion of the Semites*. London: A & C Black.

Roes, F. L., and Raymond, M. (2003). Belief in moralizing gods. *Evolution and Human Behavior, 24*, 126–135.

Rosemont, H. J., and Ames, R. (2009). *The Chinese Classic of Family Reverence: A Philosophical Translation of the Xiaojing*. Honolulu: University of Hawai'i Press.

Ross, L., and Nisbett, R. E. (1991). *The Person and the Situation: Perspectives of Social Psychology*. New York: McGraw-Hill.

Roth, L., and Kroll, J. C. (2007). Risky business: Assessing risk-preference explanations for gender differences in religiosity. *American Sociological Review, 27*, 205–220.

Rounding, K., Lee, A., Jacobson, J. A., and Ji, L. J. (2012). Religion replenishes self-control. *Psychological Science, 23*, 635–642.

Rowthorn, R. (2011). Religion, fertility and genes: A dual inheritance model. *Proceedings of the Royal Society B: Biological Sciences, 278*, 2519–2527.

Rutjens, B., van der Pligt, J., and van Harreveld, F. (2010). Deus or Darwin: Randomness and belief in theories about the origins of life. *Journal of Experimental Social Psychology, 46*, 1078–1080.

Ryan, E. G. (2012, November). Arizona is this close to electing an openly bisexual woman to Congress. *Jezebel*. Available at http://jezebel.com/5958864/arizona-is-thisclose-to-openly-electing-bisexual-atheist-woman-to-congress (accessed 03/12/2013).

Sanderson, S. K., and Roberts, W. W. (2008). The evolutionary forms of the religious life: A cross-cultural, quantitative analysis. *American Anthropologist, 110*, 454–466.

Saroglou, V. (2011). Believing, bonding, behaving, and belonging: The big four religious dimensions and cultural variation. *Journal of Cross-Cultural Psychology, 42*, 1320–1340.

Saslow, L. R., Willer, R., Feinberg, M., Piff, P. K., Clark, K., Keltner, D., and Saturn, S. R. (2013). My brother's keeper? Compassion predicts generosity more among less religious individuals. *Social Psychological and Personality Science, 4*, 31–38.

Schaller, M., and Neuberg, S. L. (2008). Intergroup prejudices and intergroup conflicts. In *Foundations of Evolutionary Psychology*, ed. C. Crawford and D. L. Krebs, pp. 399–412. Mahwah, NJ: Lawrence Erlbaum Associates.

Schjoedt, U., Stødkilde-Jørgensen, H., Geertz, A. W., and Roepstorff, A. (2009). Highly religious participants recruit areas of social cognition in personal prayer. *Social Cognitive and Affective Neuroscience, 4*, 199–207.

Schloss, J. P. (2008). He who laughs best: Involuntary religious affect as a solution to recursive cooperative defection. In *The Evolution of Religion: Studies, Theories, and Critiques*, ed. J. Bulbulia, R. Sosis, C. Genet, R. Genet, E. Harris, and K. Wyman, pp. 197–207. Santa Margarita, CA: Collins Foundation Press.

Schloss, J. P. (2009). Evolutionary theories of religion: Science set free or naturalism run wild? In *The Believing Primate: Scientific, Philosophical, and Theological Perspectives on the Origin of Religion*, ed. J. P. Schloss and M. J. Murray, pp. 1–15. Oxford, UK: Oxford University Press.

Schloss, J. P., and Murray, M. J. (2011). Evolutionary accounts of belief in supernatural punishment: A critical review. *Religion, Brain and Behavior, 1*, 46–99.

Schmidt, K. (2000). "Zuerst kam der Tempel, dann die Stadt." Vorläufiger Bericht zu den Grabungen am Göbekli Tepe und am Gürcütepe 1995–1999. *Istanbuler Mitteilungen*, *50*, 5–41.

Seabright, P. (2004). *The Company of Strangers: A Natural History of Economic Life*. Princeton, NJ: Princeton University Press.

Sedikides, C., and Gebauer, J. E. (2010). Religiosity as self-enhancement: A meta-analysis of the relation between socially desirable responding and religiosity. *Personality and Social Psychology Review*, *14*, 17–36.

Shariff, A. F. (2011). Big gods were made for big groups: Commentary on Schloss and Murray. *Religion, Brain and Behavior*, *1*, 89–93.

Shariff, A. F., and Norenzayan, A. (2007). God is watching you: Priming god concepts increases prosocial behavior in an anonymous economic game. *Psychological Science*, *18*, 803–809.

———. (2011). Mean gods make good people: Different views of god predict cheating behavior. *International Journal for the Psychology of Religion*, *21*, 85–96.

———. (2012). Religious priming effects are sensitive to religious group boundaries. Unpublished data, University of Oregon.

Shariff, A., Norenzayan, A., and Henrich, J. (2010). The birth of high gods. In *Evolution, Culture, and the Human Mind*, ed. M. Schaller, A. Norenzayan, S. J. Heine, T. Yamagishi, and T. Kameda, pp. 119–136. New York: Psychology Press.

Shariff, A. F., and Rhemtulla, M. (2012). Divergent effects of belief in heaven and hell on national crime rates. *PLoS ONE*, *7*, e39048.

Sheikh, H., Ginges, J., Coman, A., and Atran, S. (2012). Religion, group threat, and sacred values. *Judgment and Decision Making*, *7*, 110–118.

Shenhav, A., Rand, D. G., and Greene, J. D. (2012). Divine intuition: Cognitive style influences belief in God. *Journal of Experimental Psychology: General*, *141*, 423–428.

Sidanius, J., and Kurzban, R. (2003). Evolutionary approaches to political psychology. In *Handbook of Political Psychology*, ed. D. O. Sears, L. Huddy, and R. Jervis, pp. 146–181. Oxford, UK: Oxford University Press.

Sigmund, K., de Silva, H., Traulsen, A., and Hauert, C. (2010). Social learning promotes institutions for governing the commons. *Nature*, *466*, 861–863.

Sinaceur, M., and Heath, C. (2005). Emotional and deliberative reactions to a public crisis: Mad cow disease in France. *Psychological Science*, *16*, 247–254.

Sinclair, L., and Kunda, Z. (1999). Reactions to a black professional: Motivated inhibition and activation of conflicting stereotypes. *Journal of Personality and Social Psychology*, *77*, 885–904.

Singer, P. (2011). *The Expanding Circle: Ethics, Evolution and Moral Progress*. Princeton, NJ: Princeton University Press.

Slingerland, E. (2013). Body and mind in early China: An integrated humanities-science approach. *Journal of the American Academy of Religion, 81*, 6–55.

Slingerland, E., and Collard, M. (eds.). (2012). *Creating Consilience: Integrating Science and the Humanities.* Oxford, UK: Oxford University Press.

Slingerland, E., Henrich, J., and Norenzayan, A. (in press). The evolution of pro-social religions. In *Cultural Evolution,* ed. P. Richerson and M. Christiansen. Cambridge, MA: MIT Press.

Slone, D. J. (2004). *Theological Incorrectness: Why Religious People Believe What They Shouldn't.* Oxford, UK: Oxford University Press.

Smith, R. J. (1996). Biology and body size in human evolution: statistical inference misapplied. *Current Anthropology, 37*(3), 451–481.

Snarey, J. (1996). The natural environment's impact upon religious ethics: a cross-cultural study. *Journal for the Scientific Study of Religion, 80*, 85–96.

Soler, M. (2012). Costly signaling, ritual and cooperation: Evidence from Candomblé, an Afro-Brazilian religion. *Evolution and Human Behavior, 33*, 346–356.

Solt, F., Habel, F., and Grant, J. T. (2011). Economic inequality, relative power, and religiosity. *Social Science Quarterly, 92*, 447–465.

Soltis, J., Boyd, R., and Richerson, P. J. (1995). Can group-functional behaviors evolve by cultural group selection? An empirical test. *Current Anthropology, 63*, 473–494.

Sosis, R. (2000). Religion and intra-group cooperation: Preliminary results of a comparative analysis of utopian communities. *Cross-Cultural Research, 34*, 70–87.

———. (2005). Does religion promote trust? The role of signaling, reputation, and punishment. *Interdisciplinary Journal of Research on Religion, 1*, 1–30.

———. (2006). Religious behaviors, badges, and bans: Signaling theory and the evolution of religion. In *Where God and Science Meet: How Brain and Evolutionary Studies Alter Our Understanding of Religion, Volume 1: Evolution, Genes, and the Religious Brain,* ed. P. McNamara, pp. 61–86. Westport, CT: Praeger Publishers.

Sosis, R., and Alcorta, C. (2003). Signaling, solidarity, and the sacred: The evolution of religious behavior. *Evolutionary Anthropology, 12*, 264–274.

Sosis, R., and Bressler, E. (2003). Cooperation and commune longevity: A test of the costly signaling theory of religion. *Cross-Cultural Research, 37*, 211–239.

Sosis, R., Kress, H., and Boster, J. (2007). Scars for war: Evaluating alternative signaling explanations for cross-cultural variance in ritual costs. *Evolution and Human Behavior, 28*, 234–247.

Sosis, R., and Ruffle, B. J. (2003). Religious ritual and cooperation: Testing for a relationship on Israeli religious and secular kibbutzim. *Current Anthropology, 44*(5), 713–722.

Sperber, D. (1996). *Explaining Culture: A Naturalistic Approach*. Cambridge, MA: Blackwell.

Sperber, D., Clément, F., Heintz, C., Mascaro, O., Mercier, H., Origgi, G., and Wilson, D. (2010). Epistemic vigilance. *Mind and Language, 25*, 359–393.

Sprinzak, E. (2000). Israel's radical right and the countdown to the Rabin assassination. In *The Assassination of Yitzhak Rabin*, ed. Y. Peri, pp. 96–128. Stanford, CA: Stanford University Press.

Sripada, C. S., and Stich, S. (2005). A framework for the psychology of norms. In *Innateness and the Structure of the Mind*, vol. 2, ed. P. Carruthers, S. Laurence, and S. Stich, pp. 280–301. Oxford, UK: Oxford University Press.

Stark, R. (1996). *The Rise of Christianity: How the Obscure, Marginal, Jesus Movement Became the Dominant Religious Force*. Princeton, NJ: HarperOne.

———. (2001). Gods, rituals, and the moral order. *Journal for the Scientific Study of Religion, 40*, 619–636.

———. (2002). Physiology and faith: Addressing the "universal" gender difference in religious commitment. *Journal for the Scientific Study of Religion, 41*, 495–507.

Steele, P. R., and Allen, C. J. (1994). *Handbook of Inca Mythology*. Santa Barbara, CA: ABC-CLIO.

Stevens, M. (2005). The role of eyespots as anti-predator mechanisms, principally demonstrated in the Lepidoptera. *Biological Reviews, 80*, 573–588.

Swanson, G. E. (1966). *The Birth of the Gods*. Ann Arbor: University of Michigan Press.

Taves, A. (2009). *Religious Experience Reconsidered: A Building-block Approach to the Study of Religion and Other Special Things*. Princeton, NJ: Princeton University Press.

Taylor, C. (2007). *A Secular Age*. Cambridge, MA: Belknap Harvard.

Tetlock, P. (2003). Thinking the unthinkable: Sacred values and taboo cognitions. *Trends in Cognitive Science, 7*, 320–324.

Thote, A. (2009). Shang and Zhou funeral practices: Interpretation of material vestiges. In *Early Chinese Religion: Part One: Shang through Han (1250 BC–22 AD)*, ed. J. Lagerwey and M. Kalinowski, pp. 103–142. Leiden: Brill.

Tilich, P. (1951). *Systematic Theology*. Chicago: University of Chicago Press.

Tilly, C. (1975). *The Formation of National States in Western Europe*. Princeton, NJ: Princeton University Press.

Tong, F., Nakayama, K., Moscovitch, M., Weinrib, O., and Kanwisher, N. (2000). Response properties of the human fusiform face area. *Cognitive Neuropsychology, 17*, 257–279.

Tonnies, F. (2001). *Community and Civil Society*, trans. J. Harris and M. Hollis. Cambridge, UK: Cambridge University Press.

Tracy, J. L., Hart, J., and Martens, J. P. (2011). Death and science: The existential underpinnings of belief in intelligence design and discomfort with evolution. *PLoS ONE, 6*, e17349.

Trimble, D. E. (1997). The religious orientation scale: Review and meta-analysis of social desirability effects. *Educational and Psychological Measurement, 57*, 970–986.

Trivers, R. L. (1971). The evolution of reciprocal altruism. *The Quarterly Review of Biology, 46*, 35–57.

Turchin, P. (2003). *Historical Dynamics: Why States Rise and Fall.* Princeton, NJ: Princeton University Press.

———. (2007). *War and Peace and War: The Rise and Fall of Empires.* New York: Plume.

———. (2010). Warfare and the evolution of social complexity: A multilevel-selection approach. *Structure and Dynamics, 4*, 1–37.

Turiel, E. (1983). *The Development of Social Knowledge: Morality and Convention.* Cambridge, UK: Cambridge University Press.

Tuzin, D. (2001). *Social Complexity in the Making: A Case Study among the Arapesh of New Guinea.* London: Routledge.

Tversky, A., and Kahneman, D. (1983). Extension versus intuitive reasoning: The conjunction fallacy in probability judgment. *Psychological Review, 90*, 293–315.

Underhill, R. (1975). Economic and political antecedents of monotheism: A cross-cultural study. *American Journal of Sociology, 80*, 841–861.

Vail, K. E., III, Arndt, J., and Abdollahi, A. (2012) Exploring the existential function of religion and supernatural agent beliefs among Christians, Muslims, Atheists, and Agnostics. *Personality and Social Psychology Bulletin, 38*, 1288–1300.

Valdesolo, P., Ouyang, J., and DeSteno, D. (2010). The rhythm of joint action: Synchrony promotes cooperative ability. *Journal of Experimental Social Psychology, 46*(4), 693–695.

Van Vugt, M., De Cremer, D., and Janssen, D. P. (2007). Gender differences in cooperation and competition: The male-warrior hypothesis. *Psychological Science, 18*, 19–23.

van Wolkenten, M., Brosnan, S. F., and de Waal, F.B.M. (2007). Inequity responses of monkeys modified by effort. *Proceedings of the National Academy of Sciences, 104*, 18854–18859.

Voight, B. F., Kudaravalli, S., Wen, X., and Pritchard, J. K. (2006). A map of recent positive selection in the human genome. *PLoS Biology, 4*, e72.

Walter, T., and Davie, G. (1998). The religiosity of women in the modern West. *British Journal of Sociology, 49*, 640–660.

Ward, C. (1984). Thaipusam in Malaysia: A psycho-anthropological analysis of ritual trance, ceremonial possession and self-mortification practices. *Ethos, 12,* 307–334.

Warneken, F., and Tomasello, M. (2009). Varieties of altruism in children and chimpanzees. *Trends in Cognitive Sciences, 13,* 397–482.

Waytz, A., Cacioppo, J. T., and Epley, N. (2010a). Who sees human? The stability and importance of individual differences in anthropomorphism. *Perspectives on Psychological Science, 5,* 219–232.

Waytz, A., and Epley, N. (2012). Social connection enables dehumanization. *Journal of Experimental Social Psychology, 48,* 70–76.

Waytz, A., Gray, K., Epley, N., and Wegner, D. M. (2010b). Causes and consequences of mind perception. *Trends in Cognitive Sciences, 14,* 383–388.

Whitehouse, H. (2004). *Modes of Religiosity: Towards a Cognitive Explanation of the Sociopolitical Dynamics of Religion.* Walnut Creek, CA: AltaMira Press.

Wilkinson, G. S. (1990, February). Food sharing in vampire bats. *Scientific American,* 76–82.

Wilkinson, R. H. (2003). *Complete Gods and Goddesses of Ancient Egypt.* London: Thames and Hudson.

Willard, A. K., and Norenzayan, A. (in press). Intuitive biases increase belief in God, in paranormal beliefs, and in belief in life's purpose. *Cognition.*

Wilson, D. S. (2002). *Darwin's Cathedral.* Chicago: Chicago University Press.

———. (2007). *Evolution for Everyone.* New York: Delacorte Press.

Wilson, E. O. (1998). *Consilience: The Unity of Knowledge.* New York: Knopf.

———. (2012). *The Social Conquest of Earth.* New York: Liveright.

Wilson, T. D., and Schooler, J. W. (1991). Thinking too much: Introspection can reduce the quality of preferences and decisions. *Journal of Personality and Social Psychology, 60*(2), 181–192.

Wiltermuth, S. S., and Heath, C. (2009). Synchrony and cooperation. *Psychological Science, 20*(1), 1–5.

Wong, B., and Loy, H. C. (2004). War and ghosts in Mozi's political philosophy. *Philosophy East and West, 54*(3), 343–363.

Wright, R. (2009). *The Evolution of God.* New York: Little Brown.

Xygalatas, D. (in press). Effects of religious setting on cooperative behaviour: A case study from Mauritius. *Religion, Brain and Behavior.*

Xygalatas, D., Mitkidis, P., Fischer, R., Reddish, P., Skewes, J., Geertz, A. W., Roepstorff, A., and Bulbulia, J. (in press). Extreme rituals promote prosociality. *Psychological Science.*

Zhong, C. B., Bohns, V. B., and Gino, F. (2010). A good lamp is the best police: Darkness increases dishonesty and self-interested behavior. *Psychological Science, 21,* 311–314.

Zuckerman, M., Silberman, J., and Hall, J. A. (2013). *The relation between intelligence and religiosity: A meta-analysis and some proposed explanations.* Unpublished manuscript, University of Rochester.

Zuckerman, P. (2007). Atheism: Contemporary numbers and patterns. In *The Cambridge Companion to Atheism*, ed. M. Martin, pp. 47–65. Cambridge, UK: Cambridge University Press.

———. (2008). *Society without God.* New York: New York University Press.

———. (2011, February). The top mistakes atheists make. *The Huffington Post.* Available at http://www.huffingtonpost.com/phil-zuckerman/mistakes-atheists -make-th_b_822252.html (accessed 03/12/2013).

Index